CHA

Spe

well

# CHAMBERS

# Spell Well

Compiled by
**E. M. Kirkpatrick**
**and C. M. Schwarz**

Second edition with
new material by
**E. M. Kirkpatrick**

# CHAMBERS

CHAMBERS
An imprint of Larousse plc
43-45 Annandale Street
Edinburgh EH7 4AZ

First published 1980
This edition 1996

ISBN 0 550 71313 1

Typeset by Roger King Graphic Studios
Printed in England by Clays Ltd, St Ives plc

# Preface

All but the most brilliant of spellers — and few people claim to be in that class — have to check the spelling of certain words from time to time. Some of us have a few blind spots, such as *correspondence*, which we can never remember how to spell. Others — although otherwise intelligent and educated! — are poor spellers generally.

Of course ordinary dictionaries can be used to check the spelling of words but that involves sifting through information which is not at that moment required. Chambers *Spell Well* has been designed for ease of reference so that people can find quickly and easily the words which they have difficulty in spelling.

It provides in a simple, easy-to-follow, form the common words that are likely to cause spelling problems. We have deliberately not included words such as *aardvark* which the ordinary user is unlikely to want to use. If people do require help with spelling such words they will find them in one of our wide range of dictionaries.

In response to user reaction, some new material has been added for the 1996 edition, including place names which often present spelling difficulties.

# About this guide

The words in Chambers *Spell Well* are clearly listed in alphabetical order.

Those parts of speech which are liable to cause spelling problems are listed under the relevant word, e.g.

### Adverbs

| | | |
|---|---|---|
| basic | public | wilful |
| *adv* basically | *adv* publicly | *adv* wilfully |

### Plurals

| | | |
|---|---|---|
| factory | monkey | potato |
| *pl* factories | *pl* monkeys | *pl* potatoes |
| piano | crisis | thief |
| *pl* pianos | *pl* crises | *pl* thieves |

Where more than one plural is allowable both have been given, e.g.

referendum
    *pl* referenda, referendums

banjo
    *pl* banjos, banjoes

### Parts of verbs

| | | | |
|---|---|---|---|
| gallop | refer | swim | light |
| galloped | referred | swam | lit, lighted |
| galloping | referring | swum | lighting |
| | | swimming | |

The part of the verb that is given first under the headword, e.g. *galloped*, *referred*, *swam*, is the past tense of the verb as in

> The horse galloped along the road.
> He referred to the subject briefly.
> The boy swam the river yesterday.

Where more than one form is allowable both have been given, e.g. *lit*, *lighted* as in

She lit (*or* lighted) the candles.

Where three parts of a verb are listed under the headword the second part listed is the past participle, e.g. *swum* as in

The boy has swum the river three times.

Where only two parts of a verb are listed the past participle is the same as the past tense as in

The horse has galloped along the road.
He has already referred to the subject.

The part of the verb given last in every case is the present participle, e.g. *galloping, referring, swimming, lighting* as in

The horse was galloping along the road.
He is not referring to her.
He is swimming well.
She is lighting the candles.

Many verbs in English can be spelled with either *-ize* or *-ise* as the ending. Which you use is a matter of choice. This guide allows both spellings in the headword — the parts of the verb follow the headword although only the *-z-* form is given.

Words which are very commonly misspelled and so are known pitfalls, e.g. **accommodation, assassinate, occasionally, immediate**, are printed in **bold type**.

Underneath certain words are sentences or phrases in *italic type*. This is to help the user distinguish between words which are liable to be confused, e.g.

illegible

*untidy and illegible handwriting*

eligible

*an eligible bachelor: eligible for the job*

| canvas | canvass |
|---|---|
| *canvas for painting:* | *to canvass for votes* |
| *a canvas tent* | |

| check | cheque |
|---|---|
| *a police check on cars:* | *a bank cheque* |
| *to check the oil:* | |
| *to check a sum* | |

| it's | its |
|---|---|
| = it is | *its leg* |
| *It's fine* | |

To provide further assistance these words are listed in alphabetical order at the end of the book with the words with which they are liable to be confused.

## American spelling

There are some common variations between British and American spelling:

| *British English* | *American English* |
|---|---|
| **-our** as in **colour, humour** | **-or** as in **color, humor** |
| **-re** as in **centre, theatre, metre** | **-er** as in **center, theater, meter** |
| **-ae-** as in **haemoglobin, anaemia** | **-e-** as in **hemoglobin, anemia** |
| NB There is a growing tendency in British English for the **ae** in such words to become **e** as in **medieval, encyclop(a)edia**. | |
| **-ogue** as in **catalogue** | **-og** as in **catalog** |
| NB Many words of this type can be spelled either **-ogue** or **-og** in American English as **prologue/prolog, dialogue/dialog**. | |
| **-ll-** as in **travelling, equalled** | **-l-** as in **traveling, equaled** |
| **-pp-** as in **kidnapped, worshipping** | **-p-** as in **kidnaped, worshiping** |
| **-l-** as in **skilful, wilful** | **-ll-** as in **skillful, willful** |

## Pronunciation guide

| | | | |
|---|---|---|---|
| a | as in **hat** | ō | as in **toe** |
| ä | as in **path** | ŏŏ | as in **book** |
| ā | as in **play** | ōō | as in **moon** |
| e | as in **leg** | ow | as in **shout** |
| ē | as in **clean** | u | as in **run** |
| i | as in **stick** | ū | as in **tune** |
| ī | as in **side** | ə | as in **infant** |
| ö | as in **fall** | sh | as in **ship** |

A stress mark ' indicates that the syllable following is pronounced with most emphasis.

## Abbreviations

| | | | |
|---|---|---|---|
| *adv* | adverb | *compar* | comparative |
| *pl(s)* | plural(s) | *superl* | superlative |

# A

a

*a boy: a house: a usual event*

aback

abacus

*pl* abacuses

abandon

  abandoned

  abandoning

abase

  abased

  abasing

abasement

abashed

abate

  abated

  abating

abatement

**abattoir**

abbess

  *pl* abbesses

abbey

  *pl* abbeys

abbot

abbreviate

  abbreviated

  abbreviating

**abbreviation**

abdicate

  abdicated

  abdicating

abdication

abdomen

abdominal

abduct

abduction

abet

abetted

abetting

abeyance

abhor

  abhorred

  abhorring

abhorrence

abhorrent

abide by

  abided by

  abode by

  abiding by

abiding

ability

  *pl* abilities

abject

ablaze

able

  *adv* ably

ablutions

abnormal

  *adv* abnormally

abnormality

  *pl* abnormalities

aboard

  *aboard ship*

abode

abolish

abolition

abolitionist

abominable

  *adv* abominably

abominate

  abominated

  abominating

abomination

aboriginal

aborigine

abort

abortion

abortive

abound

about

above

abrasion

abrasive

  *adv* abrasively

abreast

abridge

  abridged

  abridging

abridgement,

  abridgment

abroad

*He goes abroad on holiday: There's a rumour abroad*

abrupt

abruptness

**abscess**

  *pl* abscesses

abscond

abseil

  abseiled

  abseiling

**absence**

absent

absentee

absenteeism

absent-minded

absolute

  *adv* absolutely

absoluteness

absolution

absolve

  absolved

  absolving

absorb

absorbent
absorption
abstain
abstainer
abstemious
abstention
abstinence
abstract
abstruse
 *adv* abstrusely
absurd
absurdity
 *pl* absurdities
abundance
abundant
abuse
 abused
 abusing
abusive
 *adv* abusively
abysmal
 *adv* **abysmally**
abyss
 *pl* abysses
acacia
academic
 *adv*
 academically
academy
 *pl* academies
accede
 acceded
 acceding
accelerate
 accelerated
 accelerating
acceleration
**accelerator**
accent

accentuate
 accentuated
 accentuating
accept
 *to accept a present:*
 *to accept his*
 *decision*
acceptable
acceptance
access
 *access to the*
 *motorway: He has*
 *access to his*
 *children: access*
 *information*
accessed
accessing
accessibility
accessible
 *adv* accessibly
accession
accessory
 *pl* **accessories**
accident
accidental
 *adv* accidentally
acclaim
acclamation
acclimatization,
 -isation
acclimatize,
 -ise
 acclimatized
 acclimatizing
**accommodate**
 accommodated
 accommodating
**accommodation**
**accompaniment**

accompanist
accompany
 accompanied
 accompanying
accomplice
accomplish
accomplished
accomplishment
accord
accordance
according
accordingly
accordion
accost
account
accountability
accountable
accountant
accoutrements
accredited
accrue
 accrued
 accruing
**accumulate**
 accumulated
 accumulating
**accumulation**
accumulator
accuracy
**accurate**
 *adv* accurately
accursed
accusation
accuse
 accused
 accusing
accuser
**accustomed**
ace

acetylene
ache
  ached
  aching
**achieve**
  achieved
  achieving
achievement
acid
acidity
**acknowledge**
  acknowledged
  acknowledging
**acknowledgement,**
**acknowledgment**
acme
  *the acme of*
  *perfection*
acne
  *acne on his face*
acorn
acoustic
  *adv* acoustically
acoustics
**acquaint**
**acquaintance**
**acquiesce**
  acquiesced
  acquiescing
**acquiescence**
**acquire**
  acquired
  acquiring
acquisition
acquisitive
**acquit**
  acquitted
  acquitting
**acquittal**

acre
**acreage**
acrid
acrimonious
acrimony
acrobat
acrobatic
  *adv* acrobatically
acronym
**across**
acrostic
act
action
actionable
activate
  activated
  activating
active
  *adv* actively
activity
  *pl* activities
actor
actress
  *pl* actresses
actual
  *adv* actually
actuary
  *pl* actuaries
actuate
  actuated
  actuating
acumen
acupuncture
acute
  *adv* acutely
acuteness
ad
  *an ad in the paper*
adage

adamant
Adam's apple
adapt
adaptable
adaptation
adapter
  *the adapter of a*
  *play for TV*
adaptor
  *an adaptor for an*
  *electrical plug*
add
  *to add two*
  *numbers*
  added
  adding
addendum
  *pl* addenda
adder
addict
addicted
addiction
addictive
addition
  *the addition of the*
  *numbers: an*
  *addition to the*
  *family*
**additional**
  *adv* additionally
additive
**address**
  *pl* addresses
  addressed
  addressing
addressee
adenoids
adept
adequacy

adequate
  *adv* adequately
adhere
  adhered
  adhering
adherence
adherent
adhesion
adhesive
adjacent
adjectival
  *adv* adjectivally
adjective
adjoin
  adjoined
  adjoining
adjourn
adjournment
adjudicate
  adjudicated
  adjudicating
adjudication
adjudicator
adjunct
adjust
adjustable
adjustment
adjutant
ad-lib
  ad-libbed
  ad-libbing
administer
  administered
  administering
administrate
  administrated
  administrating
administration
administrative

administrator
admirable
  *adv* admirably
admiral
admiralty
admiration
admire
  admired
  admiring
admirer
  admiring
**admissible**
  *adv* admissibly
admission
admit
  admitted
  admitting
**admittance**
admonish
admonition
admonitory
ado
**adolescence**
**adolescent**
adopt
adoption
adoptive
adorable
  *adv* adorably
adoration
adore
  adored
  adoring
adorn
adornment
adrift
adroit
adulation
adult

adulterate
adulterated
adulterating
adulteration
adulterer
adulteress
  *pl* adulteresses
adultery
advance
  advanced
  advancing
advancement
advantage
**advantageous**
advent
adventitious
adventure
adventurer
adventurous
adverb
adverbial
  *adv* adverbially
adversary
  *pl* adversaries
adverse
  *in adverse
  circumstances*
  *adv* adversely
adversity
  *pl* adversities
advert
advertise
  advertised
  advertising
**advertisement**
advice

  *She gave him good
  advice: an advice
  from the bank*

advisability
advisable
advise
  *to advise him to go*
  advised
  advising
advisory
advocate
  advocated
  advocating
adze
aeon, eon
**aerate**
  aerated
  aerating
**aerial**
aerie
  *see* eyrie
aerobatics
aerodrome
aeroplane
aerosol
**aesthetic**
  *That colour
  scheme is not very
  aesthetic*
  *adv* aesthetically
affability
affable
  *adv* affably
affair
affect
  *Will her
  nervousness affect
  her playing?*
affectation
affection
affectionate
  *adv* affectionately

affidavit
affiliate
  affiliated
  affiliating
**affiliation**
affinity
  *pl* affinities
affirm
affirmation
affirmative
affix
afflict
affliction
affluence
affluent
  *the affluent society*
afford
**afforestation**
affray
affront
Afghan
afloat
afoot
aforesaid
afraid
aft
after
aftermath
afternoon
afterthought
afterwards
again
against
agate
age
  aged
  aging, ageing
ageism
ageist

agency
  *pl* agencies
agenda
  *pl* agendas
agent
**aggravate**
  aggravated
  aggravating
  aggravation
**aggregate**
aggression
**aggressive**
  *adv* aggressively
aggrieved
**aghast**
agile
  *adv* agilely
agility
agitate
  agitated
  agitating
agitation
agitator
agnostic
**agnosticism**
ago
agog
agonized, -ised
agonizing, -ising
agony
**agoraphobia**
agree
  **agreed**
  agreeing
agreeable
  *adv* agreeably
agreement
agricultural
  *adv* agriculturally

5

agriculture
aground
ague
ahead
aid
*aid for the poor:*
*come to their aid*
aide
*the president's aide*
AIDS
ail
*What ails her?*
ailed
ailing
aileron
aim
aimless
air
*fresh air*
aired
airing
airborne
aircraft
airless
airport
airy
*adv* airily
aisle
*the aisle in the*
*church*
ajar
akimbo
akin
alacrity
alarm
alarming
alarmist
alas!
albatross

*pl* albatrosses
albino
*pl* albinos
album
alchemy
**alcohol**
alcoholic
alcoholism
alcove
alderman
ale
*two pints of ale*
alert
alfalfa
alfresco
algae
algebra
algebraic
alias
*pl* aliases
alibi
*pl* **alibis**
alien
alienate
alienated
alienating
alight
alighted, alit
alighting
**align**
aligned
aligning
**alignment**
alike
alimentary
alit
*see* alight
alive
alkali

alkaline
all
*all of you: all in red*
Allah
allay
*to allay his fears*
allayed
allaying
allegation
**allege**
alleged
alleging
allegiance
allegorical
*adv* allegorically
allegory
*Pilgrim's Progress*
*is an allegory*
*pl* allegories
**allergic**
allergy
*an allergy to*
*certain foods*
*pl* allergies
alleviate
alleviated
alleviating
alleviation
alley
*a bowling alley: He*
*ran down the alley*
*pl* alleys
alliance
**alligator**
alliterate
*Sand, sea and sun*
*alliterate*
alliterated
alliterating

alliteration
allocate
 allocated
 allocating
allocation
allot
 allotted
 allotting
**allotment**
allow
 allowed
 allowing
allowable
allowance
alloy
all right
allude
 *He did not allude to the matter*
 alluded
 alluding
allure
 allured
 alluring
allusion
 *He made no allusion to the matter*
alluvial
ally
 *pl* allies
 allied
 allying
almanac
almighty
**almond**
almost
alms
aloft

alone
along
aloof
aloofness
aloud
alpha
alphabet
alphabetical
 *adv* alphabetically
alpine
**already**
alsatian
also
altar
 *the bridegroom at the altar*
alter
 *to alter your plans: to alter a dress*
 altered
 altering
alteration
 *alteration to my plans: alteration to my dress*
altercation
 *The altercation ended in blows*
al'ternate
 *adv* alternately
 *alternately hot and cold*
'alternate
 alternated
 alternating
alternative
 *adv* alternatively
 *You could go by bus — alternatively*

 *you could go by train*

**although**
altimeter
altitude
alto
altogether
altruism
altruistic
 *adv* altruistically
**aluminium**
always
Alzheimer's (disease)
am
 *see* be
amalgam
amalgamate
 amalgamated
 amalgamating
amalgamation
amass
amateur
 *an amateur golf player*
amateurish
 *an amateurish attempt at building a shed*
amaze
 amazed
 amazing
amazement
ambassador
ambassadress
 *pl* ambassa-dresses
amber
ambidexterous,

7

ambidextrous
ambiguity
 *pl* ambiguities
**ambiguous**
ambition
ambitious
amble
 ambled
 ambling
ambrosia
ambulance
ambush
 *pl* ambushes
amenable
amend
 *to amend the law*
amendments
amenity
 *pl* amenities
**amethyst**
amiable
 *an amiable young man*
 *adv* amiably
amicable
 *on amicable terms: an amicable separation*
 *adv* amicably
amid, amidst
amiss
amity
ammonia
**ammunition**
amnesia
amnesty
 *pl* amnesties
amoeba
amok, amuck

run amok
among, amongst
 *Divide the chocolate among all four*
amoral
 *She is quite amoral — she doesn't know right from wrong*
amorous
amorousness
amount
amp, ampère
amphibian
amphibious
amphitheatre
ample
 *adv* amply
amplification
amplifier
amplify
 amplified
 amplifying
amplitude
amputate
 amputated
 amputating
amputation
amuck
 *see* amok
amulet
amuse
 amused
 amusing
amusement
an
 *an art: an orange: an honour*

**anachronism**
anachronistic
anaemia
anaemic
**anaesthetic**
anaesthetist
anagram
analgesic
analogous
analogy
 *pl* analogies
**analyse**
 analysed
 analysing
**analysis**
anarchist
anarchy
anathema
anatomical
 *adv* anatomically
anatomist
anatomy
**ancestor**
ancestral
ancestress
 *pl* ancestresses
**ancestry**
anchor
 anchored
 anchoring
anchorage
anchovy
 *pl* anchovies
ancient
ancillary
anecdotal
anecdote
anemometer
**anemone**

aneroid
barometer
angel
*an angel from heaven: Be an angel and help me with this*

angelic
*adv* angelically
angelica
anger
angered
angering
angina
angle
*an angle of 90°: a new angle on the story: to angle for a job: to angle the camera*

angled
angling
angler
Anglican
anglicize, -ise
anglicized
anglicizing
Anglo-Saxon
angora
angry
*adv* **angrily**
**anguish**
anguished
angular
animal
animate
animated
animating
animation

animosity
aniseed
ankle
annals
*The Annals of the Parish: in the annals of crime*

an'nex
*to annex a country*
'annex, annexe
*build an annexe to the house*

**annihilate**
annihilated
annihilating
**annihilation**
anniversary
*pl* anniversaries
annotate
annotated
annotating
annotation
announce
announced
announcing
**announcement**
announcer
annoy
annoyed
annoying
annoyance
annual
*pl* annuals
*Christmas annuals*
*adv* annually
annuity
*pl* annuities
annul
**annulled**

annulling
**annulment**
anoint
anomalous
anomaly
*pl* anomalies
anon
anonymity
**anonymous**
anorak
anorexia
(nervosa)
another
answer
**answered**
answering
answerable
ant
*He was bitten by an ant*

antagonism
antagonist
antagonistic
*adv* antagonisti-
cally
antagonize, -ise
antagonized
antagonizing
**Antarctic**
antecedent
antediluvian
antelope
antenatal
antenna
*pl* antennae,
antennas
anteroom
anthem
anthology

*pl* anthologies
**anthracite**
anthrax
anthropoid
anthropological
anthropologist
anthropology
**antibiotic**
anticipate
  anticipated
  anticipating
anticipation
anticlimax
anticlockwise
antics
anticyclone
antidepressant
antidote
antifreeze
antihistamine
antipathy
antipodes
antiquarian
antiquated
  *antiquated ideas*
antique
  *an antique table: a*
  *valuable antique*
antiseptic
antisocial
**antithesis**
  *pl* antitheses
antler
anvil
**anxiety**
  *pl* anxieties
anxious
any
anybody

anyhow
anyone
anything
anywhere
apart
**apartheid**
apartment
apathetic
  *adv* apathetically
apathy
ape
  aped
  aping
aperture
apex
  *pl* apexes,
  apices
aphid
apiary
  *pl* apiaries
apices
  *see* apex
apiece
aplomb
apocalypse
apocryphal
apologetic
  *adv* apologeti-
  cally
apologize, -ise
  apologized
  apologizing
apology
  *pl* apologies
apoplectic
apoplexy
apostle
apostrophe
apothecary

*pl* apothecaries
appal
  appalled
  **appalling**
apparatus
apparel
apparent
  *adv* **apparently**
apparition
appeal
  appealed
  appealing
appear
  appeared
  appearing
**appearance**
appease
  appeased
  appeasing
**appendicitis**
appendix
  *pl* appendixes,
  appendices
appertain
  appertained
  appertaining
appetite
appetizing, -ising
applaud
applause
apple
appliance
applicable
applicant
application
apply
  applied
  applying
appoint

appointment
apportion
 apportioned
 apportioning
apposite
appraisal
appraise
 appraised
 appraising
appreciable
 adv appreciably
**appreciate**
 appreciated
 appreciating
appreciation
apprehend
apprehension
apprehensive
 adv
  apprehensively
apprentice
apprenticeship
approach
 pl approaches
approachable
approbation
appropriate
 adv
  appropriately
 appropriated
 appropriating
**approval**
approve
 approved
 approving
approximate
 adv
  approximately
approximation

apricot
April
apron
apropos of
apse
apt
 adv aptly
aptitude
aquamarine
aquarium
 pl aquaria
aquatic
aqueduct
aquiline
Arab
arable
arbiter
**arbitrary**
 adv arbitrarily
arbitrate
 arbitrated
 arbitrating
**arbitration**
arbitrator
arbour
arc
 the arc of a circle:
 arc lamp
arcade
arch
 pl arches
archaeological
archaeologist
**archaeology**
archaic
archangel
archbishop
archer
archery

archipelago
 pl archipelagos,
  archipelagoes
architect
**architectural**
 adv
  architecturally
architecture
archives
**Arctic**
ardent
ardour
arduous
arduousness
are
 see be
area
 pl areas
arena
aren't = are not
argosy
 pl argosies
arguable
 adv **arguably**
argue
 argued
 arguing
argument
argumentative
 adv argumenta-
  tively
aria
 pl arias
arid
arise
 arose
 A problem arose
 arisen
 A problem has

*arisen*
arising
aristocracy
aristocrat
aristocratic
  *adv*
    aristocratically
arithmetic
arithmetical
  *adv*
    arithmetically
ark
  *Noah's ark*
arm
armada
  *pl* armadas
armadillo
  *pl* armadillos
armaments
armchair
armistice
armorial
armour
armoured
armoury
army
  *pl* armies
aroma
  *pl* aromas
aromatherapist
aromatherapy
aromatic
arose
  *see* arise
around
arouse
  aroused
  arousing
arrange

arranged
arranging
**arrangement**
arras
array
  arrayed
  arraying
arrears
arrest
**arrival**
arrive
  arrived
  arriving
arrogance
arrogant
arrow
arsenal
arsenic
arson
art
artful
  *adv* artfully
artless
artefact, artifact
arterial
artery
  *pl* arteries
artesian well
arthritic
arthritis
**artichoke**
article
articulate
  articulated
  articulating
articulation
artifact
  *see* artefact
artificial

  *adv* artificially
artificiality
artillery
artisan
artist
  *a portrait artist: a concert artist*
artiste
  *a circus artiste*
artistic
  *adv* artistically
artistry
as
asbestos
**ascend**
ascended
ascending
ascendancy,
  ascendency
ascendant,
  ascendent
ascent
  *the ascent of the mountain: ascent to the throne*
ascertain
ascetic
  *Monks lead ascetic lives*
  *adv* ascetically
ascribe
  ascribed
  ascribing
ash
ashamed
ashen
ashes
ashore
aside

asinine
ask
askance
askew
asleep
asp
asparagus
aspect
asperity
**asphalt**
asphyxia
**asphyxiate**
  asphyxiated
  asphyxiating
**asphyxiation**
aspidistra
aspiration
aspire
  aspired
  aspiring
aspirin
ass
  *pl* asses
assail
  assailed
  assailing
assailant
**assassin**
**assassinate**
  assassinated
  assassinating
  assassination
assault
assay
  *an assay of gold*
assemble
  assembled
  assembling
assembly

  *pl* assemblies
assent
  *The Queen gave her assent to the new Bill*
assert
assertion
assertive
  *adv* assertively
assess
**assessment**
assessor
asset
  *pl* assets
assiduous
assign
  assigned
  assigning
assignation
**assignment**
**assimilate**
  assimilated
  assimilating
  assimilation
assist
**assistance**
assistant
assizes
**associate**
  associated
  associating
  association
assorted
assortment
assuage
  assuaged
  assuaging
assume
  assumed

assuming
assumption
assurance
assure
  assured
  assuring
asterisk
**asthma**
**asthmatic**
  *adv* asthmatically
astonish
astonishment
astound
**astrakhan**
astral
astray
astride
astringent
astrologer
astrological
  *adv* astrologically
astrology
  *Astrology deals with the signs of the zodiac*
astronaut
astronomer
astronomical
  *adv* astronomically
astronomy
  *He is studying physics and astronomy*
astute
asunder
asylum

at
ate *see* eat
atheism
**atheist**
athlete
athletic
  *adv* athletically
athletics
atlas
  *pl* atlases
atmosphere
atmospheric
  *adv*
   atmospherically
atmospherics
atoll
atom
atomic
atone
  atoned
  atoning
atonement
**atrocious**
atrocity
  *pl* atrocities
**attach**
  attached
  attaching
attaché-case
attachment
attack
attacker
attain
attainable
attainment
attempt
attend
attendance
**attendant**

attention
attentive
  *adv* attentively
attic
attire
  attired
  attiring
**attitude**
attorney
  *pl* attorneys
attract
attraction
attractive
  *adv* attractively
attributable
attribute
  attributed
  attributing
aubergine
auburn
auction
auctioneer
audacious
audacity
audibility
audible
  *adv* audibly
audience
audio-typist
audio-visual
audit
  audited
  auditing
audition
auditor
auditorium
  *pl* auditoriums,
   auditoria
auditory

augment
augmentation
augur
  augured
  auguring
'August
au'gust
auk
aunt
  *her aunt and uncle*
aural
  = of hearing
  *Her aural facilities*
  *were impaired*
auspices
auspicious
austere
  *adv* austerely
austerity
authentic
authenticate
  authenticated
  authenticating
authenticity
author
authoritarian
authoritative
authority
  *pl* authorities
authorization,
  -isation
authorize, -ise
  authorized
  authorizing
autobiographical
autobiography
  *pl* autobiogra-
   phies
autocrat

autocue
autograph
**automatic**
  *adv*
    automatically
automation
automaton
  *pl* automatons,
    automata
autonomous
autonomy
autopilot
autopsy
  *pl* autopsies
**autumn**
autumnal
auxiliary
  *pl* auxiliaries
avail
  availed
  availing
availability
available
avalanche
avarice
avaricious
avenge
  avenged
  avenging
avenger
avenue
average
  averaged
  averaging
averse
  *I'm not averse to*
   *work*
aversion
avert

aviary
  *pl* aviaries
aviation
aviator
avid
avidity
avoid
avoidable
  *adv* avoidably
avoidance
avoirdupois
avow
avowal
await
awake
awaken
  awakened
  awakening
award
aware
awareness
away
awe
awesome
**awful**
  *adv* awfully
awfulness
**awkward**
  *adv* awkwardly
awkwardness
awl
  *the cobbler's awl*
awning
awoke
awry
axe
  *pl* axes
  *axes for chopping*
  *wood*

axed
axing
axis
  *turning on an axis*
axle
azure


**B**

babble
  babbled
  babbling
baboon
baby
  *pl* babies
babyhood
babysit
  babysat
  babysitting
babysitter
**bachelor**
bachelorhood
bacillus
  *pl* bacilli
back
backer
backgammon
background
backing
backward
backwards
bacon
bacteria
bacterial
bacteriologist
bacteriology
bad
  *a bad boy*
  *compar* worse

*superl* worst
bade *see* bid
badger
  badgered
  badgering
badminton
baffle
  baffled
  baffling
bag
  bagged
  bagging
**bagatelle**
**baggage**
baggy
Baghdad
bagpipes
Bahamas
bail
  *to pay bail: to bail him out of prison*
  bailed
  bailing
**bailiff**
bait
  baited
  *He baited his line*
  baiting
baize
bake
  baked
  baking
baker
bakery
  *pl* bakeries
balance
  balanced
  balancing
balcony

*pl* balconies
bald
balderdash
bale
  *a bale of cotton*
baleful
  *adv* balefully
bale out
  *to bale out of an aircraft: to bale out water*
  baled out
  baling out
balk, baulk
  balked, baulked
  balking, baulking
ball
  *a ball of wool: a tennis ball: a formal ball*
ballad
ballast
**ballerina**
ballet
  *ballet shoes*
ballistic
**balloon**
ballot
  *to vote in a secret ballot*
  balloted
  balloting
balm
balmy
balsa (wood)
balustrade
bamboo
bamboozle

bamboozled
bamboozling
ban
  *pl* bans
  *government bans on smoking*
  banned
  banning
banal
banality
  *pl* banalities
**banana**
band
bandage
  bandaged
  bandaging
bandeau
  *pl* bandeaux
bandit
bandy
  bandied
  bandying
bandy(-legged)
bane
bang
bangle
banish
banishment
**banister**
banjo
  *pl* banjos, banjoes
bank
banker
bankrupt
**bankruptcy**
banner
banns
  *marriage banns*

16

**banquet**
bantam
banter
bantering
baptism
baptismal
baptize, -ise
  baptized
  baptizing
bar
  barred
  barring
barb
barbarian
barbaric
  *adv* barbarically
barbarity
  *pl* barbarities
**barbecue**
  barbecued
  barbecuing
barbed
barber
bard
bare
  *to bare his teeth*
  bared
  baring
bare
  *bare legs*
barely
bareness
bargain
  bargained
  bargaining
barge
  barged
  barging
baritone

bark
barley
barn
  *hay in the barn*
barnacle
**barometer**
baron
  *He has the title of baron: Baron Smith of Baberton*
baroness
  *pl* baronesses
baronet
baronetcy
barracks
barrage
barrel
barren
  *barren fields: a barren woman*
barrenness
barricade
  barricaded
  barricading
barrier
barring
**barrister**
barrow
barter
  bartered
  bartering
basalt
base
  *This paint has an oil base: the base of his spine: to use the office as a base: to base an argument on facts*
based

basing
baseball
basement
bashful
  *adv* bashfully
basic
  *adv* **basically**
basil
basilisk
basin
**basis**
  *pl* bases
bask
basket
basket-ball
bass [bās]
  *the bass singer*
  *pl* basses
  *the basses in the choir*
bass [bas]
  *pl* bass
  *The fisherman caught several bass*
**bassoon**
baste
  basted
  basting
bastion
bat
  batted
  batting
batch
  *pl* batches
bated
  *with bated breath*
bath
  *to bath the baby*

bathed
bathing
bathe
*to bathe in the sea:*
*to bathe a wound*
bathed
bathing
batik
batman
baton
*a policeman's*
*baton*
batsman
**battalion**
batten
*The joiner put up a*
*batten*
batter
battered
battering
battery
*pl* batteries
battle
battled
battling
battle-axe
battlement
bauble
baulk *see* balk
bawl
*The child began to*
*bawl*
bay
bayed
baying
bayonet
bazaar, bazar
*an Eastern bazaar:*
*a church bazaar*

be
*to be helpful*
am, is, are
was, were
been
*he has been: they*
*have been*
being
*He is being funny:*
*a human being*
beach
*a sandy beach*
*pl* beaches
beacon
bead
beadle
beagle
beak
beaker
beam
bean
*a French bean*
bear
*a brown bear: I*
*can't bear the*
*noise: to bear the*
*strain: to bear*
*children*
bore
*He bore it*
borne
*I have borne it*
bearing
bearable
beard
bearded
bearer
bearing
beast

beastliness
beastly
beat
*to beat someone at*
*tennis*
beat
*He beat her*
beaten
*He has beaten her*
beatific
*adv* beatifically
beau [bō]
*Her latest beau is*
*very handsome*
**beautiful**
*adv* beautifully
beautify
beautified
beautifying
beauty
*pl* beauties
beaver
beaver away
beavered away
beavering away
becalmed
became *see*
become
because
beck
beckon
beckoned
beckoning
become
became
*He became a*
*doctor*
become
*He has become a*

18

*doctor*
becoming
becoming
bed
  bedded
  bedding
bedlam
bedraggled
bedridden
bee
  *a honey bee*
beech
  *a beech tree*
  *pl* beeches
beef
beefeater
beefy
been
  *see* be
beer
  *a pint of beer*
beet
  *sugar beet*
beetle
beetling
beetroot
befall
  befell
  *What befell him?*
  befallen
  *What has befallen you?*
  befalling
befit
  befitted
  befitting
before
beforehand
**befriend**

beg
  begged
  begging
began
  *see* begin
beget
  begot
  begotten
beggar
  beggared
  beggaring
beggarly
begin
  began
  *It began to rain*
  begun
  *It has begun to rain*
  beginning
begrudge
  begrudged
  begrudging
**beguile**
  beguiled
  beguiling
begun
  *see* begin
behalf
behave
  behaved
  behaving
**behaviour**
behead
behest
behind
behold
  beheld
  beholding
beholden
being *see* be

belabour
  belaboured
  belabouring
belated
belch
**beleaguer**
  beleaguered
  beleaguering
belfry
  *pl* belfries
belie
  belied
  belying
belief
  *to show his belief in God*
**believe**
  *to believe in God*
  believed
  believing
belittle
  belittled
  belittling
bell
  *a church bell*
belle
  *the belle of the ball*
bellicose
**belligerent**
bellow
  *Bulls bellow*
bellows
belly
  *pl* bellies
belong
  belonged
  belonging
  belongings
beloved

below
  *below the level*
belt
belying
  *see* belie
bemoan
  bemoaned
  bemoaning
bench
  *pl* benches
bend
  bent
  bending
beneath
benediction
benefactor
beneficial
  *adv* beneficially
beneficiary
  *pl* beneficiaries
benefit
  **benefited**
  benefiting
benevolence
benevolent
benign
bent
  *see* bend
**bequeath**
  bequeathed
  bequeathing
bequest
berate
  berated
  berating
bereaved
bereavement
bereft
beret

*She wore a blue beret*
berry
  *a holly berry*
  *pl* berries
**berserk**
berth
  *a berth on a ship*
  berthed
  berthing
beryl
beseech
beset
  beset
  besetting
beside
  *beside the tree*
besides
  *Others, besides him, will come*
**besiege**
  besieged
  besieging
besotted with
bespoke
best
  *see* good
bestial
  *adv* bestially
bestir
  bestirred
  bestirring
bestow
bet
  bet, *(rare)* betted
  betting
betray
  betrayed
  betraying

betrayal
betroth
betrothal
betrothed
better
  bettered
  bettering
better
  *see* good
betting
  *see* bet
between
  *Divide the chocolate between you and your sister: between London and New York*

bevel
**bevelled**
  bevelling
beverage
bevy
  *pl* bevies
bewail
  bewailed
  bewailing
beware
bewilder
  bewildered
  bewildering
**bewitch**
beyond
**bias**
  biased, biassed
  biasing,
    biassing
bib
bible

20

biblical
bibliographer
bibliography
  *pl*
    bibliographies
bibliophile
bicentenary
biceps
bicker
  bickered
  bickering
bicycle
bid
  bid, bade [bad]
  *He bid £10: He*
  *bade him farewell*

  bidding
bidet
biennial
  *adv* biennially
bier
  *a funeral bier*
big
  *compar* bigger
  *superl* biggest
bigamist
**bigamous**
bigamy
bigger, biggest
  *see* big
bight
  = a bay
  *the Great*
  *Australian Bight*
bigot
**bigoted**
bigotry
bike
bikini

  *pl* bikinis
bilateral
bilberry
  *pl* bilberries
bile
bilious
biliousness
bilge
**bilingual**
bill
billet
  billeted
  billeting
billet doux
billiards
billow
bin
binary
bind
  bound
  *books bound in*
  *leather: to be*
  *bound to lose*

  binding
bingo
binoculars
biodegradable
biographer
biographical
biography
  *pl* biographies
biological
  *adv* biologically
biologist
biology
birch
  *pl* birches
bird
Biro ®

birth
  *the birth of her*
  *child*
birthday
**biscuit**
bisect
bishop
bishopric
bison
bit
  *see* bite
bitch
  *pl* bitches
bite
  *Did the dog bite*
  *the man?*

  bit
  *The dog bit me*
  bitten
  *The dog has bitten*
  *me*
bitter
bivouac
  **bivouacked**
  bivouacking
bi-weekly
bizarre
  *clowns wearing*
  *bizarre costumes:*
  *We met in bizarre*
  *circumstances*

blab
  blabbed
  blabbing
black
blackboard
blacken
  blackened
  blackening

blackguard
blackmail
  blackmailed
  blackmailing
blackmailer
bladder
blade
blame
  blamed
  blaming
blameless
**blancmange**
bland
blandishments
blank
blanket
  blanketed
  blanketing
blare
  blared
  blaring
blarney
blaspheme
  blasphemed
  blaspheming
**blasphemous**
**blasphemy**
blast
blast-off
blatant
blaze
  blazed
  blazing
blazer
blazon
  blazoned
  blazoning
bleach
  *pl* bleaches

bleak
bleakness
**bleary**
bleat
bleed
  bled
  bleeding
bleep
blemish
  *pl* blemishes
blend
blender
bless
  blessed
  blessing
blew
  *see* blow
blight
blind
blindfold
blindness
blink
blinkers
bliss
blissful
  *adv* blissfully
blister
  blistered
  blistering
blithe
  *adv* blithely
**blitz**
blizzard
bloated
bloater
blob
bloc
  *the Eastern bloc of
  nations*

block
  *a block of wood: a
  block of flats: to
  block a pipe*
blockade
  blockaded
  blockading
blond
  *blond hair*
blonde
  *She's a beautiful
  blonde*
blood
bloodhound
bloodshed
bloody
bloom
  bloomed
  blooming
blossom
  blossomed
  blossoming
blot
  blotted
  blotting
blotch
  *pl* blotches
blotchy
blotter
blouse
blow
  blew
  *He blew the
  trumpet*
  blown
  *He has blown the
  trumpet*
  blowing
blowy

22

blowzy
blubber
  blubbered
  blubbering
bludgeon
  bludgeoned
  bludgeoning
blue
  *a blue sky*
blueprint
bluff
blunder
  blundered
  blundering
blunderbuss
  *pl*
    blunderbusses
blunt
blur
  blurred
  blurring
blurt out
blush
  *pl* blushes
bluster
  blustered
  blustering
boa
boa constrictor
boar
  *a wild boar*
board
  *a board of
  directors: a
  wooden board: to
  board a ship: to
  board up a
  window: to board
  at a guest house*
boarder

boast
  *to boast about his
  achievements*
boastful
  *adv* boastfully
boat
boater
boating
boatswain,
  bosun
bob
  bobbed
  bobbing
bobbin
bobsleigh
bode
  boded
  boding
bodice
**bodily**
bodkin
body
  *pl* bodies
bodyguard
boffin
bog down
  bogged down
  bogging down
bogey
  *pl* bogeys
boggle
  boggled
  boggling
bogus
boil
  boiled
  boiling
boiler
boisterous

bold
bollard
bolster up
  bolstered up
  bolstering up
bolt
bomb
  bombed
  bombing
bombard
bombardment
bombastic
bomber
bombshell
bond
bondage
bone
**bonfire**
bonnet
bonny
  *a plump, bonny
  baby*
bonus
  *pl* bonuses
bony
  *bony elbows: bony
  fist*
boo
  booed
  booing
booby
book
bookie
  *to bet with a
  bookie*
book-keeping
booklet
boom
  boomed

booming
boomerang
boon
boor
*an ill-mannered boor*

boorish
boost
*to boost his self-confidence: to boost his resistance to polio*

booster
boot
bootee
*a baby's bootee*

booth
*pl* booths
booty
*booty from the wrecked ship*

border
bordered
bordering
bore
*see* bear
bore
*He's a tiresome bore: to bore a hole: to bore him with a long speech*

bored
*a bored listener*

boring
boredom
born
*His mother died when he was born*

borne

*see* bear
borough
*Boroughs have royal charters*

borrow
borzoi
bosom
boss
*pl* bosses
bosun
*see* boatswain
botanical
*adv* botanically
botanist
botany
botch
both
bother
bothered
bothering
bothy
*pl* bothies
bottle
bottled
bottling
bottleneck
bottom
boudoir
bough
*the bough of a tree*

bought
*see* buy
boulder
bounce
bounced
bouncing
bouncer
bound
*see* bind

bound
bounded
*The dog bounded over to us*

bounding
boundary
*pl* boundaries
boundless
bounteous
bountiful
bounty
*pl* bounties
**bouquet**
*a bouquet of flowers*

**bourgeois**
bout
**boutique**
bovine
bow [bow]
*to bow one's head*

bowed
bowing
bow [bō]
*a bow in her hair*

bowels
bower
bowl
bowler
bowls
box
*pl* boxes
boxer
boy
*a fair-haired boy*

**boycott**
boycotted
boycotting
boyhood

boyish
boyishness
bra
brace
  braced
  bracing
bracelet
braces
bracing
bracken
bracket
  **bracketed**
  bracketing
brackish
bradawl
brae (*Scots*)
  *a steep brae*
brag
  bragged
  bragging
braid
**braille**
brain
  brained
  braining
brainwave
brainy
braise
  braised
  braising
brake
  *to put on the car*
  *brake: to brake*
  *going round a*
  *corner*

  braked
  braking
bramble
bran

branch
  *pl* branches
brand
brandish
brand-new
brandy
  *pl* brandies
brass
  *pl* brasses
brassière
  *What size of*
  *brassière?*
brassy
brat
bravado
brave
  *adv* bravely
  braved
  braving
bravery
bravo
brawl
brawn
brawny
bray
  *The ass began to*
  *bray*
  brayed
  braying
brazen
brazen it out
  brazened it out
  brazening it out
brazier
  *a brazier of burning*
  *coal*
brazil-nut
breach
  *a breach of the*

peace: a breach in
the defences: to
breach their
defence

  *pl* breaches
bread
  *a loaf of bread*
**breadth**
breadwinner
break
  *to break a leg*
  broke
  *He broke a cup*
  broken
  *He has broken a*
  *cup*
  breaking
breakable
breakage
breaker
breakfast
break-in
bream
breast
breath
  *a breath of air: take*
  *a breath*
**breathalyser**
breathe
  *to breathe in*
  breathed
  breathing
breathless
bred
  *see* breed
breech

  *the breech of a*
  *gun: a breech*
  *delivery of a child*

breeches
breed
  bred
  *He bred cocker spaniels*
  breeding
breeze
breezy
brethren
brevity
brew
brewery
  *pl* breweries
briar, brier
bribe
  bribed
  bribing
bribery
bric-à-brac
brick
bridal
  *bridal party*
bride
bridegroom
bridesmaid
bridge
  bridged
  bridging
bridle
  *a horse's bridle: to bridle in anger*
  bridled
  bridling
**brief**
briefs
brier
  *see* briar
brigade
brigand

bright
brighten
  brightened
  brightening
brilliance
brilliant
brim
  brimmed
  brimming
brimful
brimstone
brine
bring
  brought
  bringing
brink
briny
brioche
brisk
bristle
  bristled
  bristling
bristly
brittle
broach
  *to broach the subject*
  broached
  broaching
broad
broadcast
  broadcast
  broadcasting
broaden
  broadened
  broadening
brocade
**broccoli**
**brochure**

brogue
broil
broke, broken
  *see* break
broker
bronchitic
**bronchitis**
brontosaurus
bronze
  bronzed
brooch
  *a silver brooch*
  *pl* brooches
brood
brook
broom
broth
brother
brotherhood
brother-in-law
  *pl* brothers-in-law
brotherly
brought
  *see* bring
brow
browbeat
  browbeat
  browbeating
brown
brownie
  *pl* brownies
browse
  browsed
  browsing
**bruise**
  bruised
  bruising
brunette

brunt
brush
  *pl* brushes
**brusque**
  *adv* brusquely
brusqueness
Brussels sprouts
brutal
  *adv* brutally
brutality
brute
brutish
bubble
  bubbled
  bubbling
bubbly
**buccaneer**
buccaneering
buck
bucket
buckle
  buckled
  buckling
buckler
buckshot
bud
  budded
  budding
Buddhism
**Buddhist**
budge
  budged
  budging
**budgerigar**
budget
  **budgeted**
  budgeting
budgie
buff

buffalo
  *pl* buffaloes
buffer
buffet ['boǒfā]
  *the station buffet: a*
  *buffet supper*
buffet ['bufit]
  *Heavy waves buffet*
  *the boat*
  buffeted
  buffeting
buffoon
buffoonery
bug
  bugged
  bugging
bugbear
bugle
bugler
build
  built
  building
builder
built-up
bulb
bulbous
bulge
  bulged
  bulging
bulimia
bulk
bulky
bulldog
bulldoze
  bulldozed
  bulldozing
bulldozer
bullet
**bulletin**

bullion
bullock
bull's-eye
bully
  *pl* bullies
  bullied
  bullying
bulrush
  *pl* bulrushes
bulwark
bumble-bee
bump
bumper
bumpkin
**bumptious**
bumptiousness
bunch
  *pl* bunches
bundle
  bundled
  bundling
bung
**bungalow**
  *pl* bungalows
bungle
  bungled
  bungling
**bunion**
bunk
bunk-bed
bunker
bunkum
bunny
  *pl* bunnies
bunting
buoy
  *a mooring buoy*
buoyancy
**buoyant**

bur *see* burr
burden
  burdened
  burdening
bureau
  *pl* bureaux,
    bureaus
**bureaucracy**
  *pl* bureaucracies
bureaucratic
burger
burgh
  *Burgh is a Scots
  form of borough*
burglar
burglary
  *pl* burglaries
burgle
  burgled
  burgling
burial
buried
  *see* bury
burlesque
burly
burn
  burnt, burned
  burning
burner
burnish
burr, bur
burrow
burst
  burst
  bursting
bury
  *to bury the corpse*
  buried
  burying

bus
  *pl* buses
bush
  *pl* bushes
bushy
busier, busiest
  *see* busy
**business**
  *pl* businesses
busk
busker
bust
bustle
  bustled
  bustling
busy
  *compar* busier
  *superl* busiest
  *adv* busily
but
  *no-one but her: But
  I didn't know*
butcher
butler
butt
  *to butt in*
butter
buttercup
butterfly
  *pl* butterflies
butterscotch
buttocks
button
  **buttoned**
  buttoning
buttonhole
buttress
  *pl* buttresses
buxom

buy
  *to buy a new car*
  bought
  buying
buyer
buzz
buzzard
buzzer
by
  *written by him:
  Stand by me!*
bye
  *a bye in cricket*
bye-law, by-law
by-election
bygone
bypass
  bypassed
  bypassing
bystander

C

cab
cabaret
**cabbage**
cabin
cabinet
cable
  cabled
  cabling
cache
  *a cache of jewels*
cackle
  cackled
  cackling
cacophonous
cacophony
cactus

28

*pl* cacti,
  cactuses
cad
cadaverous
caddie
  *a golf caddie*
  *pl* caddies
caddy
  *a tea caddy*
  *pl* caddies
cadence
cadet
cadge
  cadged
  cadging
cadger
café
**cafeteria**
  *pl* cafeterias
**caffeine**
caftan
  *see* kaftan
cage
  caged
  caging
cagey, cagy
cairn
cairngorm
Cairo
cajole
  cajoled
  cajoling
cajolery
Cajun
cake
  caked
  caking
calamine
calamitous

calamity
  *pl* calamities
calcium
calculate
  calculated
  calculating
calculation
**calculator**
calculus
**calendar**
calf
  *a cow and her calf:
  the calf of his leg*
  *pl* calves
calibrate
  calibrated
  calibrating
calibre
calico
call
calligraphy
callipers, calipers
callosity
callous
  *hard-hearted and
  callous*
callow
callus
  *a callus on the skin*
  *pl* calluses
calm
calmness
calorie
calorimeter
calumny
  *pl* calumnies
calve
  *when will the cow
  calve?*

calved
calving
calypso
  *pl* calypsos
camber
came
  *see* come
camel
cameo
  *pl* cameos
camera
  *pl* cameras
camomile
**camouflage**
  camouflaged
  camouflaging
camp
**campaign**
  campaigned
  campaigning
campanology
camping
campsite
campus
  *pl* campuses
can
  could
  *He could go now*
can
  canned
  *They canned the
  tomatoes*
  canning
canal
canary
  *pl* canaries
canasta
cancan
cancel

**cancelled**
cancelling
cancer
cancerous
candid
candidacy
candidate
candied
candle
candlestick
candlewick
candour
candy
  pl candies
cane
  caned
  caning
canine
caning
canister
canker
**cannabis**
canned
  see can
cannelloni
cannery
  pl canneries
**cannibal**
cannibalism
cannon
  a cannon in battle
cannonball
cannon into
  cannoned into
  cannoning into
cannot
canoe
  pl canoes
canon

a deacon and a
canon: a canon of
the saints: a law or
canon

cañon
  see canyon
canonization,
  -isation
canonize, -ise
  canonized
  canonizing
canopy
  pl canopies
cant

jargon and cant: a
cant or slope: Did
the boat cant?

  canted
  canting
can't
  = cannot
  I can't go
cantankerous
cantata
  pl cantatas
canteen
canter
  cantered
  cantering
cantilever bridge
canton
canvas

canvas for
painting: a canvas
tent

  pl canvases
**canvass**

to canvass for
votes

canvassed
canvassing
canyon, cañon
cap
  capped
  capping
**capability**
  pl capabilities
capable
capacious
capacitor
capacity
  pl capacities
cape
caper
  capered
  capering
capercaillie,
  capercailzie
**capillary**
  pl capillaries
capital
capitalism
**capitalist**
capitalistic
capitalize, -ise
  capitalized
  capitalizing
capitulate
  capitulated
  capitulating
capitulation
capon
capped
  see cap
caprice
capricious
capsize
  capsized

capsizing
capstan
capsule
captain
 captained
 captaining
captaincy
 *pl* captaincies
caption
captious
**captivate**
 captivated
 captivating
captive
captivity
captor
capture
 captured
 capturing
car
carafe
caramel
carat
 *18 carat gold*
**caravan**
caravanserai
caraway
**carbohydrate**
carbolic
carbon
carbuncle
**carburettor,**
 **carburetter**
carcase, carcass
card
cardboard
cardiac
cardigan
cardinal

cardiology
care
 cared
 caring
carefree
careful
 *adv* carefully
carefulness
careless
carelessness
**career**
 careered
 careering
carer
**caress**
 *pl* caresses
 caressed
 caressing
caretaker
careworn
cargo
 *pl* cargoes
Caribbean
caribou
caricature
caricaturist
**caries**
carillon
carmine
carnage
carnation
carnival
carnivore
carnivorous
carol
 carolled
 carolling
carouse
 caroused

carousing
carp
carpenter
carpentry
carpet
 carpeted
 carpeting
**carriage**
carried
 *see* carry
carrier
carrion
carrot
 *grated carrot*
carry
 carried
 carrying
cart
 *a horse and cart*
cartilage
 *cartilage in the knee*
cartography
carton
 *a carton of milk*
cartoon
 *a Walt Disney cartoon*
cartoonist
cartridge
 *a cartridge for a gun: film cartridge*
cartwheel
carve
 carved
 carving
cascade
 cascaded
 cascading

case
  cased
  casing
casement
cash
  *to cash a cheque:*
  *ready cash*
cashew
**cashier**
  cashiered
  cashiering
cashmere
casino
  *pl* casinos
cask
casket
casserole
**cassette**
cassock
cast
  *the cast of a play: a*
  *cast in his eye: to*
  *cast a play: to cast*
  *a glance*

  cast
  casting
**castanets**
castaway
caste
  *a social caste*
caster
  *see* castor
castigate
  castigated
  castigating
castle
cast-off
castor, caster
castor-oil

castor, caster
  sugar
castrate
  castrated
  castrating
casual
  *adv* casually
**casualty**
  *pl* casualties
cat
cataclysm
catacomb
**catalogue**
  catalogued
  cataloguing
catalyst
catamaran
catapult
cataract
**catarrh**
catastrophe
catastrophic
  *adv*
    catastrophically
catch
  caught
  catching
catchment
catchy
**catechism**
categorical
  *adv* categorically
category
  *pl* categories
cater
  catered
  **catering**
caterer
caterpillar

caterwauling
cathedral
catherine-wheel
cathode ray tube
catholic
Catholic
catkin
cattle
caucus
caught
  *see* catch
cauldron
**cauliflower**
cause
  caused
  causing
causeway
caustic
  *adv* caustically
cauterize, -ise
  cauterized
  cauterizing
caution
cautionary
**cautious**
cavalcade
cavalier
  *Cavaliers and*
  *Roundheads: a*
  *cavalier attitude*
cavalry
  *infantry and*
  *cavalry*
cave
cave in
  caved in
  caving in
cavern
cavernous

caviare, caviar

cavil
  cavilled
  cavilling

cavity
  *pl* cavities

cavort

caw

cayenne

CD-player

cease
  ceased
  ceasing

ceasefire

ceaseless

cedar

cede
  ceded
  ceding

Ceefax ®

**ceiling**
  *He painted the
  ceiling white*

celandine

celebrate
  celebrated
  celebrating

celebration

celebrity
  *pl* celebrities

celery

celestial

celibacy

celibate

cell

  *a prison cell: a
  battery cell: a living
  cell: a monk's cell*

cellist

cello

**Cellophane** ®

cellular
  *cellular blankets*

celluloid

cellulose
  *cellulose paint*

cement

**cemetery**
  *pl* cemeteries

cenotaph

censor
  *a film censor: to
  censor letters*

censored

censoring

censorious

censure
  *to censure a
  naughty child*

censured

censuring

census
  *pl* censuses

cent
  *a dollar and a cent*

centaur

**centenarian**
  *She is a
  centenarian*

centenary
  *She celebrated her
  centenary*
  *pl* centenaries

centennial

centigrade

**centigramme**

**centilitre**

**centimetre**

centipede

central
  *adv* centrally

centralization,
  -isation

centralize, -ise
  centralized
  centralizing

centre

centrifugal

century
  *pl* centuries

ceramic

cereal
  *breakfast cereal:
  barley and other
  cereals*

cerebral

ceremonial

ceremonious

ceremony
  *pl* ceremonies

cerise

certain

certainly

**certainty**
  *pl* certainties

certificate

certify
  certified
  certifying

cessation

cesspool

chafe
  *My shoes chafe my
  heels: to chafe at
  the delay*

chafed

chafing
chaff
  *to chaff each other*
  *good-naturedly*
  chaffed
  chaffing
chaffinch
  *pl* chaffinches
chagrin
chain
  chained
  chaining
chair
  chaired
  chairing
chairman
chalet
chalice
chalk
chalky
challenge
  challenged
  challenging
chamber
chamberlain
chameleon
chamois,
  shammy
champ
**champagne**
champion
  championed
  championing
championship
chance
  chanced
  chancing
chancel
**chancellor**

chancery
chancy
chandelier
change
  changed
  changing
**changeable**
changeling
channel
  **channelled**
  channelling
chant
chanty
  *see* shanty
**chaos**
**chaotic**
  *adv* chaotically
chap
chapel
chaperone
  chaperoned
  chaperoning
chaplain
chapped
chapter
char
  charred
  charring
charabanc
character
**characteristic**
  *adv* character-
    istically
characterization,
  -isation
characterize, -ise
  characterized
  characterizing
charade

charcoal
charge
  charged
  charging
charger
chariot
charioteer
charitable
  *adv* charitably
charity
  *pl* charities
charlatan
charm
charming
charnel-house
chart
  charted
  *They have charted*
  *the coastline*
  charting
charter
  chartered
  *We chartered a*
  *plane*
  chartering
charwoman
chary
chase
  chased
  *The dog chased the*
  *cat*
  chasing
**chasm**
chassis
chaste
  *a chaste woman*
chasten
  chastened
  chastening

chastise
  chastised
  chastising
chastisement
chastity
chat
  chatted
  chatting
château
  *pl* châteaux
chattels
chatter
  chattered
  chattering
chatterbox
chatty
  *adv* chattily
**chauffeur**
cheap
  *at a cheap price*
cheapen
  cheapened
  cheapening
cheat
check
  *a police check on
  cars: to check the
  oil: to check a sum*
checked
  *a checked dress*
checkmate
check-out
cheek
cheeky
  *adv* cheekily
cheep
  *the cheep of a bird:
  to cheep merrily*
  cheeped

cheeping
cheer
  cheered
  cheering
cheerful
  *adv* cheerfully
cheerio
cheerless
cheery
  *adv* cheerily
cheese
cheeseparing
**cheetah**
chef
chemical
  *adv* chemically
chemist
chemistry
cheque
  *a bank cheque*
chequered
  *a chequered career*
**cherish**
cheroot
cherry
  *pl* cherries
cherub
  *pl* cherubs,
    cherubim
chess
chest
chesterfield
chestnut
cheviot
chevron
chew
chic [shēk]
chicanery
chick

chicken
chicken out
  chickened out
  chickening out
chickenpox
chicory
chide
  chided
  chiding
**chief**
chiefly
chieftain
chiffon
chihuahua
**chilblain**
child
  *pl* children
childhood
childish
childlike
children
  *see* child
Chile
chill
chilli, chili
  *chilli pepper: chili
  con carne*
  *pl* chillies,
    chilies
chilly
  *a chilly wind*
chime
  chimed
  chiming
chimney
  *pl* chimneys
chimpanzee
chin
china

35

chinchilla
chink
**chintz**
chip
  chipped
  chipping
chipmunk
chipolata
chiropodist
**chiropody**
chiropractor
chirp
chirpy
  adv chirpily
chirrup
  chirruped
  chirruping
**chisel**
  chiselled
  chiselling
chit
chit-chat
chivalrous
chivalry
chive
**chlorinate**
  chlorinated
  chlorinating
chlorine
**chloroform**
chock-a-block
chock-full
chocolate
choice
choir
  a church choir: a
  children's choir
choke
  choked

choking
cholera
cholesterol
choose
  to choose a book
chose
  He chose a book
chosen
  He has chosen a
  book
choosing
chop
  chopped
  chopping
chopper
choppy
chopsticks
choral
chord
  a musical chord:
  the chord of a
  circle
chore
**choreographer**
**choreography**
chorister
chortle
  chortled
  chortling
chorus
  pl choruses
chose, chosen
  see choose
chow
christen
  christened
  christening
Christian
Christianity

Christmas
chromatic
chrome
chromium
chronic
  adv **chronically**
chronicle
chronicler
chronological
  adv
  chronologically
chronometer
chrysalis
**chrysanthemum**
chubby
chuck
chuckle
  chuckled
  chuckling
chum
chunk
church
  pl churches
churlish
churn
chute
  a rubbish chute:
  The child slid
  down the chute
chutney
  pl chutneys
cider
cigar
**cigarette**
cinder
cinema
**cinnamon**
cipher
circa

circle
circled
circling
circuit
**circuitous**
circular
circulate
circulated
circulating
circulation
circumference
circumlocution
circumspect
circumstances
circumstantial
circumstantiate
circumstantiated
circumstantiating
circumvent
circus
pl circuses
cirrus clouds
**cistern**
citadel
citation
cite

to cite as proof: to
cite as a divorce
co-respondent

cited
citing
citizen
citizenship
citric acid
citrus fruit
city
pl cities
civic
civics

civil
adv civilly
**civilian**
civility
pl civilities
civilization,
-isation
civilize, -ise
civilized
civilizing
clad
claim
claimed
claiming
claimant
clairvoyance
clairvoyant
clamber
clambered
clambering
clammy
clamorous
clamour
clamp
clam up
clammed up
clamming up
clan
clandestine
adv clandestinely
clang
clanger
clank
clannish
clap
clapped
clapping
claret
clarify

clarified
clarifying
clarinet
clarinettist
clarity
clash
pl clashes
class
pl classes
classic
adv classically
classical
classification
classify
classified
classifying
clatter
clattered
clattering
clause
**claustrophobia**
claustrophobic
claw
clay
clayey
claymore
clean
cleaned
cleaning
cleaner
cleanliness
cleanness
cleanse
cleansed
cleansing
clear
cleared
clearing
clearance

clearly
clearness
cleavage
cleave
cleaver
clef
cleft
cleg
clematis
clemency
clement
clench
clergy
clergyman
clerical
clerk
clever
cleverness
cliché
click
**client**
**clientele**
cliff
climate
climatic
climax
  *pl* climaxes
climb
climber
clinch
  *pl* clinches
cling
  clung
  clinging
clinic
clinical
  *adv* clinically
clink
clip

clipped
clipping
clipper
**clique**
cloak
cloche
clock
clockwise
clockwork
clod
clodhopper
clog
  clogged
  clogging
cloister
cloistered
close [klōs]
  *adv* closely
close [klōz]
  closed
  closing
closeness
closet
closet with
  closeted with
  closeting with
close-up
closure
clot
  clotted
  clotting
cloth
  *pl* cloths
  *dish cloths*
clothe
  clothed
  clothing
clothes
  *bedclothes:*

  *children's clothes*
clothing
cloud
cloudy
clove
cloven-hoofed
clover
clown
cloy
  cloyed
  cloying
club
  clubbed
  clubbing
cluck
clue
  *pl* clues
clump
clumsiness
clumsy
  *adv* clumsily
clung
  *see* cling
cluster
  clustered
  clustering
clutch
  *pl* clutches
clutter
  cluttered
  cluttering
coach
  *pl* coaches
coagulate
  coagulated
  coagulating
coal
**coalesce**
  coalesced

coalescing
coalfield
coalition
coarse
*coarse sand: a coarse sense of humour*

*adv* coarsely
coarsen
  coarsened
  coarsening
coarseness
coast
coastal
coaster
coastguard
coat
  coated
  coating
coax
cob
cobalt
cobble
  cobbled
  cobbling
cobbler
cobra
cobweb
cocaine
cochineal
cock
cockade
cockatoo
cockatrice
**cockerel**
cocker spaniel
cockle
cockleshell
cockpit

cockroach
  *pl* cockroaches
cocksure
cocktail
cocky
  *adv* cockily
**cocoa**
**coconut**
cocoon
  cocooned
  cocooning
cod
coddle
  coddled
  coddling
code
codicil
co-driver
coeducation
coerce
  coerced
  coercing
coercion
coercive
coeval
coexist
coexistence
**coffee**
coffer
coffin
cog
cogency
cogent
cogitate
  cogitated
  cogitating
**cognac**
cognizance,
  -isance

cohere
  cohered
  cohering
coherence
coherent
cohesion
cohesive
cohort
coiffure
coil
  coiled
  coiling
coin
  coined
  coining
coinage
coincide
  coincided
  coinciding
**coincidence**
coincidental
coke
**colander**
cold
coldness
coleslaw
colic
**collaborate**
  collaborated
  collaborating
collaboration
collaborator
collage
  *The children made a collage*
collapse
  collapsed
  collapsing
**collapsible**

39

collar
  collared
  collaring
collarbone
collate
  collated
  collating
collateral
collation
**colleague**
collect
collection
collective
  *adv* collectively
collector
college
  *college and
  university*
collegiate
collide
  collided
  colliding
collie
collier
colliery
  *pl* collieries
collision
colloquial
  *adv* colloquially
colloquialism
collusion
cologne
colon
**colonel**
colonial
colonist
colonization,
  -isation
colonize, -ise

colonized
colonizing
colonnade
colony
  *pl* colonies
**colossal**
colour
  coloured
  colouring
colourful
  *adv* colourfully
colourless
colt
column
coma
  *in a deep coma*
comatose
comb
combat
  combated
  combating
combatant
combination
combine
  combined
  combining
combine
  harvester
combustible
combustion
come
  came
  *He came today*
come
  *He has come*
coming
comedian
comedy
  *pl* comedies

comeliness
comely
comet
comfort
comfortable
  *adv* comfortably
comic
comical
  *adv* comically
coming
  *see* come
comma
  *a comma or a full
  stop*
command
commandeer
  commandeered
  commandeering
commander
commandment
commando
  *pl* commandoes
**commemorate**
  commemorated
  commemorating
commemoration
commemorative
commence
  commenced
  commencing
commencement
commend
commendable
commendation
commensurate
comment
commentary
  *pl*
    commentaries

**commentator**
commerce
**commercial**
  *adv*
  commercially
**commiserate**
  commiserated
  commiserating
  commiseration
  commissariat
**commission**
  commissioned
  commissioning
**commissionaire**
  *a cinema*
  *commissionaire*
commissioner
  *the High*
  *Commissioner*
commit
  **committed**
  committing
**commitment**
**committal**
**committee**
commodious
commodity
  *pl* commodities
commodore
common
commoner
commonplace
Commonwealth
commotion
communal
commune
  communed
  communing
**communicate**

communicated
communicating
communication
communicative
communion
communiqué
communism
communist
community
  *pl* communities
commute
  commuted
  commuting
**commuter**
compact
**companion**
companionable
  *adv*
  companionably
company
  *pl* companies
comparable
  *adv* comparably
**comparative**
  *adv*
  comparatively
compare
  compared
  comparing
**comparison**
compartment
compass
  *a compass to find*
  *the direction*
  *pl* compasses
  *The climbers*
  *carried compasses*
compasses
  *Use compasses to*

draw a circle
compassion
compassionate
  *adv* compassion-
  ately
**compatibility**
**compatible**
  *adv* compatibly
compatriot
compel
  **compelled**
  compelling
compensate
  compensated
  compensating
compensation
compère
compete
  competed
  competing
competence
competent
competition
**competitive**
competitor
compilation
compile
  compiled
  compiling
compiler
complacency
complacent
complain
  complained
  complaining
complaint
complement
  *the complement of*
  *a verb: the*

*complement of an angle: make up a full complement*

complementary
*complementary angles: a complementary amount*

complete
  *adv* completely
completed
completing
completeness
completion
complex
  *pl* complexes
complexion
complexity
  *pl* complexities
compliance
compliant
complicate
  complicated
  complicating
complication
complicity
complied
  *see* comply
compliment
  *a compliment to a beautiful woman*

complimentary
  *complimentary remark: complimentary ticket*

comply
  complied
  complying

component
compose
  composed
  composing
composite
composition
compositor
compost
composure
compound
comprehend
comprehensible
comprehension
comprehensive
  *adv* comprehensively
compress
compression
comprise
  comprised
  comprising
compromise
  compromised
  compromising
compulsion
compulsive
  *adv* compulsively
compulsory
  *adv* compulsorily
compunction
computation
compute
  computed
  computing
**computer**
computerization, -isation
computerize,

-ise
computerized
computerizing
comrade
con
  **conned**
  conning
concave
**conceal**
  concealed
  concealing
**concealment**
concede
  conceded
  conceding
**conceit**
**conceited**
conceivable
  *adv* conceivably
**conceive**
  conceived
  conceiving
concentrate
  concentrated
  concentrating
concentration
concentric
concept
conception
concern
concerning
concert
  *a musical concert*
concerted
concertina
concerto
  *pl* concertos
**concession**
conciliate

conciliated
conciliating
conciliation
conciliatory
concise
conciseness
conclude
  concluded
  concluding
conclusion
conclusive
  *adv* conclusively
concoct
concoction
concord
concourse
concrete
concur
  concurred
  concurring
  concurrence
**concurrent**
**concussion**
condemn
  **condemned**
  condemning
condemnation
condemnatory
condensation
condense
  condensed
  condensing
**condescend**
condescending
condescension
condiment
condition
  conditioned
  conditioning

conditional
  *adv*
    conditionally
condole
  condoled
  condoling
  condolences
condom
condone
  condoned
  condoning
conducive
conduct
conduction
conductor
conductress
  *pl*
    conductresses
conduit
cone
coney
  *see* cony
confectioner
**confectionery**
confederacy
confederate
confederation
confer
  conferred
  conferring
**conference**
confess
confession
**confetti**
confidant
  *the king's trusted*
  *confidant*
confidante
  *She was the*

  *queen's confidante*
confide
  confided
  confiding
confidence
confident
  *confident of*
  *success*
confidential
  *adv*
    confidentially
confine
  confined
  confining
confinement
confines
confirm
confirmation
confiscate
  confiscated
  confiscating
confiscation
conflagration
conflict
confluence
conform
conformation
conformity
confound
confront
confrontation
confuse
  confused
  confusing
confusion
**congeal**
  congealed
  congealing
congenial

*adv* congenially
congenital
conger eel
congested
congestion
conglomeration
congratulate
  congratulated
  congratulating
**congratulations**
congratulatory
congregate
  congregated
  congregating
congregation
congregational
congress
  *pl* congresses
congruent
congruity
congruous
conical
conifer
conjectural
conjecture
  conjectured
  conjecturing
conjugal
conjugate
  conjugated
  conjugating
conjugation
conjunction
**conjunctivitis**
conjure
  conjured
  conjuring
conjuror
conman

connect
connection
conned
  *see* con
connive at
  connived at
  conniving at
**connoisseur**
**connotation**
conquer
  conquered
  conquering
conqueror
conquest
**conscience**
  *a bad conscience*
**conscientious**
  *a conscientious*
  *worker*
conscientiousness
**conscious**

  *Is the patient*
  *conscious now?: a*
  *conscious*
  *decision:*
  *conscious of his*
  *disability*

consciousness
conscript
conscription
consecrate
  consecrated
  consecrating
consecration
consecutive
  *adv*
    consecutively
consensus
consent

consequence
consequent
consequential
**consequently**
conservation
conservationist
conservative
conservatory
  *pl*
  conservatories
conserve
  conserved
  conserving
consider
  considered
  considering
considerable
  *adv*
    considerably
considerate
  *adv*
    considerately
consideration
consign
**consignment**
consist
consistency
consistent
**consolation**
console
  consoled
  consoling
consolidate
  consolidated
  consolidating
consolidation
consonant
'consort
  *the Queen's*

*consort*

con'sort
  *to consort with*
  *criminals*

**conspicuous**

conspiracy
  *pl* conspiracies

conspirator

conspire
  conspired
  conspiring

constable

constabulary

constancy

constant

constellation

consternation

constipation

constituency
  *pl*
    constituencies

constituent

**constitute**
  constituted
  constituting

constitutional
  *adv*
    constitutionally

constrain

constraint

constrict

construct

construction

constructive
  *adv*
    constructively

consul

  *He is British consul*
  *in Spain*

consulate

consult

consultant

consultation

consume
  consumed
  consuming

**consumer**

consummate
  consummated
  consummating

consumption

contact

contagious

contain
  contained
  containing

container

contaminate
  contaminated
  contaminating

contamination

contemplate
  contemplated
  contemplating

contemplation

contemporary

contempt

contemptible
  *adv* contemptibly

contemptuous

contend

content

contented

contention

contentious

contentment

contents

contest

contestant

context

**continent**

continental

contingency
  *pl* contingencies

contingent

continual
  *in continual pain:*
  *There have been*
  *continual attempts*
  *on his life*

  *adv* continually

continuance

continuation

continue
  continued
  continuing

continuity

**continuous**
  *a continuous line*
  *of cars*

  *adv* continuously

contort

contortion

contortionist

contour

contraband

contraception

**contraceptive**

contract

contraction

contractor

contradict

contradiction

**contradictory**

contralto
  *pl* contraltos

contraption

contrary
contrast
contravene
  contravened
  contravening
contravention
contretemps
contribute
  contributed
  contributing
contribution
contributor
contrite
  *adv* contritely
contrition
contrivance
contrive
  contrived
  contriving
control
  **controlled**
  controlling
controllable
**controller**
controls
**controversial**
  *adv*
    controversially
controversy
  *pl* controversies
conundrum
conurbation
**convalesce**
  convalesced
  convalescing
convalescence
**convalescent**
convection
convector

convene
  convened
  convening
convener
convenience
**convenient**
convent
convention
conventional
  *adv*
    conventionally
converge
  converged
  converging
convergence
convergent
conversation
conversational
  *adv* conversation-
    ally
converse
  conversed
  conversing
conversion
convert
**convertible**
convex
convey
  **conveyed**
  conveying
conveyance
conveyor belt
convict
conviction
convince
  convinced
  convincing
convivial
  *adv* convivially

conviviality
convocation
**convolvulus**
convoy
  convoyed
  convoying
convulse
  convulsed
  convulsing
convulsion
convulsive
  *adv* convulsively
cony, coney
coo
  cooed
  cooing
cook
cooker
cookery
cooking
cool
  *adv* **coolly**
coolness
coop
  *a chicken coop*
cooper
**co-operate**
  co-operated
  co-operating
co-operation
**co-operative**
  *adv* co-
    operatively
co-opt
  co-opted
  co-opting
coop up
  cooped up
  cooping up

co-ordinate
  co-ordinated
  co-ordinating
co-ordination
coot
cope
  coped
  coping
coping-stone
copious
copper
copperplate
coppice
copra
copse
copy
  *pl* copies
  copied
  copying
copyright
coquette
coquettish
coracle
coral
  *a coral reef: a*
  *necklace of coral*
cord
  *the cord of a*
  *dressing-gown:*
  *spinal cord: vocal*
  *cords*
cordial
  *adv* cordially
cordiality
cordite
cordon
cordon bleu
cordon off
  cordoned off

cordoning off
**corduroy**
core
  cored
  coring
**co-respondent**
  *the co-respondent*
  *in a divorce case*
corgi
  *pl* corgis
coriander
cork
corkscrew
corm
cormorant
corn
cornea
  *pl* corneas
corner
  cornered
  cornering
corner-stone
cornet
  *He plays the*
  *cornet: ice-cream*
  *cornet*
cornflour
  *to thicken the*
  *sauce with*
  *cornflour*
cornflower
  *a pretty blue*
  *cornflower*
cornice
corollary
  *pl* corollaries
**coronary**
  *pl* coronaries
coronation

coroner
coronet
  *a baron's coronet*
corporal
corporate
corporation
corps [kör]
  *corps of an army:*
  *corps de ballet*
  *pl* corps
corpse
  *dead as a corpse*
  *pl* corpses
corpulence
corpulent
corpuscle
corral
  *cattle in the corral:*
  *a corral of wagons*
correct
correction
corrective
correspond
**correspondence**
correspondent
  *a letter from a*
  *regular*
  *correspondent*
**corridor**
corrigendum
  *pl* corrigenda
**corroborate**
  corroborated
  corroborating
corroboration
corroborative
corrode
  corroded
  corroding

corrosion
corrosive
**corrugated**
corrupt
corruptible
corruption
corset
cortège
cosh
  pl coshes
cosmetic
cosmic
cosmonaut
**cosmopolitan**
cosset
  cosseted
  cosseting
cost
  cost
  *That coat cost £30: That has cost him his life*
  costed
  *Have you costed the research project?*
  costing
costermonger
costliness
costly
costume
cosy
  adv cosily
cot
coterie
cottage
cottager
cotton
cottonwool

couch
  pl couches
couch grass
couchant
cougar
cough
could
  see can
coulomb
council
  *the town council*
**councillor**
  *a town councillor*
counsel
  *He was her counsel in the divorce case*
counsel
  *to counsel him to stay*
  counselled
  counselling
counsellor
  *a marriage guidance counsellor*
count
countenance
  countenanced
  countenancing
counter
  countered
  countering
counteract
**counterfeit**
counterfoil
countermand
counterpane
counterpart
countersign

countess
  pl countesses
countless
country
  pl countries
countryside
county
  pl counties
coup
  *The president was killed in the coup*
couple
  coupled
  coupling
couplet
coupon
courage
**courageous**
courgette
courier
course
  *the course of the river: in the course of time: in due course*
coursing
court
**courteous**
courtesy
  *He behaved with politeness and courtesy*
courtier
courtly
court-martial
  pl
    courts-martial
courtship
courtyard

cousin
couture
cove
coven
covenant
covenanter
cover
  covered
  covering
coverage
coverlet
covert
covet
  coveted
  coveting
covetous
covetousness
covey
  *pl* coveys
coward
cowardice
cowardly
cowboy
cowed
cower
  cowered
  cowering
cowherd
cowl
cowslip
cox
coxcomb
coxswain
coy
coyote
crab
crabbed
crack
cracker

crackle
  crackled
  crackling
cradle
  cradled
  cradling
craft
craftsman
crafty
  *adv* craftily
crag
craggy
cram
  crammed
  cramming
cramp
  cramped
  crampon
cranberry
  *pl* cranberries
crane
crank
cranky
cranny
  *pl* crannies
crape
  *see* crêpe
crash
  *pl* crashes
crass
crate
crater
cravat
crave
  craved
  craving
crawl
crayfish
crayon

craze
crazy
  *adv* crazily
creak
  *the creak of the
  stairs: The beams
  began to creak*
cream
  creamed
  creaming
creamy
crease
  creased
  creasing
create
  created
  creating
creation
creative
creator
creature
**crèche**
credentials
credibility
credible
  *adv* credibly
credit
  **credited**
  crediting
creditable
creditor
credulity
credulous
creed
creek
  *fishing-boats in the
  creek: canoeing in
  the creek*
creep

crept
creeping
creeper
cremate
  cremated
  cremating
cremation
**crematorium**
Creole
**creosote**
crêpe, crape
crept
  *see* creep
**crescent**
cress
crest
crestfallen
crevasse
  *a crevasse in the ice*
crevice
  *a crevice in the rock*
crew
crewcut
crib
  cribbed
  cribbing
cribbage
crick
cricket
cricketer
cried
  *see* cry
crier
cries
  *see* cry
crime
criminal

*adv* criminally
crimson
cringe
  cringed
  cringing
crinkle
  crinkled
  crinkling
crinkly
crinoline
cripple
  crippled
  crippling
**crisis**
  *pl* crises
crisp
crispy
criss-cross
**criterion**
  *pl* criteria
critic
critical
  *adv* critically
criticism
criticize, -ise
  criticized
  criticizing
croak
croaky
crochet ['krōshā]
  *to crochet a shawl*
**crocheted**
  crocheting
crock
crockery
**crocodile**
crocus
  *pl* crocuses
croft

crofter
croissant
crone
crony
  *pl* cronies
crook
crooked
crookedness
croon
  crooned
  crooning
crooner
crop
  cropped
  cropping
cropper
croquet
cross
  *pl* crosses
  crossed
  crossing
cross-examine
  cross-examined
  cross-examining
crossing
crossness
crossroads
cross-section
crotchet
  *a musical crotchet*
crotchety
crouch
croup
**croupier**
crow
  crowed,
  *(old)* crew
  *The baby crowed:*

*The cock crew*
crowing
crowbar
crowd
crowded
crown
**crucial**
 *adv* crucially
crucible
crucifix
 *pl* crucifixes
**crucifixion**
crucify
 crucified
 crucifying
crude
 *adv* crudely
crudeness
crudity
cruel
 *adv* **cruelly**
cruelty
**cruise**
 cruised
 cruising
cruiser
crumb
crumble
 crumbled
 crumbling
crumbly
crumpet
crumple
 crumpled
 crumpling
crunch
crusade
crusader
crush

crust
crustacean
crusty
crutch
 *pl* crutches
crux
cry
 *pl* cries
 cried
 crying
crypt
**cryptic**
 *adv* cryptically
crystal
crystalline
crystallization,
 -isation
crystallize, -ise
 crystallized
 crystallizing
cub
cube
cubic
**cubicle**
cuckoo
 *pl* cuckoos
cucumber
cud
cuddle
 cuddled
 cuddling
cudgel
cue
 *a cue in billiards:*
 *The actor missed*
 *his cue*
cuff
 *pl* cuffs
cufflinks

**cuisine**
cul-de-sac
culinary
cull
culminate
 culminated
 culminating
culmination
culpable
culprit
cult
cultivate
 cultivated
 cultivating
cultivation
cultural
culture
cultured
cumbersome
cumin
cummerbund
cumulative
cumulus
cunning
cup
 cupped
 cupping
cupboard
**cupful**
 *pl* cupfuls
Cupid
cupidity
cupola
cup-tie
cur
**curable**
curate
curator
curb

to act as a curb on
his extravagances:
*Curb your desires!*

curd

curdle
curdled
curdling

cure
cured
curing

curfew

curio
*pl* curios

**curiosity**
*pl* curiosities

**curious**

curl

curlew

curling

curly

currant
*currants and
sultanas: black and
red currants*

**currency**
*pl* currencies

current
*a current of air: an
electric current: the
current financial
year: a current
account: That
rumour is current*

**curriculum**
*pl* curricula,
curriculums

**curriculum vitae**
*pl* curricula
vitae

curry
*pl* curries
curried
currying

curse
cursed
cursing

cursor

cursory
*adv* cursorily

curt

curtail
curtailed
curtailing

curtailment

curtain

curtness

curtsy, curtsey
*She made a curtsy
to the queen*
*pl* curtsies,
curtseys
curtsied
curtsying,
curtseying

curvature

curve
curved
curving

cushion
cushioned
cushioning

cushy

custard

custodian

custody

custom

**customary**
*adv* customarily

customer

cut
cut
cutting

cute
*adv* cutely

cuteness

cuticle

cutlass
*pl* cutlasses

cutlery

cutlet

cutting

cuttlefish

cut-up

cyanide

cyberspace

cyclamen

cycle
cycled
cycling

cyclist

cyclone

cygnet
*a swan and her
cygnet*

cylinder

cylindrical
*adv* cylindrically

cymbal
*He plays the
cymbals*

**cynic**

cynical
*adv* cynically

**cynicism**

**cynosure**

cypress
*pl* cypresses

Cyprus
cyst
cystitis
czar
*see* tsar
Czech

**D**

dab
 dabbed
 dabbing
dabble
 dabbled
 dabbling
**dachshund**
dad
daddy
 *pl* daddies
dado
 *pl* dadoes,
 dados
**daffodil**
daft
dagger
**dahlia**
daily
 *pl* dailies
daintiness
dainty
 *adv* daintily
dairy
 *milk from the dairy*
 *pl* dairies
**dais**
 *pl* daises
daisy
 *pl* daisies
dale

dalliance
dally
 dallied
 dallying
dam
 *to dam a river*
 dammed
 *He dammed up the river*
 damming
**damage**
 damaged
 damaging
damask
dame
dammed
 *see* dam
damn
 *to damn a soul: Damn! I've dropped it*
 damned
 *a damned soul: that damned dog*
 damning
damnable
damnation
damned
 *see* damn
damp
dampen
 dampened
 dampening
damper
dampness
damsel
damson
dance
 danced

dancing
dancer
dandelion
**dandruff**
danger
dangerous
dangle
 dangled
 dangling
Danish
dank
dapper
dappled
dare
 dared
 daring
daredevil
dark
darken
 darkened
 darkening
darkness
darling
darn
dart
dartboard
dash
 *pl* dashes
dashing
dastardly
data
 *sing* datum
date
 dated
 dating
datum
 *see* data
daub
 daubed

daubing
daughter
daughter-in-law
 pl daughters-in-
 law
daunt
dauntless
dawdle
 dawdled
 dawdling
dawn
day
daydream
daze
 dazed
 dazing
dazzle
 dazzled
 dazzling
deacon
deaconess
 pl deaconesses
dead
deaden
 deadened
 deadening
deadline
deadliness
deadly
deadness
deaf
deafen
 deafened
 deafening
deafness
deal
 dealt
 dealing
dealer

dean
dear
 *a dear friend: The*
 *shoes are too dear*
dearly
dearness
dearth
death
deathly
debar
 debarred
 debarring
debase
 debased
 debasing
 debasement
**debatable**
debate
 debated
 debating
**debauched**
debauchery
debilitate
 debilitated
 debilitating
**debility**
debit
 debited
 debiting
debonair
débris, debris
debt
debtor
début, debut
debutante
decade
decadence
decadent
decanter

decapitate
 decapitated
 decapitating
decathlon
decay
 decayed
 decaying
decease
**deceased**
**deceit**
deceitful
 *adv* deceitfully
**deceive**
 deceived
 deceiving
deceiver
decelerate
 decelerated
 decelerating
December
decency
decent
deception
deceptive
 *adv* deceptively
decibel
decide
 decided
 deciding
decidedly
**deciduous**
decimal
decimalization,
 -isation
decimalize, -ise
 decimalized
 decimalizing
decimate
 decimated

54

decimating
**decipher**
deciphered
deciphering
decision
decisive
*adv* decisively
deck
declaim
declaimed
declaiming
declamation
declamatory
declaration
declare
declared
declaring
decline
declined
declining
decode
decoded
decoding
decommission
decommissioned
decommissioning
decompose
decomposed
decomposing
decomposition
décor, decor
decorate
decorated
decorating
decoration
decorative
*adv* decoratively
decorator
decorous

decorum
decoy
**decoyed**
decoying
**decrease**
decreased
decreasing
decree
**decreed**
decreeing
decrepit
decry
*to decry modern youth*
decried
decrying
dedicate
dedicated
dedicating
dedication
deduce
deduced
deducing
deduct
deduction
deed
deep
deepen
deepened
deepening
deer
*He shot a deer*
*pl* deer
deface
defaced
defacing
defacement
defamation
defamatory

defame
defamed
defaming
default
defaulter
**defeat**
defeated
defeating
defect
defection
defective
defence
defenceless
defend
**defendant**
defensible
defensive
*adv* defensively
defer
deferred
deferring
deference
deferential
*adv* deferentially
defiance
defiant
deficiency
*pl* deficiencies
deficient
deficit
defied
*see* defy
defile
defiled
defiling
defilement
define
defined
defining

**definite**
  *adv* **definitely**
definition
definitive
  *adv* definitively
deflate
  deflated
  deflating
deflation
deflect
deflection
deform
deformed
deformity
  *pl* deformities
defraud
defray
  defrayed
  defraying
defrost
deft
defunct
defy
  **defied**
  defying
degenerate
  degenerated
  degenerating
degenerative
degradation
degrade
  degraded
  degrading
degree
**dehydrate**
  dehydrated
  dehydrating
dehydration
deify

deified
deifying
**deign**
deigned
deigning
deity
  *pl* deities
dejected
dejection
delay
  delayed
  delaying
delectable
  *adv* delectably
delegate
  delegated
  delegating
delegation
delete
  deleted
  deleting
deleterious
deletion
Delhi
**deliberate**
  *adv* deliberately
  deliberated
  deliberating
deliberation
delicacy
  *pl* delicacies
delicate
  *adv* delicately
**delicatessen**
**delicious**
delight
delighted
delightful
  *adv* delightfully

delinquency
**delinquent**
**delirious**
delirium
deliver
delivered
delivering
deliverance
delivery
  *pl* deliveries
dell
delphinium
delta
delude
deluded
deluding
deluge
deluged
deluging
delusion
  *He's under the*
  *delusion that he's*
  *Napoleon*
delve
delved
delving
demand
demean
demeaned
demeaning
**demeanour**
demented
demise
demo
demob
demobbed
demobbing
demobilization,
-isation

demobilize, -ise
  demobilized
  demobilizing
democracy
  *pl* democracies
democrat
democratic
  *adv*
  democratically
demolish
demolition
demon
demonstrable
  *adv*
  demonstrably
**demonstrate**
  demonstrated
  demonstrating
demonstration
demonstrative
demonstrator
demoralize, -ise
  demoralized
  demoralizing
demote
  demoted
  demoting
demotion
demur
  demurred
  demurring
demure
  *adv* demurely
demureness
den
denial
denied
  *see* deny
denier

denigrate
  denigrated
  denigrating
denim
denizen
denomination
denominational
denominator
denote
  denoted
  denoting
denounce
  denounced
  denouncing
dénouement
dense
  *adv* densely
denseness
density
  *pl* densities
dent
dental
dentist
dentistry
denture
denudation
denude
  denuded
  denuding
**denunciation**
deny
  **denied**
  denying
**deodorant**
deodorize, -ise
  deodorized
  deodorizing
depart
department

departure
depend
dependable
**dependant**
  *His wife and*
  *children are his*
  *dependants*
**dependence**
dependent
  *His wife is*
  *dependent on him*
depict
depilatory
deplete
  depleted
  depleting
depletion
deplorable
  *adv* deplorably
deplore
  deplored
  deploring
deploy
  deployed
  deploying
depopulated
deport
deportation
deportment
depose
  deposed
  deposing
deposit
deposition
depository
  *pl* depositories
depot, depôt
depraved
depravity

deprecate
*to deprecate her behaviour*
deprecated
deprecating
deprecation
depreciate
*The pound will depreciate*
depreciated
depreciating
depreciation
depredation
depress
depression
deprivation
deprive
deprived
depriving
**depth**
deputation
deputize, -ise
deputized
deputizing
deputy
*pl* deputies
derail
derailed
derailing
**derailment**
deranged
derangement
derby
derelict
dereliction
deride
derided
deriding
derision

derisive
*adv* derisively
derivation
derivative
derive
derived
deriving
**dermatitis**
dermatologist
dermatology
**derogatory**
*adv* derogatorily
derrick
descant
**descend**
descended
descending
**descendant**
*He is a descendant of Queen Victoria*
descendent
*a descendent slope*
descent
describe
described
describing
description
descriptive
descry
*to descry a ship at sea*
descried
descrying
desecrate
desecrated
desecrating
desecration
deselect
de'sert

*to desert from the army: to desert one's family*
'desert
*a desert island*
deserter
desertion
deserve
deserved
deserving
deservedly
**desiccate**
desiccated
desiccating
**desiccation**
design
designed
designing
designate
designated
designating
designation
desirability
desirable
*adv* desirably
desire
desired
desiring
desirous
desist
desk
desolate
desolated
desolation
despair
despaired
despairing
despatch
*see* dispatch

desperado
  *pl* desperadoes,
  desperados
**desperate**
  *adv* desperately
desperation
despicable
  *adv* despicably
despise
  despised
  despising
despite
despoil
  despoiled
  despoiling
despoliation
despondency
despondent
despot
despotic
  *adv* despotically
despotism
dessert
  *the dessert course*
destination
destined
destiny
destitute
destroy
  destroyed
  destroying
destroyer
destructible
destruction
destructive
desultory
  *adv* desultorily
**detach**
  detached

detaching
**detachable**
detachment
detail
  detailed
  detailing
detain
  detained
  detaining
detect
detection
detective
detector
détente
detention
deter
  **deterred**
  deterring
**detergent**
deteriorate
  deteriorated
  deteriorating
deterioration
determination
determine
  determined
  determining
**deterrent**
detest
detestable
  *adv* detestably
detestation
detonate
  detonated
  detonating
detonator
detour
detoxification
detract

detraction
detriment
detrimental
**deuce**
devastate
  devastated
  devastating
devastation
**develop**
  **developed**
  developing
  developer
**development**
deviate
  deviated
  deviating
deviation
device
  *a device for boring
  holes*
devil
devilish
devilry
devious
devise
  *to devise a plan*
  devised
  devising
devoid
devolution
  *the devolution of
  power from central
  government*
devolve
  devolved
  devolving
devote
  devoted
  devoting

devotee
devotion
devour
devout
devoutness
dew
*the morning dew*
dewy
dexterity
dexterous,
dextrous
**diabetes**
**diabetic**
diabolic
diabolical
*adv* diabolically
diadem
diagnose
diagnosed
diagnosing
**diagnosis**
*pl* diagnoses
diagnostic
diagonal
*adv* diagonally
diagram
diagrammatic
dial
dialled
dialling
dialect
dialectal
**dialogue**
dialysis
diameter
diametric
*adv*
diametrically
diamond

diaphanous
**diaphragm**
**diarrhoea**
diary
*Make a note in
your diary*
*pl* diaries
diatribe
dice
dictate
dictated
dictating
dictation
dictator
dictatorial
*adv* dictatorially
diction
dictionary
*pl* dictionaries
did
*see* do
die
*to die young*
died
*He died young*
dying
*dying young*
diesel
diet
dieted
dieting
dietetic
differ
differed
differing
**difference**
**different**
differentiate
differentiated

differentiating
differentiation
difficult
difficulty
*pl* difficulties
diffidence
diffident
diffuse
dig
dug
digging
digest
digestible
digestion
digestive
digger
digit
digital
digitalis
dignified
dignitary
*pl* dignitaries
dignity
digress
digression
dike, dyke
**dilapidated**
dilatation
dilate
dilated
dilating
dilatory
**dilemma**
**dilettante**
diligence
diligent
dilly-dally
dilly-dallied
dilly-dallying

dilute
  diluted
  diluting
dilution
dim
  dimmed
  dimming
dimension
dimensional
**diminish**
**diminution**
diminutive
dimness
dimple
din
  dinned
  dinning
dine
  dined
  dining
dinghy
  *a sailing dinghy*
  *pl* dinghies
dinginess
dingy
  *dark and dingy*
dinner
**dinosaur**
dint
diocesan
diocese
dip
  dipped
  dipping
**diphtheria**
**diphthong**
diploma
  *pl* diplomas
diplomacy

diplomat
diplomatic
  *adv*
  diplomatically
dire
direct
  directed
  directing
direction
directly
directness
director
directory
  *pl* directories
dirge
dirt
dirtiness
dirty
  *adv* dirtily
  dirtied
  dirtying
disability
  *pl* disabilities
disable
  disabled
  disabling
disablement
disabuse
  disabused
  disabusing
disadvantage
disadvantaged
**disadvan-**
  **tageous**
disaffected
disagree
  **disagreed**
  disagreeing
  **disagreeable**

  *adv*
  disagreeably
**disagreement**
disallow
disappear
  **disappeared**
  disappearing
**disappearance**
**disappoint**
  disappointed
  disappointment
**disapproval**
disapprove
  disapproved
  disapproving
disarm
disarming
disarrange
  disarranged
  disarranging
  disarrangement
disarray
disaster
**disastrous**
disband
**disbelief**
  *He looked at me in
  disbelief*
**disbelieve**
  *to disbelieve a
  story*
  disbelieved
  disbelieving
disburse
disc, disk
discard
discern
discernible
  *adv* discernibly

discerning
discernment
discharge
discharged
discharging
disciple
disciplinarian
disciplinary
**discipline**
disclaim
disclaimer
disclose
disclosed
disclosing
disclosure
disco
discoloration,
discolouration
discolour
discoloured
discolouring
discomfiture
discomfort
disconcert
disconnect
disconnection
disconsolate
*adv*
disconsolately
discontent
discontented
discontentment
discontinue
discontinued
discontinuing
discord
discordant
**discothèque**
discount

discourage
discouraged
**discouraging**
discouragement
discourse
discoursed
discoursing
**discourteous**
discover
discovered
discovering
discoverer
discovery
*pl* discoveries
discredit
discredited
discrediting
discreditable
discreet
**discrepancy**
*pl* discrepancies
discretion
discriminate
discriminated
discriminating
**discrimination**
discus
*He throws the
discus*
discuss
*to discuss a
problem*
**discussion**
disdain
disdained
disdaining
disdainful
*adv* disdainfully
**disease**

diseased
disembark
disembarkation
disembodied
disengage
disengaged
disengaging
disentangle
disentangled
disentangling
disfavour
disfigure
disfigured
disfiguring
disfigurement
disgorge
disgorged
disgorging
disgrace
disgraced
disgracing
disgraceful
*adv*
disgracefully
disgruntled
**disguise**
disguised
disguising
disgust
disgusted
dish
*pl* dishes
dishearten
disheartened
disheartening
**dishevelled**
dishonest
dishonesty
dishonour

**dishonourable**
  *adv*
  dishonourably
**disillusion**
  disillusioned
  disillusioning
  disillusionment
disinclined
disinfect
**disinfectant**
disinherit
  **disinherited**
  disinheriting
disintegrate
  disintegrated
  disintegrating
  disintegration
disinterested
disjointed
disk
  *see* disc
dislike
  disliked
  disliking
dislocate
  dislocated
  dislocating
  dislocation
dislodge
  dislodged
  dislodging
disloyal
  *adv* disloyally
disloyalty
dismal
  *adv* dismally
dismantle
  dismantled
  dismantling

dismay
  dismayed
  dismaying
dismember
  dismembered
  dismembering
  dismemberment
dismiss
**dismissal**
dismount
disobedience
disobedient
disobey
  **disobeyed**
  disobeying
disobliging
disorder
  disordered
  disorderliness
  disorderly
disown
**disparage**
  disparaged
  disparaging
  disparagement
disparity
  *pl* disparities
dispassionate
  *adv*
    dispassionately
dispatch,
  despatch
  *pls* dispatches,
    despatches
dispel
  **dispelled**
  dispelling
dispensable
dispensary

  *pl*
    dispensaries
dispensation
dispense
  dispensed
  dispensing
  dispenser
dispersal
disperse
  dispersed
  dispersing
dispirited
displace
  displaced
  displacing
  displacement
display
  displayed
  displaying
displease
  displeased
  displeasing
displeasure
disposable
**disposal**
dispose
  disposed
  disposing
disposition
**dispossess**
disproportionate
  *adv* disproportion-
    ately
disprove
disputable
disputation
dispute
  disputed
  disputing

disqualification
disqualify
  disqualified
  disqualifying
disquiet
disquieting
disregard
disrepair
disreputable
  *adv* disreputably
disrepute
disrespect
disrespectful
  *adv*
    disrespectfully
disrupt
disruption
disruptive
**dissatisfaction**
**dissatisfy**
  dissatisfied
  dissatisfying
**dissect**
dissemble
  dissembled
  dissembling
**disseminate**
  disseminated
  disseminating
  dissemination
dissension
**dissent**
  dissented
  dissenting
dissenter
dissertation
disservice
dissident
**dissimilar**

dissimilarity
  *pl*
  dissimilarities
dissimulate
  dissimulated
  dissimulating
dissipate
  **dissipated**
  dissipating
**dissipation**
**dissociate**
  dissociated
  dissociating
  dissociation
**dissolute**
dissolution
dissolve
  dissolved
  dissolving
**dissonance**
dissonant
**dissuade**
  dissuaded
  dissuading
distaff
distance
distant
distaste
distasteful
  *adv* distastefully
distemper
distend
distension
distil
  **distilled**
  distilling
distillation
**distillery**
  *pl* distilleries

distinct
distinction
distinctive
**distinguish**
distinguished
distort
distortion
distract
distraction
**distraught**
distress
distribute
  distributed
  distributing
distribution
district
distrust
distrustful
  *adv* distrustfully
disturb
disturbance
**disuse**
disused
ditch
  *pl* ditches
dither
  dithered
  dithering
ditto
ditty
  *pl* ditties
divan
dive
  dived
  diving
diver
diverge
  diverged
  diverging

divergence
divergent
diverse
diversify
  diversified
  diversifying
diversion
diversity
divert
divest
divide
  divided
  dividing
dividend
divination
divine
  divined
  divining
divinity
  *pl* divinities
divisibility
**divisible**
division
divisional
divisive
divisor
divorce
  divorced
  divorcing
divorcee
divulge
  divulged
  divulging
dizziness
dizzy
do
  does, do
  did
  *He did it*

done
  *He has done it*
doing
docile
  *adv* docilely
docility
dock
docker
docket
doctor
  doctored
  doctoring
doctrinal
doctrine
document
**documentary**
  *pl*
    documentaries
dodder
doddery
dodge
  dodged
  dodging
dodo
  *pl* dodos,
    dodoes
doe
  *a buck and a doe*
doer
does
  *see* do
doff
dog
  dogged
  dogging
dogged
  *adv* doggedly
**doggerel**
dogma

dogmatic
  *adv*
    dogmatically
doily, doyley
  *a doily for a cake*
doing
  *see* do
doldrums
dole
doleful
  *adv* dolefully
dolefulness
dole out
  doled out
  doling out
dollar
dolly
  *a child's dolly: a
  dolly bird*
  *pl* dollies
dolphin
dolt
domain
dome
domestic
  *adv*
    domestically
domesticated
domesticity
domicile
dominance
dominant
dominate
  dominated
  dominating
domination
domineer
  domineered
**domineering**

dominion
domino
  *pl* dominoes
don
  donned
  donning
**donate**
  donated
  donating
donation
done
  *see* do
donkey
  *pl* donkeys
donor
don't
  = do not
doom
  doomed
door
doorway
dope
  doped
  doping
dormant
dormer window
dormitory
  *pl* dormitories
dormouse
  *pl* dormice
dorsal
dose
  dosed
  dosing
doss down
dossier
dot
dotage
dote on

doted on
doting on
dotted
double
  *adv* doubly
  doubled
  doubling
double-barrelled
doublet
**doubt**
  doubted
  doubting
doubtful
  *adv* doubtfully
doubtless
dough
  *dough for bread*
doughnut
dove
dovecote
dovetail
  dovetailed
  dovetailing
dowdy
  *adv* dowdily
down
downfall
downstairs
downtrodden
downwards
dowry
  *pl* dowries
doyley
  *see* doily
doze
  dozed
  dozing
dozen
drab

draft
  *a rough draft: to draft a plan*
drag
  dragged
  dragging
dragon
  *St George and the dragon*
dragonfly
  *pl* dragonflies
dragoon
  *the dragoon guards: Did he dragoon you into going?*
  dragooned
  dragooning
drain
drainage
drake
drama
  *pl* dramas
dramatic
  *adv* dramatically
dramatist
dramatization, -isation
dramatize, -ise
  dramatized
  dramatizing
drank
  *see* drink
drape
  draped
  draping
draper
drapery
drastic

*adv* **drastically**
draught
  *a cold draught: a*
  *draught of ale*
draughtsman
**draughty**
draw
  drew
  *He drew a sketch*
  drawn
  *He has drawn a*
  *sketch*
  drawing
drawer
drawl
drawn
  *see* draw
dread
dreadful
  *adv* dreadfully
dreadfulness
dream
  dreamed,
   dreamt
  dreaming
dreamy
  *adv* dreamily
dreary
  *adv* drearily
dredge
  dredged
  dredging
dredger
dregs
drench
dress
  *pl* dresses
  dressed
  dressing

dresser
drew
  *see* draw
drey
  *pl* dreys
dribble
  dribbled
  dribbling
dried
  *see* dry
drift
driftwood
drill
drily
  *see* dry
drink
  drank
  *He drank some*
  *water*
  drunk
  *He has drunk some*
  *water*
  drinking
drip
  dripped
  dripping
drip-dry
  drip-dried
  drip-drying
drive
  drove
  *He drove her car*
  driven
  *He has driven her*
  *car*
  driving
drivel
  drivelled
  drivelling

driven
  *see* drive
driver
drizzle
drizzled
drizzling
drizzly
droll
dromedary
  *pl* dromedaries
drone
droned
droning
drool
**drooled**
drooling
droop
**drooped**
drooping
drop
dropped
dropping
droplet
droppings
dross
drought
drove
  *see* drive
drove
drown
drowsy
  *adv* drowsily
drudge
drudged
drudging
drudgery
drug
drugged
drugging

druggist
drum
  drummed
  drumming
drummer
drumstick
drunk
  *see* drink
drunkard
drunken
**drunkenness**
dry
  *adv* dryly, drily
  dried
  drying
dryad
dry-clean
  dry-cleaned
  dry-cleaning
dual
  *dual-purpose: a dual carriageway*
dub
  dubbed
  dubbing
Dubai
dubiety
**dubious**
ducal
duchess
  *pl* duchesses
duchy
  *pl* duchies
duck
  ducked
  ducking
duck
  *ducks and drakes*
duckling

duct
dud
dudgeon
  *in high dudgeon*
due
  *Your account is due: Go due south: death due to starvation*
duel
  *They fought a duel*
duellist
dues
duet
duffel-coat,
  duffle-coat
dug
  *see* dig
dug-out
duke
dukedom
dulcet
dulcimer
dull
  *adv* dully
  *He spoke dully and boringly*
dullness
duly
  *He duly arrived*
dumb
  *adv* dumbly
**dumbfound**
dumbness
dummy
  *pl* dummies
dump
dumpling
dumpy

dun
  dunned
  dunning
dunce
dune
dung
**dungarees**
dungeon
  *jailed in a dungeon*
dupe
  duped
  duping
duplicate
  duplicated
  duplicating
duplication
duplicity
durable
  *adv* durably
duration
**duress**
during
dusk
dusky
dust
duster
dusty
Dutch
dutiable
**dutiful**
  *adv* dutifully
duty
  *pl* duties
duvet
dux
  *the dux of the school*
dwarf
  *pl* dwarfs,

dwarves
dwarfed
dwarfing
dwell
  dwelled, dwelt
  dwelling
dwindle
  dwindled
  dwindling
dye
  *to dye a dress red*
  dyed
  *She dyed her dress*
  dyeing
  *dyeing a dress red*
dying
  *see* die
dyke
  *see* dike
dynamic
  *adv* dynamically
**dynamite**
dynamo
  *pl* dynamos
dynastic
dynasty
  *pl* dynasties
**dysentery**
dysgraphia
dyslexia
**dyspepsia**
dyspeptic

# E

each
eager
eagerness
eagle

ear
eardrum
earl
earliness
early
  *compar* earlier
  *superl* earliest
  *adv* early
earmark
earn
earnest
earnings
earth
earthenware
earthly
  *in this earthly life:*
  *no earthly use*
earthquake
earthy
  *an earthy sense of*
  *humour: These*
  *potatoes are very*
  *earthy*
earwig
ease
  eased
  easing
easel
easier, easiest
  *see* easy
east
Easter
easterly
  *an easterly wind*
eastern
  *eastern customs*
eastward
eastwards
easy

  *compar* easier
  *superl* easiest
  *adv* easily
eat
  ate
  *He ate a cake*
  eaten
  *He has eaten a*
  *cake*
  eating
eatable
eaten
  *see* eat
eaves
eavesdrop
  eavesdropped
  eavesdropping
ebb
ebony
ebullience
ebullient
**eccentric**
eccentricity
  *pl* eccentricities
**ecclesiastic**
ecclesiastical
echo
  *pl* echoes
eclipse
  *an eclipse of the*
  *sun: to eclipse his*
  *glory*
  eclipsed
  eclipsing
ecological
  *adv* ecologically
ecologist
ecology
**economic**

economic *(continued)* the country's economic future: an economic rent

*adv*
economically
economical
*economical use of supplies: He is extravagant; she is economical*

*adv*
economically
economics
economist
economize, -ise
economized
economizing
economy
*pl* economies
**ecstasy**
*pl* ecstasies
ecstatic
*adv* ecstatically
**eczema**
eddy
*pl* eddies
edge
edged
edging
edgeways
edgy
*adv* edgily
edible
edict
edification
edifice
edify
edified
edifying

edit
edited
editing
edition
*a new edition of his book: the evening edition of the newspaper*

editor
editorial
*adv* editorially
educate
educated
educating
education
educational
*adv*
educationally
eel
eerie
*an eerie silence: a dark eerie house*

*adv* eerily
eeriness
efface
effaced
effacing
effect
*the effect of the drug: the effect of the new lighting: The new law is not yet in effect: goods and effects: to effect a reconciliation*
effected
effecting
**effective**
*adv* effectively

effectual
*adv* effectually
effeminate
*adv* effeminately
**effervesce**
effervesced
effervescing
**effervescence**
effervescent
**efficacious**
efficacy
efficiency
**efficient**
effigy
*pl* effigies
effluent
*The factory's effluent caused disease*

effort
effortless
**effrontery**
effusive
*adv* effusively
egg
egg on
egged on
egging on
egoism
egoist
egoistic
*adv* egoistically
egotism
egotist
egotistic
*adv* egotistically
Egypt
eiderdown
eider duck

eight
eighteen
eighteenth
eighth
**eightieth**
eighty
Einstein
Eire
either
ejaculate
　ejaculated
　ejaculating
ejaculation
eject
ejection
ejector
eke out
　eked out
　eking out
**elaborate**
　elaborated
　elaborating
élan
elapse
　elapsed
　elapsing
elastic
elasticity
elated
elation
elbow
　*pl* elbows
　elbowed
　elbowing
elder
　*the elder of the*
　*(two) brothers*
elderberry
　*pl* elderberries

elderly
eldest
　*the eldest of four*
　*brothers*
elect
election
electioneer
　electioneered
　electioneering
electorate
electric
　*adv* electrically
electrical
　*adv* electrically
**electrician**
electricity
electrify
　electrified
　electrifying
electrocute
　electrocuted
　electrocuting
electrode
electron
electronic
　*adv*
　electronically
electronics
elegance
elegant
elegy
　*pl* elegies
element
elementary
elephant
elevate
　elevated
　elevating
elevation

elevator
eleven
**elevenses**
eleventh
elf
　*pl* elves
elfin
elfish
elicit
　*to elicit*
　*information*
　elicited
　eliciting
eligibility
eligible
　*an eligible*
　*bachelor: eligible*
　*for the job*
eliminate
　eliminated
　eliminating
elimination
élite
elitist
elixir
elk
ellipse
　*a geometrical*
　*ellipse*
　*pl* ellipses
elliptical
　*adv* elliptically
elm
elocution
elongate
　elongated
　elongating
elongation
elope

eloped
eloping
elopement
eloquence
eloquent
else
elsewhere
elucidate
elucidated
elucidating
**elude**
*He tried to elude his pursuers*
eluded
eluding
elusive
elves
*see* elf
emaciated
e-mail, E-mail
emanate
emanated
emanating
emanation
**emancipate**
emancipated
emancipating
emancipation
embalm
embankment
embargo
*pl* embargoes
embark
embarkation
**embarrass**
embarrassed
embarrassing
**embarrassment**
embassy

*pl* embassies
embed
embedded
embedding
embellish
embellishment
ember
embezzle
embezzled
embezzling
embezzlement
emblazon
emblazoned
emblazoning
emblem
emblematic
embodiment
embody
embodied
embodying
emboss
embrace
embraced
embracing
embrocation
embroider
embroidered
embroidering
embroidery
embroil
embroiled
embroiling
embryo
*pl* embryos
embryonic
emend
*to emend the manuscript*
emendation

emerald
emerge
emerged
emerging
**emergence**
emergency
*pl* emergencies
**emergent**
emery
emetic
emigrant
*an emigrant to America from Britain*
emigrate
emigration
*emigration from Britain*
eminence
eminent
eminently
emissary
*pl* emissaries
emission
*the emission of gases*
emit
emitted
emitting
emollient
**emolument**
emotion
**emotional**
*adv* emotionally
emotive
empathy
emperor
emphasis
*The emphasis must*

be on hygiene: *The emphasis is on the first syllable*

**emphasize, -ise**
*to emphasize its value: to emphasize the word 'new'*
emphasized
emphasizing
emphatic
*adv*
  emphatically
empire
empirical
*adv* empirically
empiricism
employ
  employed
  employing
**employee**
*He sacked his young employee*
employer
*His employer gave him a rise*
employment
empress
  *pl* empresses
emptiness
empty
  **emptied**
  emptying
emu
emulate
  emulated
  emulating
emulation
emulsion

**enable**
  enabled
  enabling
enact
enamel
  enamelled
  enamelling
enamoured of
encampment
enchant
enchanter
enchantment
enchantress
  *pl*
  enchantresses
enclose
  enclosed
  enclosing
enclosure
encompass
encore
encounter
  encountered
  encountering
**encourage**
  encouraged
  encouraging
encouragement
encroach
encroachment
encumbrance
**encyclopaedia,**
  encyclopedia
encyclopaedic,
  encyclopedic
end
endanger
  endangered
  endangering

endear
  endeared
  endearing
  endearment
**endeavour**
endemic
ending
endive
endorse
  endorsed
  endorsing
  endorsement
endow
  endowment
**endurance**
endure
  endured
  enduring
enema
enemy
  *pl* enemies
energetic
  *adv*
    **energetically**
energy
  *pl* energies
**enervate**
  enervated
  enervating
enforce
  enforced
  enforcing
  enforcement
engage
  engaged
  engaging
  engagement
engine
**engineer**

engineered
engineering
engrave
  engraved
  engraving
engross
enhance
  enhanced
  enhancing
enigma
enigmatic
  *adv*
  enigmatically
enjoy
  enjoyed
  enjoying
enjoyable
enjoyment
enlarge
  enlarged
  enlarging
enlargement
enlighten
  enlightened
  enlightening
enlightenment
enlist
enliven
  enlivened
  enlivening
enmity
enormity
enormous
**enough**
enquire
  *see* inquire
enrage
  enraged
  enraging

enrol, enroll
  enrolled
  enrolling
  enrolment
ensconce
  ensconced
  ensconcing
ensemble
ensign
ensue
  ensued
  **ensuing**
ensure
  *Great effort will*
  *ensure success*
  ensured
  ensuring
entail
  **entailed**
  entailing
entangle
  entangled
  entangling
  entanglement
enter
  entered
  entering
enterprise
enterprising
entertain
  entertained
  entertaining
  entertainer
  entertainment
enthral
  enthralled
  enthralling
enthuse
  enthused

enthusing
**enthusiasm**
enthusiast
enthusiastic
  *adv*
  enthusiastically
entice
  enticed
  enticing
enticement
entire
entirely
entirety
entitle
  entitled
  entitling
entity
entomologist
  *The entomologist*
  *studied the insects*
entomology
entrails
'entrance
en'trance
  entranced
  entrancing
entrant
entreat
  entreated
  entreating
entreaty
  *pl* entreaties
entrenched
entrust
entry
  *pl* entries
E-number
**enumerate**
  enumerated

enumerating
enumeration
enunciate
  enunciated
  enunciating
enunciation
envelop
  *The mist began to envelop the hills*
  **enveloped**
  enveloping
**envelope**
  *a brown envelope*
enviable
  *adv* enviably
envious
environment
environmental
  *adv* environmentally
environmentalist
envisage
  envisaged
  envisaging
envoy
envy
  envied
  envying
enzyme
eon
  *see* aeon
epaulet,
  epaulette
ephemeral
  *adv* ephemerally
epic
epicure
epicurean
epidemic

epiglottis
epigram
  *a witty epigram*
epigrammatic
**epilepsy**
epileptic
epilogue
episcopacy
episcopal
episcopalian
episode
episodic
epistle
epitaph
  *an epitaph on his grave*
epithet
  *'Great' was the epithet given to King Alfred*
epitome
epitomize, -ise
  epitomized
  epitomizing
epoch
equable
  *adv* equably
equal
  *adv* equally
  **equalled**
  equalling
equality
**equalize,** -ise
  equalized
  equalizing
equanimity
equate
  equated
  equating

equation
equator
equatorial
equerry
  *pl* equerries
equestrian
equidistant
equilateral
equilibrium
equine
equinoctial
equinox
equip
  **equipped**
  equipping
equipment
equitable
  *adv* equitably
equity
equivalent
equivocal
  *adv* equivocally
equivocate
  equivocated
  equivocating
era
  *pl* eras
eradicate
  eradicated
  eradicating
eradication
erase
  erased
  erasing
eraser
ere
  *ere dawn*
erect
erection

ermine
erode
  eroded
  eroding
erosion
erotic
  *erotic pictures of nudes*
  *adv* erotically
eroticism
err
  *to err is human*
  erred
  erring
errand
errant
erratic
  *an erratic driver*
  *adv* erratically
erratum
  *pl* errata
**erroneous**
error
**erudite**
  *adv* eruditely
erudition
erupt
eruption
escalate
  escalated
  escalating
escalation
**escalator**
escapade
escape
  escaped
  escaping
escapement
  *the escapement of*

*a watch*
**escapism**
escapist
escarpment
  *a rocky escarpment*
escort
escutcheon
Eskimo
  *pl* Eskimos
esoteric
esparto
especial
  *adv* especially
**espionage**
esplanade
Esq
  = Esquire
  *John Brown Esq*
essay
  *He wrote an essay on Shakespeare*
essayist
**essence**
**essential**
  *adv* essentially
establish
establishment
estate
esteem
  esteemed
  esteeming
estimate
  estimated
  estimating
estimation
**estranged**
estuary
  *pl* estuaries
etc = et cetera

etch
etching
eternal
  *adv* eternally
eternity
ether
ethereal
  *adv* ethereally
ethical
  *adv* ethically
ethics
ethnic
ethos
**etiquette**
etymological
  *adv* etymologically
etymologist
  *An etymologist is interested in words*
etymology
  *pl* etymologies
eucalyptus
  *pl* eucalypti, eucalyptuses
eulogize, -ise
  eulogized
  eulogizing
eulogy
  *pl* eulogies
euphemism
euphemistic
  *adv* euphemistically
euphonious
euphonium
euphoria
euphoric
  *adv* euphorically

eurhythmics
European
**euthanasia**
evacuate
  evacuated
  evacuating
evacuation
evacuee
evade
  evaded
  evading
evaluate
  evaluated
  evaluating
evaluation
evanescent
evangelical
evangelist
evaporate
  evaporated
  evaporating
evaporation
evasion
evasive
  *adv* evasively
eve
even
evening
evenness
event
eventful
  *adv* eventfully
eventual
  *adv* eventually
eventuality
  *pl* eventualities
ever
evergreen
evermore

every
everybody
everyone
everything
everywhere
evict
eviction
evidence
evident
**evidently**
evil
  *adv* evilly
evince
  evinced
  evincing
evocative
  *adv* evocatively
evoke
  evoked
  evoking
evolution
  *the evolution of the*
  *species: Darwin's*
  *theory of evolution*
evolutionary
evolve
  evolved
  evolving
ewe
  *a ram and a ewe*
ewer
exact
exacting
exactness
**exaggerate**
  exaggerated
  exaggerating
**exaggeration**
exalt

exaltation
exalted
examination
examine
  examined
  examining
examiner
example
**exasperate**
  exasperated
  exasperating
exasperation
excavate
  excavated
  excavating
excavation
excavator
**exceed**
**exceedingly**
excel
  excelled
  excelling
excellence
excellency
**excellent**
except

  *Nobody except*
  *John went: We*
  *enjoyed it except*
  *for the rain*

excepting
exception
exceptional
  *adv*
  exceptionally
excerpt
excess

  *an excess of*
  *alcohol*

*pl* excesses
**excessive**
  *adv* excessively
exchange
  exchanged
  exchanging
**exchequer**
ex'cise
  excised
  excising
'excise
excision
excitable
  *adv* excitably
excite
  excited
  exciting
excitement
exciting
exclaim
  exclaimed
  exclaiming
**exclamation**
exclamatory
exclude
  excluded
  excluding
exclusion
exclusive
  *adv* exclusively
**excommunicate**
**excommunication**
excrement
excrescence
excrete
  excreted
  excreting
excruciating
excursion

excuse
  excused
  excusing
execrable
  *adv* execrably
execute
  executed
  executing
execution
executioner
  *He was put to*
  *death by the*
  *executioner*
executive
executor
  *executor of his will*
exemplary
exemplify
  exemplified
  exemplifying
exempt
exemption
**exercise**
  *ballet exercises:*
  *exercises in*
  *spelling: to*
  *exercise your body*

  exercised
  exercising
exert
exertion
**exhaust**
  exhausted
  exhausting
  exhaustion
  exhaustive
**exhibit**
  exhibited
  exhibiting

**exhibition**
exhibitionism
exhibitionist
exhibitor
**exhilarate**
  exhilarated
  exhilarating
exhort
exhortation
exhumation
exhume
  exhumed
  exhuming
exigency
  *pl* exigencies
exigent
exile
  exiled
  exiling
exist
existence
exit
  exited
  exiting
exodus
  *pl* exoduses
exonerate
  exonerated
exoneration
exorbitance
exorbitant
**exorcism**
exorcist
**exorcize,** -ise
  *to exorcize the*
  *house of spirits*
  exorcized
  exorcizing
exotic

*adv* exotically
expand
*Metals expand when heated*
expanse
expansion
expansive
*a talkative and expansive person*
expatiate
*to expatiate about an experience*
expatiated
expatiating
expatriate
expect
expected
expecting
expectancy
expectant
expectation
expedience
expediency
expedient
expedite
expedited
expediting
expedition
expeditious
expel
expelled
expelling
expend
*to expend energy*
expenditure
expense
expensive
*expensive clothes*
*adv* expensively

experience
experienced
experiencing
experiment
experimental
*adv* experimentally
expert
expertise
**expiate**
*to expiate a crime*
expiated
expiating
expire
expired
expiring
expiry
explain
explained
explaining
**explanation**
explanatory
expletive
explicable
*adv* explicably
explicit
explode
exploded
exploding
exploit
exploited
exploiting
exploitation
exploration
explore
explored
exploring
explorer
explosion

explosive
exponent
export
exportation
expose
exposed
exposing
exposition
exposure
expound
express
expression
expressive
*adv* expressively
expropriate
expropriated
expropriating
expropriation
expulsion
expurgate
expurgated
expurgating
**exquisite**
*adv* exquisitely
extant
*Cannibalism is still extant in a few areas*
extempore
extemporize, -ise
extemporized
extemporizing
extend
extension
extensive
*adv* extensively
extent
extenuate
extenuated

extenuating
extenuation
exterior
exterminate
  exterminated
  exterminating
extermination
external
  *adv* externally
extinct
  *The dodo is*
  *extinct: That*
  *volcano is now*
  *extinct*

extinction
**extinguish**
extinguisher
extol
  extolled
  extolling
extort
extortion
extortionate
  *adv*
  extortionately
extra
extract
extraction
extradite
  extradited
  extraditing
extradition
**extraneous**
**extraordinary**
  *adv*
  extraordinarily
extrasensory
extravagance
**extravagant**

extravert
  *see* extrovert
extreme
  *adv* extremely
extremist
extremity
  *pl* extremities
extricate
  extricated
  extricating
extrovert,
  extravert
exuberance
exuberant
exude
  exuded
  exuding
exult
exultant
exultation
eye
  eyed
  eyeing
eyebrow
eyelash
eyelid
eyewitness
eyrie, eyry, aerie
  *an eagle's eyrie*

## F

fable
fabric
fabricate
  fabricated
  fabricating
fabrication
**fabulous**

façade
face
  faced
  facing
facet
**facetious**
facetiousness
facial
  *adv* facially
facile
  *adv* facilely
facilitate
  facilitated
  facilitating
facility
  *pl* facilities
facsimile
fact
faction
factious
factor
factory
  *pl* factories
factotum
faculty
  *pl* faculties
fad
faddy
fade
  faded
  fading
**faeces**
faerie, faery
  *Spenser wrote the*
  *Faerie Queen: the*
  *magical land of*
  *faerie*

fag
faggot

**Fahrenheit**
fail
  failed
  failing
failure
fain
  *Fain would he die
  for love*
faint
  *She felt faint and
  collapsed: a faint
  noise: to faint in
  the heat*
faintness
fair
  *Children enjoy a
  fair: She has fair
  hair: a fair attempt*
fairness
fairy
  *the fairy on the
  Christmas tree:
  fairy stories*
  *pl* fairies
faith
faithful
  *adv* faithfully
faithfulness
faithless
faithlessness
fake
  faked
  faking
falcon
falconry
fall
  fell
  *He fell off the wall*
  fallen

*He has fallen off
the wall*
falling
**fallacious**
fallacy
  *pl* fallacies
fallen
  *see* fall
fallibility
**fallible**
fallow
false
  *adv* falsely
falsehood
falseness
falsification
falsify
  falsified
  falsifying
falter
  faltered
  faltering
fame
**familiar**
familiarity
familiarize, -ise
  familiarized
  familiarizing
family
  *pl* families
famine
famished
famous
fan
  fanned
  fanning
**fanatic**
fanatical
  *adv* fanatically

fancier
fanciful
fancy
  *pl* fancies
fancied
fancying
fanfare
fang
fanlight
fantastic
  *adv* fantastically
fantasy
  *pl* fantasies
far
  *compar* farther
  *superl* farthest
farce
**farcical**
fare
  *bus fare: How did
  you fare?*
  fared
  faring
farewell
farm
farmer
farrow
farther, farthest
  *see* far
farthing
fascia
**fascinate**
fascinated
fascinating
fascination
fascist
fashion
fashioned
fashioning

fashionable
  adv fashionably
fast
fasten
  fastened
  fastening
fastidious
fastness
fat
  compar fatter
  superl fattest
fatal
  adv fatally
fatality
  pl fatalities
fate
  a fate worse than
  death
fated
fateful
  adv fatefully
father
father-in-law
  pl fathers-in-law
fathom
  fathomed
  fathoming
**fatigue**
fatness
fatten
  fattened
  fattening
**fatuous**
fault
faultless
faulty
faun
  A faun is an
  imaginary creature

fauna
favour
  favoured
  favouring
favourable
  adv favourably
favourite
favouritism
fawn
  fawn in colour: a
  deer and its fawn:
  Courtiers fawn on
  the king
fax
  faxed
  faxing
fear
fearful
  adv fearfully
fearless
  adv fearlessly
feasibility
feasible
  adv feasibly
feast
feat
  a difficult feat
feather
feathery
feature
  featured
  featuring
**February**
fed
  see feed
federal
federated
**federation**
fee

feeble
  adv feebly
feebleness
feed
  fed
  feeding
feel
  felt
  feeling
**feeler**
feet
  see foot
**feign**
  Did she feign
  sleep?
  feigned
  feigning
feint
  a feint in fencing
felicitous
felicity
  pl felicities
feline
fell
  see fall
fell
  felled
  He felled the tree
  felling
fellow
fellowship
felon
felony
  pl felonies
felt
  see feel
felt
female
feminine

*adv* femininely
femininity
feminism
feminist
femur
fen
fence
  fenced
  fencing
fend
fender
ferment
  *to ferment beer: in a ferment of excitement*
fermentation
fern
**ferocious**
ferocity
ferret
  ferreted
  ferreting
ferrule
ferry
  *pl* ferries
  ferried
  ferrying
fertile
fertility
fertilization, -isation
fertilize, -ise
  fertilized
  fertilizing
fertilizer, -iser
fervent
fervour
fester
  festered

festering
festival
festive
  *adv* festively
festivity
  *pl* festivities
festoon
  **festooned**
  festooning
fetch
fête
  *a stall at the summer fête*
fetid, foetid
fetish
  *pl* fetishes
fetlock
fetters
fettle
**feud**
**feudal**
feudalism
fever
**fevered**
feverish
few
fez
  *pl* fezzes
fiancé
  *He is her fiancé*
fiancée
  *She is his fiancée*
**fiasco**
  *pl* fiascos
fib
  fibbed
  fibbing
**fibre**
fibreglass

fibrous
fickle
fickleness
fiction
**fictitious**
fiddle
  fiddled
  fiddling
fidelity
fidget
  fidgeted
  fidgeting
field
field-marshal
**fiend**
fiendish
**fierce**
  *adv* fiercely
fierceness
**fiery**
fifteen
fifteenth
fifth
fiftieth
fifty
fig
fight
  fought
  fighting
fighter
figment
figurative
  *adv* figuratively
figure
figured
figurehead
filament
filch
file

filed
*She filed the letter*
filing
**filial**
filigree
fill
filled
*We filled the bucket*
filling
filler
fillet
fillip
filly
*pl* fillies
film
filter
filtered
filtering
filth
filthy
fin
final
*a final separation*
*adv* finally
finale
*the finale at the end of the concert*
finality
finalization, -isation
finalize, -ise
finalized
finalizing
finance
financed
financing
financial
*adv* financially

financier
finch
*pl* finches
find
found
*He found the ball*
finding
fine
fined
fining
finery
**finesse**
finger
fingered
fingering
fingerprint
finish
finished
finite
Finnish
**fiord, fjord**
fir
*a fir tree: a fir cone*
fire
fired
firing
fireworks
firm
firmament
firmness
first
first aid
firstly
firth
fiscal
fish
*pl* fish
fisherman
fishmonger

fishy
fission
*nuclear fission*
fissure
*a fissure in the rock*
fist
fisticuffs
fit
*compar* fitter
*superl* fittest
fitted
fitting
fitful
*adv* fitfully
fitness
five
fix
fixedly
fixture
fizz
fizzle out
fizzled out
fizzling out
fizzy
fjord
*see* fiord
**flabbergasted**
flabbiness
flabby
**flaccid**
flag
flagged
flagging
flagellation
flagon
flagrancy
flagrant
flail

flailed
flailing
flair
*a flair for
dressmaking*
flak
flake
flaked
flaking
flamboyance
**flamboyant**
flame
flamed
**flaming**
flamingo
*pl* flamingos,
flamingoes
**flammable**
*Flammable
material burns
easily*
flan
flange
flank
flannel
**flannelette**
flap
flapped
flapping
flare
*a flare as a signal:
Did the fire flare
up?*
flared
flaring
flash
*pl* flashes
flashy
*adv* flashily

flask
flat
*compar* flatter
*superl* flattest
flatness
flatten
flattened
flattening
flatter
**flattered**
flattering
flattery
flatulence
flatulent
flaunt
**flavour**
flavoured
flavouring
flaw
flawed
flawless
flax
flay
flayed
flaying
flea
*bitten by a flea*
fleck
flecked
fled
*see* flee
fledged
**fledgling**
flee
*to flee from the
enemy*
fled
fleeing
fleece

fleeced
fleecing
fleecy
fleet
fleeting
fleetness
flesh
fleshy
flew
*see* fly
flex
flexibility
flexible
flick
flicker
flickered
flickering
flight
flightiness
flighty
flimsy
flinch
fling
flung
flinging
flint
flip
flipped
flipping
flippancy
**flippant**
flipper
flirt
flirtation
flirtatious
flit
flitted
flitting
float

floated
floating
flock
*flocks of sheep*
floe
*an ice floe*
flog
flogged
flogging
flood
flooded
flooding
floodlighting
floor
floored
flooring
flop
flopped
flopping
floppy
flora
floral
florid
florist
flotation
flotilla
flotsam
flounce
flounced
flouncing
flounder
floundered
floundering
flour
*Bread is made with flour*
floury
*floury potatoes: My hands are floury*

flourish
*pl* flourishes
flourished
flourishing
flout
flouted
flouting
flow
*a flow of blood: to flow smoothly*
flowed
flowing
flower
*a beautiful flower: Will that bush flower this year?*
flowered
flowering
flowery
*a flowery material: flowery language*
flown
*see* fly
fluctuate
fluctuated
fluctuating
fluctuation
flu
*a flu epidemic*
flue
*The sweep cleaned the flue*
fluency
**fluent**
fluff
fluffy
**fluid**
fluke
flung

*see* fling
**fluoridate**
fluoridation
**fluoride**
fluoridize, -ise
fluoridized
fluoridizing
flurry
*pl* flurries
flurried
flurrying
flush
*pl* flushes
fluster
flustered
flustering
flute
fluted
flutter
fluttered
fluttering
flux
fly
*pl* flies
flew
*The bird flew away: He flew the plane*
flown
*The bird has flown away: He has flown the plane*
flyover
foal
foaled
foaling
foam
foamed
foaming
fob

fob off
  fobbed off
  fobbing off
focal
fo'c'sle
  *see* forecastle
focus
  *pl* focuses, foci
  focused,
    focussed
  focusing,
    focussing
fodder
**foe**
foetid
  *see* fetid
foetus
fog
foggy
foil
  foiled
  foiling
foist
fold
folder
**foliage**
folk
folklore
folksong
follow
  followed
  following
follower
folly
  *pl* follies
foment
  *to foment trouble*
fond
fondle

fondled
fondling
fondness
font
  *the baptismal font*
food
fool
  fooled
  fooling
foolhardy
**foolish**
**foolishness**
foolproof
foolscap
foot
  *pl* feet
  *These shoes hurt
  my feet*
football
footing
footlights
footprint
footstep
footwear
for
forage
  foraged
  foraging
foray
forbade
  *see* forbid
forbear
  forbore
  forbearing
forbearance
forbearing
forbid
  forbade
  *He forbade me to*

go
forbidden
  *He has forbidden
  me to go*
forbidding
forbore
  *see* forbear
force
  forced
  forcing
forceful
  *adv* forcefully
forceps
**forcible**
  *adv* forcibly
ford
fore
  *well to the fore*
forearm
foreboding
forecast
  forecast
  forecasting
forecastle,
  fo'c'sle
forefather
forefinger
forefront
foregone
  *a foregone
  conclusion*
foreground
forehead
foreign
**foreigner**
foreleg
forelock
foreman
  *pl* foremen

foremost
**forensic**
forerunner
foresee
  foresaw
  *He foresaw the
  problem*
  foreseen
  *He has foreseen
  the problem*
  foreseeing
foreshore
foresight
forest
forestall
  forestalled
  forestalling
forester
forestry
foretaste
foretell
  foretold
  foretelling
forethought
foretold
  *see* foretell
forewarn
forewoman
  *pl* forewomen
foreword
  *Who wrote the
  foreword to the
  book?*
**forfeit**
  forfeited
  forfeiting
  forfeiture
forgave
  *see* forgive

forge
forged
forging
forgery
  *pl* forgeries
forget
  forgot
  *He forgot it*
  forgotten
  *He has forgotten it*
  forgetting
forgetful
  *adv* forgetfully
forgetfulness
forgive
  forgave
  *He forgave her*
  forgiven
  *He has forgiven her*
  forgiving
forgiveness
forgo
  forgoing
  forgone
  *He has forgone
  privileges*
  forwent
  *He forwent
  privileges*
forgot, forgotten
  *see* forget
fork
forlorn
form
formal
  *adv* formally
formality
  *pl* formalities
format

formation
formative
former
formerly
formidable
  *adv* formidably
formula
  *pl* formulae,
  formulas
formulate
  formulated
  formulating
formulation
forsake
  forsook
  *She forsook
  religion*
  forsaken
  *She has forsaken
  religion*
  forsaking
forswear
  forswore
  *He forswore
  alcohol*
  forsworn
  *He has forsworn
  alcohol*
  forswearing
fort
  *They besieged the
  fort*
forte
  *Singing is his forte*
forth
  *issuing forth:
  giving forth*
forthcoming
forthright

**forthwith**
**fortieth**
fortification
fortify
  fortified
  fortifying
fortitude
fortnight
fortnightly
fortress
  *pl* fortresses
**fortuitous**
fortunate
  *adv* **fortunately**
fortune
forty
  *He spent forty
  pounds*
forum
  *pl* forums
forward
  *forward not
  backward*
forwards
forwent
  *see* forgo
fossil
foster
  fostered
  fostering
fought
  *see* fight
foul
  *the foul smell of
  tobacco: foul
  weather*
found
  *see* find
found

founded
  *He founded the
  business*
founding
foundation
founder
  foundered
  foundering
foundling
foundry
  *pl* foundries
fount
  *the fount of
  knowledge*
fountain
four
  *Four and four
  makes eight*
fourteen
fourteenth
fourth
  *He was fourth in
  the race*
fowl
  *fish and fowl*
fox
  *pl* foxes
foxglove
foxtrot
foxy
**foyer**
fracas
  *pl* fracas
fraction
fractional
  *adv* fractionally
fractious
fracture
  fractured

fracturing
fragile
fragment
fragmentary
fragrance
fragrant
frail
**frailty**
  *pl* frailties
frame
  framed
  framing
framework
franc
  *the French franc*
franchise
frank
  *a frank statement:
  frank and honest*
frank
  *to frank a letter*
frankfurter
**frankincense**
frantic
  *adv* frantically
fraternal
fraternity
fraternization,
  -isation
fraternize, -ise
  fraternized
  fraternizing
**fraud**
fraudulent
**fraught**
fray
  frayed
  fraying
freak

freakish
freckle
free
**freedom**
freelance
freely
freeze
  *to freeze*
  *vegetables*
froze
*She froze the meat*
frozen
*She has frozen the*
*peas*
freezing
**freight**
freighter
French
frenetic
  *adv* frenetically
frenzied
frenzy
**frequency**
  *pl* frequencies
frequent
fresco
  *pl* frescoes,
    frescos
fresh
freshen
  freshened
  freshening
fret
  fretted
  fretting
fretful
  *adv* fretfully
fretwork
friar

friary
  *pl* friaries
friction
Friday
**fridge**
fried
  *see* fry
**friend**
friendliness
friendly
friendship
frieze
  *a ceiling frieze*
frigate
fright
frighten
  frightened
  frightening
frightful
  *adv* frightfully
frigid
frigidity
frill
frilly
fringe
  fringed
  fringing
frippery
  *pl* fripperies
Frisbee ®
frisk
frisky
  *adv* friskily
fritter
  frittered
  frittering
frivolity
  *pl* frivolities
frivolous

frizzy
fro
frock
frog
frogman
  *pl* frogmen
frolic
  frolicked
  frolicking
  frolicsome
from
frond
front
frontage
frontier
frontispiece
frost
frosted
frosty
  *adv* frostily
froth
frothy
frown
froze, frozen
  *see* freeze
frugal
  *adv* frugally
frugality
fruit
**fruiterer**
fruitful
  *adv* fruitfully
fruition
fruitless
  *adv* fruitlessly
frump
frumpish
frustrate
  frustrated

frustrating
frustration
fry
  fried
  frying
**fuchsia**
fuddle
  fuddled
  fuddling
fudge
**fuel**
  fuelled
  fuelling
**fugitive**
fugue
fulcrum
  *pl* fulcrums,
  fulcra
fulfil
  **fulfilled**
  fulfilling
**fulfilment**
full
**fullness**
fully
fulmar
fulminate
  fulminated
  fulminating
fulsome
  *adv* fulsomely
fumble
  fumbled
  fumbling
fume
  fumed
  fuming
fumes
**fumigate**

fumigated
fumigating
fumigation
fun
function
  functioned
  functioning
functional
  *adv* functionally
fund
fundamental
  *adv*
    fundamentally
funeral
  *He attended her
  funeral*
funereal
  *solemn, funereal
  music*
funfair
fungus
  *pl* fungi,
  funguses
funicular railway
funnel
funny
  *adv* funnily
fur
  *a fur coat: a cat's
  fur*
furbish
**furious**
furlong
furnace
furnish
furnishings
**furniture**
furore
furrier

furrow
furry
further
  **furthered**
  furthering
furthermore
furthest
furtive
  *adv* furtively
fury
fuse
  fused
  fusing
**fuselage**
fusion
fuss
  fussed
  fussing
fussy
  *adv* fussily
fusty
futile
  *adv* futilely
futility
future
fuzz
fuzzy

G

gabble
  *the noisy gabble of
  the crowd: to
  gabble noisily*

  gabbled
  gabbling
gaberdine
gable
  *the gable of a*

*house*
gadget
Gaelic
gaff
  *a fishing gaff: blow the gaff*
gaffe
  *a social gaffe*
gag
  gagged
  gagging
gaggle
**gaiety**
gaily
  *see* gay
gain
  gained
  gaining
gait
  *a shuffling gait*
gaiter
gala
galaxy
  *pl* galaxies
gale
gall
gallant
gallantry
gallbladder
galleon
  *a Spanish galleon*
gallery
  *pl* galleries
galley
  *pl* galleys
galling
gallon
  *a gallon of petrol*
gallop

**galloped**
galloping
gallows
galore
galoshes
galvanize, -ise
galvanized
galvanizing
galvanometer
gambit
gamble
  *to gamble on a horse*
gambled
gambling
gambol
  *The lambs gambol*
gambolled
gambolling
game
gamekeeper
gaming
gammon
gamut
gander
Gandhi
gang
ganger
gangrene
gangrenous
gangster
gang up
  ganged up
  ganging up
gangway
gannet
gantry
  *pl* gantries
gaol

*see* jail
gaoler
  *see* jailer
gap
gape
  gaped
  gaping
garage
  garaged
  garaging
garb
garbage
garbed
garbled
garden
  gardened
  gardening
gardener
gargantuan
gargle
  gargled
  gargling
gargoyle
garish
garland
**garlic**
garment
garnet
garnish
  *pl* garnishes
garret
**garrison**
  garrisoned
  garrisoning
garrotte
  garrotted
  garrotting
garrulity
garrulous

garter
gas
  pl gases
  gassed
  gassing
gaseous
gash
  pl gashes
gasometer
gasp
gastric
gastritis
gastronomic
gate
  a garden gate
**gâteau**
  pl gâteaux
gatecrash
gatecrasher
gather
  gathered
  gathering
gauche
gaucho
  pl gauchos
gaudiness
gaudy
  adv gaudily
**gauge**
  gauged
  gauging
gaunt
gauntlet
gauze
gave
  see give
gavotte
gawky

adv gawkily
gay
  adv gaily
gaze
  gazed
  gazing
gazelle
gazette
  gazetted
  gazetting
**gazetteer**
gear
gear to
  geared to
  gearing to
geese
  see goose
**geisha**
gelatine
gelatinous
gelding
gem
gender
gene
genealogical
genealogist
genealogy
  pl genealogies
genera
  see genus
general
  adv generally
generalization,
  -isation
generalize, -ise
  generalized
  generalizing
generate
  generated

generating
generation
**generator**
generosity
generous
genesis
genetic
  adv genetically
genetics
genial
  adv genially
genie
  a magic genie
genius
  He is clever but not
  a genius
  pl geniuses
genocide
genteel
  a genteel tea-party
  adv genteelly
gentile
  He is a gentile, not
  a Jew
gentility
gentle
  She has a kind,
  gentle nature: a
  gentle breeze
  adv gently
gentleman
  pl gentlemen
gentlemanly
gentleness
gentry
**genuine**
  adv genuinely
genuineness
genus

*To what genus does that plant belong?*

*pl* genera
geographical
  *adv* geographically
geography
geological
  *adv* geologically
geologist
geology
geometric
  *adv* geometrically
geometry
geranium
**gerbil**
germ
German
germane
germinate
  germinated
  germinating
  germination
**gesticulate**
  gesticulated
  gesticulating
  gesticulation
gesture
  gestured
  gesturing
get
  got
  getting
geyser
Ghanaian
ghastliness
**ghastly**

gherkin
**ghetto**
  *pl* ghettos
ghost
ghostliness
ghostly
ghoul
ghoulish
giant
giantess
gibber
  gibbered
  gibbering
gibberish
gibbet
gibbon
gibe
  *see* jibe
giblets
giddiness
giddy
gift
gifted
**gigantic**
giggle
  giggled
  giggling
gild
  *to gild a brooch: to gild the lily*
gill
gillie
gilt
  *a brooch covered in gilt*
gimcrack
gimlet
**gimmick**
gin

ginger
gingerly
**gingham**
gipsy
  *see* gypsy
**giraffe**
gird
girder
girdle
girl
girlhood
girlish
giro, Giro
  *pl* giros, Giros
girth
gist
give
  gave
  *He gave her a present*
  given
  *He has given her a present*
  giving
glacé
glacier
  *The glacier is melting*
glad
gladden
  gladdened
  gladdening
glade
gladiator
gladness
**glamorous**
glamour
glance
  glanced

glancing
gland
glandular
glare
glared
glaring
glass
*pl* glasses
glassy
*adv* glassily
glaze
glazed
glazing
glazier
*The glazier
mended the
window*
gleam
gleamed
gleaming
glean
gleaned
gleaning
glee
gleeful
*adv* gleefully
glen
glib
glibness
glide
glided
gliding
glider
glimmer
glimmered
glimmering
**glimpse**
glimpsed
glimpsing

glint
glisten
glistened
glistening
glitter
glittered
glittering
gloaming
gloat
**global**
*adv* globally
globe
globular
globule
gloom
gloomy
*adv* gloomily
glorify
glorified
glorifying
**glorious**
glory
*pl* glories
gloss
*pl* glosses
glossary
*pl* glossaries
glossy
*adv* glossily
glove
glow
glowed
glowing
glower
glowered
glowering
glucose
glue
glued

gluing
gluey
glum
glut
glutted
glutting
gluten
glutinous
*a glutinous
substance*
glutton
**gluttonous**
*gluttonous diners*
gluttony
**glycerine**
**gnarled**
**gnash**
**gnat**
**gnaw**
**gnome**
**gnu**
go
went
*He went yesterday*
gone
*He has gone away*
going
goad
go-ahead
goal
*He scored a goal*
goat
gobble
gobbled
gobbling
goblet
goblin
god
goddess

95

*pl* goddesses
godfather
godliness
godly
godmother
goggles
going
  *see* go
**goitre**
gold
golden
goldfish
golf
  golfed
  golfing
golfer
golliwog,
  gollywog
gondola
gondolier
gone
  *see* go
gong
good
  *compar* better
  *superl* best
  *adv* well
goodbye
good-day
goodly
goodness
goodwill
goose
  *pl* geese
gooseberry
  *pl* gooseberries
goosepimples
gore
  gored

goring
gorge
  gorged
  gorging
**gorgeous**
gorgon
gorgonzola
gorilla
  *A gorilla is an ape*
gorse
gory
gosling
gospel
gossamer
gossip
  **gossiped**
  gossiping
got
  *see* get
gouache
gouge
  gouged
  gouging
goulash
  *pl* goulashes
gourd
gourmand
  *He is a greedy gourmand*
gourmet
  *He likes good food and wine — he is a gourmet*
gout
govern
  governed
  governing
governess

*pl* governesses
**government**
governor
gown
grab
  grabbed
  grabbing
grace
  graced
  gracing
graceful
  *adv* gracefully
gracefulness
gracious
graciousness
gradation
  *gradation in order of difficulty*
grade
  graded
  grading
gradient
gradual
  *adv* gradually
gradualness
graduate
  graduated
  graduating
graduation
  *graduation from University*
**graffiti**
graft
Grail
grain
gram
  *see* gramme
**grammar**
grammatical

*adv*
  grammatically
gramme, gram
**gramophone**
granary
  *pl* granaries
grand
grandchild
  *pl* grandchildren
grand-daughter
**grandeur**
grandfather
grandiloquent
grandiose
grandmother
grandson
grandstand
granite
granny
  *pl* grannies
grant
granular
granule
grape
grapefruit
graph
graphic
  *adv* graphically
graphics
graphite
graphology
grapple
  grappled
  grappling
grasp
grass
  *pl* grasses
grasshopper
grassy

grate
  *a fire in the grate*
**grateful**
  *adv* gratefully
grater
gratification
gratify
  gratified
  gratifying
grating
gratis
**gratitude**
**gratuitous**
gratuity
  *pl* gratuities
grave
  *adv* gravely
gravel
graven
graveyard
gravitate
  gravitated
  gravitating
gravitation
gravity
gravy
gray
  *see* grey
graze
  grazed
  grazing
grease
  greased
  greasing
greasy
great
  *a great man: a
  great amount*
greatness

greed
greediness
greedy
  *adv* greedily
green
greenery
greenfly
greengage
greengrocer
greenhouse
greenish
greenness
greet
  greeted
  greeting
**greetings**
**gregarious**
grenade
grew
  *see* grow
grey, gray
greyhound
grid
griddle
**grief**
  *full of grief at his
  death*
grievance
**grieve**
  *to grieve over his
  death*
  grieved
  grieving
grievous
griffin, griffon
grill
  *a grill on a cooker:
  a mixed grill: to
  grill a steak*

grille
*a metal grille in a window*
grim
grimace
grimaced
grimacing
grime
grimness
grin
grinned
grinning
grind
ground
*He ground the coffee*
grinding
grinder
grindstone
grip
gripped
*He gripped her hand*
gripping
gripe
griped
*He griped about the service*
griping
gripped
*see* grip
grisly
*a grisly, horrible sight*
grist
gristle
gristly
*gristly meat*
grit

gritted
gritting
grizzled
grizzly
*a grizzly bear*
groan
groaned
groaning
groat
grocer
grocery
*pl* groceries
groggy
*adv* groggily
groin
groom
groomed
grooming
groove
groovy
grope
*to grope one's way: to grope for a handkerchief*
groped
groping
gross
grossly
grossness
**grotesque**
*adv* grotesquely
grotesqueness
grotto
*pl* grottos, grottoes
ground
*see* grind
ground
grounded

*They grounded the planes*
grounding
grounding
groundless
groundsel
groundwork
group
*a group of children: to group together*
grouped
grouping
grouse
*to shoot a grouse*
*pl* grouse
grouse
*a grouse about prices*
*pl* grouses
groused
grousing
grove
grovel
**grovelled**
grovelling
grow
grew
*He grew tall*
grown
*He has grown tall*
growing
growl
grown
*see* grow
**growth**
grub
grubbed
grubbing

grubbiness
grubby
 *adv* grubbily
grudge
 grudged
 grudging
gruel
gruelling
**gruesome**
gruff
grumble
 grumbled
 grumbling
grumpy
 *adv* grumpily
grunt
**guarantee**
 **guaranteed**
 guaranteeing
**guarantor**
**guard**
**guardian**
guava
Guernsey
guerrilla
 *guerrilla warfare*
guess
 *pl* guesses
 guessed
 guessing
**guest**
guffaw
guidance
guide
 guided
 guiding
guidebook
guideline
guild

*a guild of craftsmen*
guile
guileless
guillemot
**guillotine**
 guillotined
 guillotining
guilt
 *the guilt of the prisoner*
guilty
 *adv* guiltily
**guinea**
guinea-fowl
guinea-pig
**guise**
**guitar**
gulf
 *pl* gulfs
gull
gullet
gullible
 *adv* gullibly
gully
 *pl* gullies
gulp
gum
 gummed
 gumming
gummy
gumption
gun
 gunned
 gunning
gunfire
gunpowder
gunwale, gunnel
gurgle

gurgled
gurgling
guru
 *pl* gurus
gush
gusset
gust
gusto
gusty
 *adv* gustily
gut
 gutted
 gutting
guts
gutter
guttersnipe
guttural
 *adv* gutturally
guy
 *pl* guys
gym
**gymkhana**
gymnasium
 *pl* gymnasiums,
 gymnasia
gymnast
**gymnastics**
gynaecological
gynaecologist
gynaecology
**gypsy, gipsy**
 *pl* gypsies,
 gipsies
gyrate
 gyrated
 gyrating
gyratory

# H

haberdasher
haberdashery
habit
habitable
habitat
habitation
**habitual**
  *adv* habitually
habituate
  habituated
  habituating
hack
hackles
hackney
hackneyed
hacksaw
haddock
Hades
**haemoglobin**
**haemorrhage**
  haemorrhaged
  haemorrhaging
hag
haggard
haggis
  *pl* haggises
haggle
  haggled
  haggling
ha-ha
hail
  *hail and wind: to*
  *hail a taxi*
  hailed
  hailing
hailstone
hair

*a hair of her head*
hairdresser
hair-raising
hairy
hake
halberd
**halcyon**
hale
  *hale and hearty*
half
  *half an apple*
  *pl* halves
halfpenny
  *pl* halfpennies
halibut
halitosis
hall
hallmark
hallo
  *see* hello
hallow
  *to hallow a shrine*
Hallowe'en
hallucinate
  hallucinated
  hallucinating
**hallucination**
halo
  *a saint's halo*
  *pl* halos, haloes
halt
halter
halting
halve
  *to halve an apple*
  halved
  halving
halves
  *see* half

ham
hamburger
hamfisted
hamlet
hammer
**hammered**
hammering
hammock
hamper
  hampered
  hampering
hamster
hamstring
  hamstrung
  hamstringing
hand
handbag
handcuffs
handful
  *pl* **handfuls**
handicap
**handicapped**
handicraft
handiness
handiwork
**handkerchief**
  *pl*
   handkerchiefs,
   handkerchieves
handle
  handled
  handling
handlebars
handsome
  *adv* handsomely
handsomeness
handwriting
handy
handyman

hang
hung
*A picture hung on the wall: He hung his coat up*

hanged
*They hanged the murderer*

hanging
hangar
*a hangar for two planes*

hanger
*a coat hanger*

hanger-on
*pl* hangers-on
hangover
hank
hanker
hankered
hankering
hankie, hanky
*pl* hankies
hansom-cab
haphazard
hapless
happen
**happened**
happening
**happiness**
happy
*compar* happier
*superl* happiest
*adv* happily
happy-go-lucky
hara-kiri
**harangue**
harangued
haranguing

**harass**
harassed
harassing
harassment
harbinger
harbour
harboured
harbouring
hard
harden
hardened
hardening
hardiness
hardly
hardness
hardware
hardy
*adv* hardily
hare
*a hare and a rabbit*
harebell
hare-brained
hair-lip
harem
hark
hark back
harked back
harking back
harlequin
harm
harmful
*adv* harmfully
harmless
harmonica
harmonious
harmonium
harmonize, -ise
harmonized
harmonizing

harmony
harness
*pl* harnesses
harp
harpist
harp on
harpoon
harpsichord
harpy
*pl* harpies
harrier
harrow
harrowing
harry
harried
harrying
harsh
harshness
hart
*a hart and a hind*
harvest
harvester
hash
hassock
haste
hasten
hastened
hastening
**hasty**
*adv* hastily
hat
hatch
*pl* hatches
hatchery
*pl* hatcheries
hatchet
hatchway
hate
hated

hating
hateful
  *adv* hatefully
**hatred**
hatter
haughtiness
**haughty**
  *adv* haughtily
haul
  hauled
  hauling
**haulage**
haunch
  *pl* haunches
haunt
have
  had
  having
haven
haversack
**havoc**
haw
Hawaii
hawk
hawker
hawthorn
hay
hay fever
haystack
haywire
**hazard**
hazardous
haze
hazel
haziness
hazy
  *adv* hazily
he
head

headed
heading
**headache**
head-dress
header
heading
headlight
headline
headmaster
headmistress
  *pl*
    headmistresses
headquarters
headstrong
headway
heady
heal
  *to heal a wound*
  healed
  healing
health
healthy
  *adv* healthily
heap
  heaped
  heaping
hear
  *She cannot hear you*
  heard
  hearing
hearsay
**hearse**
heart
  *heart disease: a loving heart*
heartburn
hearten
  heartened

heartening
heartfelt
hearth
heartless
hearty
  *adv* heartily
heat
heated
heating
heath
heathen
heather
heave
  heaved
  heaving
heaven
heavenly
heave to
  hove to
  heaving to
heaviness
heavy
  *compar* heavier
  *superl* heaviest
  *adv* heavily
heckle
  heckled
  heckling
heckler
hectare
hectic
  *adv* hectically
hector
  hectored
  hectoring
he'd
  = he had, he
    would
hedge

hedged
hedging
hedgehog
hedgerow
heed
heedless
heel
*the heel of a shoe:*
*to heel a shoe*
heeled
heeling
hefty
**heifer**
**height**
heighten
**heightened**
heightening
**heinous**
heinousness
**heir**
*heir to the throne:*
*heir to a fortune*
heiress
*pl* heiresses
heirloom
held
*see* hold
**helicopter**
heliotrope
helium
he'll
= he will
hell
hellish
hello, hallo, hullo
*Hello there!: Hallo!*
*How are you?*
helm
helmet

helmsman
help
helpful
*adv* helpfully
helpfulness
helping
helpless
helplessness
helter-skelter
hem
hemmed
hemming
hemisphere
hemispherical
hemlock
hemp
hen
hence
henceforth
henchman
henna
henpecked
heptagon
heptagonal
her
herald
heraldic
heraldry
herb
**herbaceous**
herbal
**herbalist**
herbivore
herbivorous
Herculean
herd
here
*Here you are: I left*
*it here*

hereabouts
hereafter
hereby
**hereditary**
heredity
heresy
*pl* heresies
heretic
heretical
*adv* heretically
heritage
hermaphrodite
hermetically
hermit
hermitage
hero
*pl* heroes
heroic
*adv* heroically
heroin
*heroin addicts*
heroine
*the hero and*
*heroine*
**heroism**
heron
*a heron eating fish*
herring
*fried herring*
hers
herself
hertz
he's
= he is, he has
hesitancy
hesitant
**hesitate**
hesitated
hesitating

hesitation
hessian
het up
hew
*to hew down a tree*
hewed
*He hewed down a tree*
hewed, hewn
*He has hewed down a tree: He has hewn it down*
hewing
hexagon
hexagonal
**heyday**
hibernate
hibernated
hibernating
hibernation
**hiccup, hiccough**
hide
hid
*He hid the treasure*
hidden
*He has hidden the treasure*
hidebound
**hideous**
hiding
**hierarchy**
**hieroglyphics**
**hi-fi**
higgledy-
piggledy
high
*compar* higher
*at a higher level*
*superl* highest

highbrow
high fidelity
Highlands
highlight
highlighted
highlighting
highly
highness
highway
**hijack**
hijacked
hijacking
hijacker
hike
hiked
hiking
hiker
**hilarious**
hilarity
hill
hillock
hilly
hilt
him
*She killed him*
Himalayas
himself
hind
hinder
hindered
hindering
hindmost
**hindrance**
hindsight
Hindu
hinge
hinged
hinging
hint

hinterland
hip
**hippopotamus**
*pl* hippopota-
muses,
hippopotami
hire
*to hire a car*
hired
hiring
hire purchase
hirsute
his
hiss
*pl* hisses
historian
historic
historical
*adv* histor-
ically
history
*pl* histories
histrionics
hit
hit
hitting
hitch
*pl* hitches
hitchhike
hitchhiked
hitchhiking
hither
hitherto
HIV
hive
hoar
*hoar frost*
hoard
*to hoard food*

hoarding
hoarse
*She is hoarse from shouting*
*adv* hoarsely
hoary
hoax
*pl* hoaxes
hob
hobble
hobbled
hobbling
hobby
*pl* hobbies
hobby-horse
hobgoblin
hobnail
hobnob
hobnobbed
hobnobbing
hock
hockey
hocus-pocus
hod
hoe
hoed
hoeing
hog
hogged
hogging
Hogmanay
hoist
hold
held
holding
**holdall**
holder
holding
hold-up

hole
*a hole in the ground: a hole in her sock*
**holiday**
holiness
hollow
holly
**hollyhock**
**holocaust**
holster
holt
holy
homage
home
homed
homing
homelessness
homeliness
homely
home-made
homesick
homestead
homewards
homework
homicidal
homicide
homing
homoeopathic, homeopathic
homoeopathy, homeopathy
homogenization, -isation
homogenize, -ise
homogenized
homogenizing
homogenous
**homonym**

hone
honed
honing
**honest**
honesty
honey
honeycomb
honeyed
honeymoon
honeysuckle
honk
honorarium
**honorary**
*He is honorary secretary of the club*
honour
honoured
honouring
honourable
*He is an honest and honourable man*
*adv* honourably
hood
hoodwink
hoof
*pl* hooves, hoofs
hook
hookah, hooka
hooked
**hooligan**
hooliganism
hoop
*a hoop round a barrel*
hooray
hoot

hooted
hooting
hooter
Hoover ®
hoover
  hoovered
  hoovering
hop
  hopped
    *The bird hopped over*
  hopping
hope
  hoped
    *She hoped that he would come*
  hoping
hopeful
hopefully
hopefulness
hopeless
hopelessness
hopped
  *see* hop
hopper
hopscotch
horde
  *a horde of noisy children*
horizon
horizontal
hormonal
hormone
horn
hornet
hornpipe
horny
**horoscope**
horrendous

**horrible**
  *adv* horribly
horrid
horrify
  horrified
  horrifying
horror
horse
  *two dogs and a horse*
horseplay
horsepower
horseshoe
horticultural
**horticulture**
horticulturist
hosanna
hose
hosiery
hospitable
  *adv* hospitably
hospital
hospitality
hospitalization, -isation
hospitalize, -ise
host
hostage
hostel
hostelry
  *pl* hostelries
hostess
  *pl* hostesses
hostile
  *adv* hostilely
hostility
  *pl* hostilities
hot
  *compar* hotter

*superl* hottest
hotchpotch
hot dog
hotel
hotelier
hotfoot
hot-headed
hothouse
hound
hour
hourly
house
  housed
  housing
household
householder
housekeeper
housewife
hovel
hover
  hovered
  hovering
hovercraft
hove to
  *see* heave to
how
howdah
however
howl
howler
hub
hubbub
huddle
  huddled
  huddling
hue
  *the hue of the sky: a hue and cry*
huff

huffy
hug
  hugged
  hugging
huge
  *adv* hugely
hugeness
hula-hoop
hulk
hulking
hull
**hullabaloo**
hullo
  *see* hello
hum
  hummed
  humming
human
  *a human being*
humane
  *cruel, not humane*
  *adv* humanely
humanism
humanist
humanitarian
humanity
humble
  *adv* humbly
humdrum
humid
humidity
humiliate
  humiliated
  humiliating
humiliation
  *full of shame and humiliation*
humility
  *meekness and*

*humility*
humorist
**humorous**
**humour**
hump
humpbacked
humus
hunch
  *pl* hunches
hundred
hundredth
hundredweight
hung
  *see* hang
hunger
  hungered
  hungering
hungry
  *adv* hungrily
hunt
hunter
huntress
  *pl* huntresses
huntsman
  *pl* huntsmen
hurdle
  hurdled
  hurdling
hurdygurdy
hurl
hurlyburly
hurrah
hurray
**hurricane**
hurry
  **hurried**
  hurrying
hurt
hurtful

*adv* hurtfully
hurtle
  hurtled
  hurtling
husband
husbandry
hush
hush-hush
husk
husky
  *pl* huskies
hussar
hussy
  *pl* hussies
hustings
hustle
  hustled
  hustling
hut
hutch
  *pl* hutches
**hyacinth**
hyaena
  *see* hyena
hybrid
hydra
hydrant
hydraulic
hydro
hydroelectric
hydrogen
hydropathic
hydrophobia
hyena, hyaena
**hygiene**
hygienic
  *adv* hygienically
hymn
  *The choir sang a*

*hymn*
hymnal
hymnary
 *pl* hymnaries
hype
 hyped
 hyping
hyperactive
hyperbole
hypermarket
**hyphen**
**hypnosis**
hypnotic
 *adv* hypnotically
hypnotism
hypnotist
hypnotize, -ise
 hypnotized
 hypnotizing
hypochondria
**hypochondriac**
**hypocrisy**
hypocrite
hypocritical
 *adv*
 hypocritically
hypodermic
hypotenuse
hypothermia
hypothesis
 *pl* hypotheses
hypothetical
 *adv*
 hypothetically
hysterectomy
hysteria
**hysterical**
 *adv* hysterically
hysterics

108

I

ice
iced
icing
iceberg
icecream
**icicle**
icing
icon, ikon
iconoclasm
icy
 *adv* icily
I'd
 = I had, I
 should, I
 would
idea
ideal
 *adv* ideally
idealism
idealist
idealize, -ise
 idealized
 idealizing
identical
 *adv* identically
identification
identify
 identified
 identifying
Identikit ®
 (picture)
identity
 *pl* identities
**ideological**
 *adv*
 ideologically
ideology

idiocy
 *pl* idiocies
idiom
idiomatic
 *adv*
 idiomatically
**idiosyncrasy**
 *pl*
 idiosyncrasies
**idiosyncratic**
 *adv* idiosyncrati-
 cally
idiot
idiotic
 *adv* idiotically
idle
 *a slow and idle
 worker*
 *adv* idly
 *to idle away time*
 idled
 idling
idleness
idly
 *see* idle
idol
 *The pop star is her
 idol: heathen idols*
idolize, -ise
 idolized
 idolizing
idyll
**idyllic**
 *adv* idyllically
if
igloo
 *pl* igloos
igneous
ignite

ignited
igniting
ignition
ignoble
  *adv* ignobly
**ignominious**
ignominy
ignoramus
  *pl* ignoramuses
**ignorance**
ignorant
ignore
  ignored
  ignoring
iguana
ikon
  *see* icon
I'll
  = I shall, I will
ill
  *compar* worse
  *superl* worst
illegal
  *adv* illegally
illegibility
**illegible**
  *untidy and illegible
  handwriting*
  *adv* illegibly
illegitimacy
**illegitimate**
  *adv*
    illegitimately
**illicit**
  *an illicit love affair*
**illiteracy**
**illiterate**
  *He cannot read that
  letter — he is*

*illiterate*
illness
  *pl* illnesses
illogical
  *adv* illogically
illuminate
  illuminated
  illuminating
illumination
illusion
  *an optical illusion:
  an illusion of
  grandeur*
illustrate
  illustrated
  illustrating
illustration
illustrative
illustrator
illustrious
I'm
  = I am
image
imagery
imaginary
imagination
**imaginative**
  *adv*
    imaginatively
imagine
  imagined
  imagining
imbecile
imbibe
  imbibed
  imbibing
imbue
  imbued
  imbuing

**imitate**
  imitated
  imitating
**imitation**
**immaculate**
  *adv*
    immaculately
immaterial
immature
immediacy
**immediate**
  *adv* immediately
**immemorial**
immense
  *adv* immensely
immensity
immerse
  immersed
  immersing
immersion
immigrant
  *immigrants to
  Britain*
immigration
  *immigration into
  Britain*
imminent
immobile
immobility
immobilize, -ise
  immobilized
  immobilizing
**immoderate**
**immoral**
  *wicked and
  immoral*
immorality
  *wickedness and
  immorality*

109

immortal
*People die — they are not immortal*

immortality
*the immortality of God*

immortalize, -ise
immortalized
immortalizing

**immovable**
*adv* immovably

immune

immunity

immunize, -ise
immunized
immunizing

imp

impact

impair
impaired
impairing

impairment

impale
impaled
impaling

impart

impartial
*adv* impartially

impartiality

impassable

**impasse**

impassioned

impassive
*adv* impassively

impatience

impatient

impeach

**impeccable**
*adv* impeccably

**impecunious**

impede
impeded
impeding

impediment

**impel**
impelled
impelling
impending

**imperative**
*adv* imperatively

**imperceptible**
*adv* imperceptibly

imperfect

imperfection

imperial

imperialism

imperil
imperilled
imperilling

imperious

impermeable

impersonal
*adv* impersonally

impersonate
impersonated
impersonating

impersonation

impersonator

impertinence

impertinent

imperturbable

**impervious**

impetigo

impetuosity

**impetuous**
*rash and*

*impetuous*

impetus
*the impetus of the blow*

impiety

impinge
impinged
impinging

**impious**

impish

implement

implicate
implicated
implicating

implication

implicit

imply
implied
implying

impolite
*adv* impolitely

import

importance

important

importation

importunate

importune
importuned
importuning

importunity

impose
imposed
imposing

imposition

impossibility

impossible
*adv* impossibly

impostor

impotence

impotent
impound
impoverish
impracticability
impracticable
*an impracticable idea*
*adv*
  impracticably
impractical
*an impractical person*
*adv*
  impractically
impracticality
impregnable
impregnate
**impresario**
*pl* impresarios
impress
impression
impressionable
impressionism
impressive
*adv*
  impressively
imprint
imprison
  **imprisoned**
imprisoning
**imprisonment**
improbability
improbable
*adv* improbably
**impromptu**
improper
**impropriety**
*pl* improprieties
improve

improved
improving
improvement
improvidence
improvident
improvisation
improvise
improvised
improvising
impudence
impudent
impulse
impulsive
*adv* impulsively
impulsiveness
impunity
impure
impurity
*pl* impurities
imputation
impute
imputed
imputing
in
  *in the house:*
  *dressed in black:*
  *covered in dirt*
inability
**inaccessible**
*adv* inaccessibly
**inaccurate**
*adv* inaccur-
  ately
inaction
inactive
inactivity
inadequacy
*pl* inadequacies
inadequate

*adv*
  inadequately
**inadmissible**
inadvertent
inane
*adv* inanely
**inanimate**
inanity
*pl* inanities
inapplicable
**inappropriate**
*adv*
  inappropriately
inapt
*an inapt remark*
inarticulate
inasmuch as
inattention
inattentive
*adv* inattentively
inaudible
*adv* inaudibly
**inaugural**
inaugurate
inaugurated
inaugurating
inauguration
inauspicious
inborn
inbred
inbreeding
incalculable
**incandescent**
incantation
incapable
incapacitate
incapacitated
incapacitating
incapacity

incarcerate
  incarcerated
  incarcerating
incarnate
incarnation
incendiary
in'cense
  incensed
  incensing
'incense
incentive
inception
**incessant**
inch
  *pl* inches
incidence
incident
incidental
  *adv* incidentally
incinerator
**incipient**
incision
incisive
  *adv* incisively
incisiveness
incisor
incite
  incited
  inciting
incitement
incivility
  *pl* incivilities
inclemency
inclement
inclination
incline
  inclined
  inclining
include

included
including
inclusion
inclusive
  *adv* inclusively
**incognito**
incoherence
incoherent
incombustible
income
incoming
incommode
  incommoded
  incommoding
**incommunicado**
incomparable
  *adv* incomparably
incompatibility
incompatible
incompetence
incompetent
incomprehensible
  *adv* incompre-
    hensibly
incomprehension
**inconceivable**
  *adv* inconceiv-
    ably
inconclusive
  *adv* inconclus-
    ively
**incongruity**
**incongruous**
  *adv*
    incongruously
inconsequential
  *adv* inconse-
    quentially
inconsiderable

inconsiderate
  *adv*
    inconsiderately
inconsistent
inconsolable
inconspicuous
inconstancy
inconstant
incontinence
incontinent
**incontrovertible**
  *adv*
    incontrovertibly
inconvenience
inconvenient
incorporate
  incorporated
  incorporating
incorrect
**incorrigible**
  *adv* incorrigibly
incorruptible
increase
  increased
  increasing
increasingly
incredibility
incredible
  *an incredible story*
  *adv* incredibly
incredulity
**incredulous**
  *an incredulous
  person: an
  incredulous look*
increment
**incriminate**
  incriminated
  incriminating

incubate
  incubated
  incubating
incubation
**incubator**
inculcate
  inculcated
  inculcating
incumbent
incur
  **incurred**
  incurring
incurable
  *adv* incurably
incursion
**indebted**
indebtedness
indecency
indecent
indecision
indecisive
  *adv* indecisively
indeed
**indefatigable**
  *adv*
  indefatigably
indefensible
  *adv* indefensibly
**indefinable**
  *adv* indefinably
**indefinite**
  *adv* indefinitely
indelible
  *adv* indelibly
indelicacy
indelicate
  *adv* indelicately
indemnity
indent

indentation
indenture
**independence**
**independent**
**indescribable**
  *adv*
  indescribably
indestructible
indeterminate
  *adv*
  indeterminately
index
  *pl* indexes,
  indices
  *indexes of books:*
  *indices of numbers*
Indian
indicate
  indicated
  indicating
indication
indicative
indicator
indices
  *see* index
**indict** [in'dīt]
**indictment**
indifference
indifferent
indigence
indigenous
  *Tobacco is not*
  *indigenous to*
  *Britain*
indigent
  *the indigent widow*
**indigestible**
indigestion
**indignant**

indignation
indignity
  *pl* indignities
indigo
indirect
indiscreet
indiscretion
indiscriminate
  *adv* indiscrimin-
  ately
**indispensable**
  *adv*
  indispensably
indisposed
indisposition
indisputable
  *adv* indisputably
indistinct
**indistinguishable**
  *adv* indistinguish-
  ably
individual
  *adv* individually
individualism
individualist
individuality
indivisible
indoctrinate
  indoctrinated
  indoctrinating
indolence
indolent
**indomitable**
  *adv* indomitably
indoor
indoors
**indubitable**
  *adv* indubitably
induce

induced
inducing
inducement
induct
induction
inductive
**indulge**
indulged
indulging
indulgence
industrial
  *an industrial
  process: an
  industrial worker*
  (= in industry)
industrialist
industrious
  *an industrious
  child*
  (= hardworking)
**inebriated**
inebriation
inedible
ineffable
  *adv* ineffably
ineffective
  *adv* ineffectively
ineffectiveness
ineffectual
  *adv* ineffectually
**inefficiency**
inefficient
inelegance
inelegant
ineligibility
**ineligible**

  *ineligible for the
  post because of
  lack of*

  *qualifications*
inept
  *an inept attempt:
  an inept young
  man*
ineptitude
**inequality**
  *pl* inequalities
inert
inertia
**inescapable**
  *adv* inescapably
inestimable
  *adv* inestimably
inevitability
inevitable
  *adv* inevitably
**inexcusable**
  *adv*
  inexcusably
**inexhaustible**
inexorable
  *adv* inexorably
inexpensive
  *adv*
  inexpensively
inexperience
inexperienced
inexplicable
  *adv* inexplicably
inexpressible
  *adv*
  inexpressibly
inextricable
  *adv* inextricably
infallibility
**infallible**
  *adv* infallibly
infamous

infamy
infancy
infant
infanticide
infantry
**infatuated**
infatuation
infect
infection
infectious
infer
**inferred**
inferring
inference
inferior
inferiority
infernal
  *adv* infernally
inferno
  *pl* infernos
infertile
infertility
infest
infidel
infidelity
infiltrate
infiltrated
infiltrating
infiltration
infinite
  *adv* infinitely
infinitesimal
  *adv*
  infinitesimally
**infinitive**
infinity
infirm
infirmary
  *pl* infirmaries

infirmity
  *pl* infirmities
inflame
  **inflamed**
  inflaming
**inflammable**
  *Petrol is highly
  inflammable*
**inflammation**
**inflammatory**
inflate
  inflated
  inflating
inflation
**inflationary**
inflection
  *see* inflexion
inflexible
inflexion,
  inflection
inflict
infliction
influence
  influenced
  influencing
influential
  *adv* influentially
**influenza**
influx
inform
informal
  *adv* informally
informality
informant
information
informative
  *adv*
  informatively
informer

infra-red
infringe
  infringed
  infringing
infringement
infuriate
  infuriated
  infuriating
infuse
  infused
  infusing
infusion
ingenious
  *an ingenious idea*
ingenuity
ingenuous
  *young and
  ingenuous*
ingenuousness
ingot
ingrained
**ingratiate**
  ingratiated
  ingratiating
ingratitude
**ingredient**
inhabit
  inhabited
  inhabiting
**inhabitant**
inhalant
inhalation
inhale
  inhaled
  inhaling
inhaler
inherent
inherit
  inherited

inheriting
**inheritance**
inhibit
  inhibited
  inhibiting
**inhibition**
inhospitable
  *adv* inhospitably
inhuman
  *The torturing of
  prisoners is
  inhuman: a
  strange, inhuman
  laugh*

inhumane
  *inhumane
  treatment of
  animals*

  *adv* inhumanely
inimical
  *adv* inimically
inimitable
  *adv* inimitably
**iniquitous**
iniquity
  *pl* iniquities
initial
  **initialled**
  initialling
  initially
**initiate**
  initiated
  initiating
**initiation**
**initiative**
inject
injection
injudicious
injunction

115

injure
  injured
  injuring
injury
  *pl* injuries
injustice
ink
inkling
inky
inlaid *see* inlay
inland
inlay
  inlaid
  inlaying
inlet
inmate
inmost
inn
  *to stay at an inn*
**innate**
inner
innings
innkeeper
innocence
innocent
**innocuous**
innovation
innuendo
  *pl* innuendoes
**innumerable**
innumeracy
**innumerate**
**inoculate**
  inoculated
  inoculating
inoculation
inoffensive
  *adv*
    inoffensively

inopportune
  *adv*
    inopportunely
inordinate
  *adv* inordinately
inorganic
in-patient
input
inquest
inquire, enquire
  inquired,
    enquired
  inquiring,
    enquiring
inquirer, enquirer
inquiry, enquiry
  *pls* inquiries,
    enquiries
inquisition
inquisitive
  *adv* inquisitively
inquisitor
inroads
insane
  *adv* insanely
insanitary
insanity
insatiable
  *adv* insatiably
inscribe
  inscribed
  inscribing
inscription
inscrutable
  *adv* inscrutably
insect
**insecticide**
insecure
  *adv* insecurely

insecurity
insensible
insensitive
  *adv* insensitively
**inseparable**
  *adv* inseparably
insert
insertion
inset
inshore
inside
**insidious**
insight
insignia
insignificance
insignificant
**insincere**
  *adv* insincerely
insincerity
insinuate
  insinuated
  insinuating
insinuation
insipid
insist
**insistence**
insistent
insolence
insolent
insoluble
insolvent
**insomnia**
insomniac
inspect
inspection
inspector
inspiration
inspire
  inspired

inspiring
instability
instal, install
  installed
  installing
  installation
**instalment**
instance
instant
**instantaneous**
instead
instep
instigate
  instigated
  instigating
  instigation
instil
  instilled
  instilling
instinct
instinctive
  *adv* instinctively
institute
  instituted
  instituting
**institution**
institutional
instruct
instruction
instructive
  *adv* instructively
instructor
instrument
instrumental
instrumentalist
insubordinate
insubordination
insufferable
  *adv* insufferably

insufficiency
insufficient
insular
insulate
  insulated
  insulating
  insulation
insulin
insult
insuperable
  *adv* insuperably
insurance
insure
  *to insure one's life:*
  *to insure one's*
  *house against theft*
  insured
  insuring
insurgence
insurgent
insurmountable
  *adv*
    insurmountably
insurrection
intact
intake
intangible
  *adv* intangibly
integral
integrate
  integrated
  integrating
  integration
integrity
intellect
**intellectual**
  *adv*
    intellectually
intelligence

intelligent
  *bright and*
  *intelligent*
intelligentsia
intelligible
  *a scarcely*
  *intelligible account*
  *of the accident*
  *adv* intelligibly
intemperance
intemperate
  *adv*
    intemperately
intend
intense
  *adv* intensely
intensify
  intensified
  intensifying
intensity
intensive
  *adv* intensively
intent
intentional
  *adv* intentionally
inter
  interred
  interring
interact
interaction
intercede
  interceded
  interceding
**intercept**
intercession
interchange
  interchanged
  interchanging
interchangeable

intercom
intercourse
interdict
interest
interesting
interfere
  interfered
  interfering
**interference**
interim
**interior**
interject
interjection
interlock
interloper
interlude
intermediary
  *pl*
    intermediaries
**intermediate**
interment
  *the interment of the corpse*
interminable
  *adv*
    interminably
intermission
**intermittent**
intern
internal
  *adv* internally
international
  *adv*
    internationally
internee
Internet
internment
  *the internment of the prisoner*

**interpret**
  interpreted
  interpreting
**interpretation**
interpreter
**interrogate**
  interrogated
  interrogating
**interrogation**
**interrogative**
interrogator
**interrupt**
interruption
intersection
intersperse
  interspersed
  interspersing
interstice
interval
intervene
  intervened
  intervening
intervention
**interview**
intestate
intestinal
intestines
intimacy
intimate
  *adv* intimately
  intimated
  intimating
intimation
intimidate
  intimidated
  intimidating
intimidation
into
intolerable

  *adv* intolerably
intolerance
intolerant
intonation
intone
  intoned
  intoning
intoxicant
**intoxicate**
  intoxicated
  intoxicating
intoxication
intractable
intransigence
intransigent
intransitive
intrusive
  *adv* intrusively
intrepid
intrepidity
**intricacy**
  *pl* intricacies
intricate
  *adv* intricately
**intrigue**
  intrigued
  intriguing
intrinsic
  *adv* **intrinsically**
introduce
  introduced
  introducing
introduction
introductory
introspection
introspective
  *adv*
    introspectively
intrude

intruded
intruding
**intruder**
intrusion
intrusive
**intuition**
**intuitive**
  *adv* intuitively
inundate
  inundated
  inundating
  inundation
**inure**
  inured
  inuring
invade
  invaded
  invading
invader
invalid
invalidate
  invalidated
  invalidating
invalidity
invaluable
  *adv* **invaluably**
invariable
  *adv* **invariably**
invasion
invective
**inveigle**
  inveigled
  inveigling
invent
invention
inventive
inventor
inventory
  *pl* inventories

inverse
  *adv* inversely
inversion
invert
**invertebrate**
  *A worm is an*
  *invertebrate*
  *creature*
invest
investigate
  investigated
  investigating
investigation
investigator
investiture
investment
investor
**inveterate**
  *an inveterate liar*
invidious
invigilate
  invigilated
  invigilating
invigilator
invigorate
  invigorated
  invigorating
invincible
inviolable
inviolate
invisibility
invisible
  *adv* invisibly
invitation
invite
  invited
  inviting
invocation
invoice

invoke
invoked
invoking
**involuntary**
  *adv*
  involuntarily
involve
involved
involving
**involvement**
inward
inwardly
inwards
**iodine**
iota
IOU
Iowa
Iraqi
irascibility
**irascible**
  *adv* irascibly
irate
  *adv* irately
ire
**iridescence**
iridescent
iris
  *pl* irises
Irish
irk
irksome
iron
**ironed**
ironing
ironic, ironical
  *adv* ironically
ironmonger
irony
  *pl* ironies

**irrational**
  *adv* irrationally
**irregular**
irregularity
  *pl* irregularities
irrelevance
irrelevancy
**irrelevant**
**irreparable**
  *adv* irreparably
**irreplaceable**
irrepressible
  *adv* irrepressibly
irreproachable
  *adv*
    irreproachably
**irresistible**
  *adv* irresistibly
irresolute
  *adv* irresolutely
**irrespective**
  *adv*
    irrespectively
**irresponsible**
  *adv*
    irresponsibly
irreverence
irreverent
**irrevocable**
  *adv* irrevocably
irrigate
  irrigated
  irrigating
irrigation
**irritable**
  *adv* irritably
irritant
irritate
  irritated

irritating
irritation
is
  *see* be
island
islander
isle
  *Isle of Man*
isn't
  = is not
isobar
isolate
  isolated
  isolating
  isolation
**isosceles**
isotherm
Israeli
issue
  issued
  issuing
isthmus
  *pl* isthmuses
it
Italian
**italicize, -ise**
  italicized
  italicizing
italics
itch
  *pl* itches
itchy
item
**itinerant**
**itinerary**
  *pl* itineraries
it'll
  = it shall, it will
it's

= it is
  *It's fine*
its
  *its leg*
itself
I've
  = I have
ivory
ivy

**J**

jab
  jabbed
  jabbing
jabber
  jabbered
  jabbering
jack
**jackal**
**jackass**
  *pl* jackasses
jackdaw
jacket
jack-in-the-box
jack-knife
jackpot
Jacuzzi ®
jade
  jaded
jag
  jagged
  jagging
**jaguar**
jail, gaol
  *He was sent to jail/*
  *gaol*
jailer, gaoler
jam

120

*strawberry jam: in a jam: Did the machine jam?: to jam full*

jammed
jamming
jamb
*the door jamb*
jamboree
jangle
  jangled
  jangling
janitor
January
jar
  jarred
  jarring
jargon
jasmine
jaundice
jaunt
jaunty
  *adv* jauntily
javelin
jaw
jay
jaywalker
jazz
**jealous**
jealousy
jeans
Jeep ®
jeer
  jeered
  jeering
Jekyll and Hyde
jelly
  *pl* jellies
jellyfish

**jeopardize, -ise**
  jeopardized
  jeopardizing
jeopardy
jerboa
jerk
jerkin
jerky
  *adv* jerkily
jersey
  *pl* jerseys
jest
jester
jet
jetsam
jettison
  **jettisoned**
  jettisoning
jetty
  *pl* jetties
Jew
  *a Jew from Israel*
  *pl* Jews
  *Jews in the synagogue*
jewel
**jeweller, jeweler**
**jewellery, jewelry**
Jewish
jib
  *to jib at paying a lot*
  jibbed
  jibbing
jibe, gibe
  *to sneer and jibe*
  jibed, gibed
  jibing, gibing

jig
  jigged
  jigging
jigsaw
jilt
jingle
  jingled
  jingling
job
  jobbing
job centre, Jobcentre
joblessness
jockey
  *pl* jockeys
  jockeyed
  jockeying
jocular
jocularity
**jodhpurs**
jog
  jogged
  jogging
joggle
  joggled
  joggling
Johannesburg
join
  joined
  joining
joiner
joint
joist
joke
  joked
  joking
joker
jollification
jollity

jolly
  *compar* jollier
  *superl* jolliest
  *adv* jollily
jolt
joss-stick
jostle
  jostled
  jostling
jot
  jotted
  jotting
jotter
joule
journal
**journalism**
**journalist**
journey
  *pl* journeys
  journeyed
  journeying
joust
jovial
  *adv* jovially
jowl
joy
joyful
  *adv* joyfully
joyfulness
joyless
joyous
joyrider
**jubilant**
jubilation
**jubilee**
judge
  judged
  judging
judgement,

judgment
judicial
  *a judicial inquiry*
judiciary
judicious
  *a judicious choice*
  *of books*
judo
jug
  jugged
**juggernaut**
juggle
  juggled
  juggling
juggler
**jugular** (vein)
juice
juicy
ju-jitsu
jukebox
July
jumble
  jumbled
  jumbling
jumble sale
jumbo
jump
jumper
jumpy
junction
  *a road junction*
juncture
  *at this juncture*
June
jungle
junior
juniper
junk
junket

junketing
Junoesque
jurisdiction
juror
jury
  *pl* juries
just
justice
justifiable
  *adv* justifiably
justification
justify
  justified
  justifying
jut
  jutted
  jutting
jute
**juvenile**
juxtapose
  juxtaposed
  juxtaposing
juxtaposition

**K**

Kafkaesque
kaftan, caftan
kaiser
kale
**kaleidoscope**
kaleidoscopic
  *adv* kaleido-
    scopically
kangaroo
  *pl* kangaroos
kapok
karaoke
**karate**

kart
  *a go-kart*
kayak
kebab
kedgeree
keel
  keeled
  keeling
keelhaul
keen
**keenness**
keep
  kept
  keeping
keeper
keepsake
keg
kelp
kelvin
kennel
kept
  *see* keep
kerb
  *She stood on the kerb*
kernel
kerosene
kestrel
ketch
  *pl* ketches
ketchup
kettle
key
  *the key to the door*
keyboard
keyed-up
keyhole
keynote
**khaki**

Khyber
**kibbutz**
  *pl* kibbutzim
kick
kick-off
kid
kidnap
  **kidnapped**
  kidnapping
**kidnapper**
kidney
  *pl* kidneys
kill
killer
kiln
kilogramme
**kilometre**
kilowatt
kilt
kimono
  *pl* kimonos
kin
kind
kindergarten
kindle
  kindled
  kindling
kindliness
kindly
kindness
kindred
kinetic
  *adv* kinetically
king
kingdom
kingfisher
kingly
kink
kinky

kinsman
**kiosk**
kipper
kiss
  *pl* kisses
kit
kitchen
**kitchenette**
kite
kitten
kittiwake
kitty
kiwi
  *pl* kiwis
**kleptomania**
kleptomaniac
**knack**
knacker
**knackered**
knapsack
**knave**
  *the knave of hearts*
knavish
knead
  *knead the bread*
knee
  kneed
  *He kneed him in the stomach*
  kneeing
kneel
  knelt
  kneeling
knell
knelt
  *see* kneel
knew
  *see* know
knickerbockers

knickers
**knick-knack**
knife
  *pl* knives
  knifed
  knifing
knight
  *a knight in shining armour*
knighted
knighthood
knightly
  *Bravery is a knightly quality*
knit
  *to knit a cardigan*
  knitted
  knitting
knob
knock
knocker
knock-kneed
knoll
knot
  *a knot in the string*
  knotted
  knotting
knotty
  *a knotty problem*
know
  *I know her well*
  knew
  *I knew it*
  known
  *I should have known*
  knowing
knowingly
**knowledge**

**knowledgeable**
  *adv*
  knowledgeably
known
  *see* know
knuckles
knuckle under
  knuckled under
  knuckling under
koala bear
kookaburra
Koran
kosher
**kowtow**
  kowtowed
  kowtowing
kudos
kung-fu

## L

lab
label
  **labelled**
  labelling
**laboratory**
  *pl* laboratories
laborious
labour
  laboured
  labouring
  labourer
**laburnum**
**labyrinth**
lace
  laced
  lacing
lacerate
  lacerated

lacerating
laceration
lack
**lackadaisical**
  *adv*
  lackadaisically
lackey
  *pl* lackeys
**laconic**
  *adv* laconically
**lacquer**
  lacquered
  lacquering
lacrosse
lactic
lad
ladder
  **laddered**
  laddering
lade
  *a mill lade*
laden
ladies
  *see* lady
lading
ladle
  ladled
  ladling
lady
  *pl* ladies
ladybird
ladyship
lag
  lagged
  lagging
**lager**
lagoon
laid
  *see* lay

lain
  *see* lie
lair
  *a wolf's lair*
laird
laity
lake
lama
  *Tibetans respect the lama*
lamb
lame
lameness
lament
lamentable
lamentation
lamp
lampoon
  lampooned
  lampooning
lance
  lanced
  lancing
lance-corporal
land
landau
landlady
  *pl* landladies
landlord
landscape
lane
  *a country lane*
**language**
**languid**
**languish**
**languor**
**languorous**
  *adv*
    languorously

laniard
  *see* lanyard
lank
lanky
lantern
lanyard, laniard
lap
  lapped
  lapping
lapdog
lapel
lapidary
  *pl* lapidaries
lapse
  lapsed
  lapsing
lapwing
larceny
larch
  *pl* larches
lard
larder
large
largely
largeness
largesse
lariat
lark
larkspur
larva
  *pl* larvae
**laryngitis**
**larynx**
**lascivious**
laser
lash
  *pl* lashes
lass
  *pl* lasses

**lassitude**
lasso
  *pl* lassos,
    lassoes
last
lastly
Las Vegas
latch
  *pl* latches
latchkey
late
lately
latency
lateness
latent
lateral
  *adv* laterally
  *A crab moves laterally*
latex
lath
  *a lath of wood*
lathe
  *A mechanic uses a lathe*
lather
  lathered
  lathering
Latin
**latitude**
latter
latterly
  *Latterly he has grown senile*
lattice
laud
  lauded
  lauding
laudable

*adv* laudably
laugh
laughable
  *adv* laughably
**laughter**
**launch**
  *pl* launches
launder
  laundered
  laundering
**launderette**
**laundry**
  *pl* laundries
laurel
lava
lavatory
  *pl* lavatories
lavender
lavish
law
lawful
  *adv* lawfully
lawless
lawlessness
lawn
lawnmower
lawyer
lax
laxative
laxity
lay
  *see* lie
lay
  *to lay it on the table*
  laid
  *She laid it on the bed*
  laying

layabout
layby
  *pl* laybys
layer
  *two layers of cloth*
**layette**
laze
  lazed
  lazing
**laziness**
lazy
  *compar* lazier
  *superl* laziest
  *adv* lazily
lea
  *the green lea*
lead [lēd]
  *to lead into battle*
  led
  *He led me to the king*
  leading
lead [led]
  *lead pipes*
leaden
leader
leaf
  *pl* leaves
leaflet
leafy
**league**
leak
  *a gas leak: Does this kettle leak?*
leakage
lean
  leant, leaned
  leaning
**leanness**

leant
  *see* lean
leap
  leapt, leaped
  leaping
leapfrog
leapt
  *see* leap
learn
  learned, learnt
  learning
learner
lease
  leased
  leasing
leasehold
leash
  *pl* leashes
least
  *see* little
leather
  leathered
  leathering
leathery
leave
  left
  leaving
leaves
  *see* leaf
leavings
**lecherous**
lechery
lectern
lecture
  lectured
  lecturing
lecturer
led
  *see* lead

edge
**edger**
ee
*in the lee of the boat*
eech
*pl* leeches
eek
*leek soup*
eer
leered
leering
ees
eeward
eeway
eft
*see* leave
eg
egacy
*pl* legacies
egal
*adv* legally
egality
*pl* legalities
egalize, -ise
legalized
legalizing
egatee
egation
egend
**egendary**
egerdemain
eggings
eggy
egibility
**egible**
*clear, legible writing*
*adv* legibly

legion
**legionary**
legislate
legislated
legislating
legislation
legislative
legislator
legislature
legitimacy
**legitimate**
*adv* legitimately
**leisure**
leisured
leisurely
lemming
*like lemmings to the sea*
lemon
*an orange and a lemon*
lemonade
lemony
lemur
lend
lent
lending
**length**
**lengthen**
lengthened
lengthening
lengthways
**lengthy**
*adv* lengthily
leniency
lenient
lens
*pl* lenses
Lent

lent
*see* lend
lentil
**leopard**
*a tiger and a leopard*
**leotard**
leper
*a leper dressed in rags*
**leprechaun**
leprosy
less
*see* little
lessen
*to lessen the pain*
lessened
lessening
lesser
lesson
*a French lesson*
lest
let
let
letting
lethal
lethargic
*adv* lethargically
lethargy
letter
lettered
**lettering**
lettuce
**leukaemia**
levee
level
**levelled**
levelling
lever

127

leveret
leviathan
levied
*see* levy
levitate
levitated
levitating
levitation
levity
levy
*pl* levies
levied
levying
**lewd**
lewdness
lexicographer
lexicography
liability
*pl* liabilities
liable
*You are liable to slip on ice: liable for her debts*

**liaise**
liaised
liaising
**liaison**
liar
*Don't believe a liar*
libel
*guilty of libel: Did the newspaper libel him?*
libelled
libelling
libellous
liberal
*adv* liberally
liberality

liberate
liberated
liberating
liberation
libertine
liberty
*pl* liberties
librarian
library
*pl* libraries
libretto
*pl* libretti, librettos
lice
*see* louse
licence
*a TV licence: poetic licence*
license
*to license a TV*
licensed
licensing
**licensee**
**licentious**
licentiousness
lichen
lick
lid
lie
lied
*He lied about his age*
lying
lie
lay
*He lay down*
lain
*He has lain down: He'd lain there for*

*three days*
lying
**liege**
**lieu**
**lieutenant**
life
*pl* lives
lifeguard
lifeless
life-like
lifestyle
lift
lift-off
ligament
ligature
light
lit, lighted
lighting
lighten
lightened
lightening
*lightening the load*
lighter
lighthouse
lightning
*thunder and lightning*
like
liked
liking
likeable, likable
likelihood
likely
likeness
likewise
**lilac**
Lilliputian
lilt
lily

pl lilies
**limb**
**limber**
limbered
limbering
**limbo**
**lime**
**limelight**
**limit**
 **limited**
 limiting
 limitation
**limousine**
limp
limpet
limpid
linchpin
line
 lined
 lining
**lineage**
lineal
 *adv* lineally
lineament
 *the lineaments of her face*
linear
**linen**
liner
linesman
linger
 lingered
 lingering
**lingerie**
**linguist**
**linguistic**
 *adv*
 linguistically
linguistics

liniment
 *to rub some liniment on his leg*
lining
link
links
linnet
lino
**linoleum**
linseed
lint
lintel
lion
lioness
 *pl* lionesses
lionize, -ise
 lionized
 lionizing
lip
lipstick
**liquefy**
 liquefied
 liquefying
**liqueur**
 *Cointreau is an orange liqueur*
liquid
liquidate
 liquidated
 liquidating
 liquidation
 liquidator
liquor
 *whisky and other strong liquors*
**liquorice**
lisp
lissom, lissome
list

listen
 **listened**
 listening
listener
listless
lit
 *see* light
litany
 *pl* litanies
literacy
literal
 *a literal translation*
 *adv* literally
literary
 *He has literary tastes*
literate
 *He is scarcely literate*
**literature**
lithe
lithograph
litigation
**litre**
litter
 littered
 littering
little
 *compar* less
 *superl* least
liturgical
liturgy
 *pl* liturgies
live [liv]
 lived
 living
live [līv]
**livelihood**
**liveliness**

livelong
lively
  *compar* livelier
  *superl* liveliest
liven up
  livened up
  livening up
liver
livery
  *pl* liveries
livestock
livid
living
living-room
lizard
llama
  *The llama is of the camel family*
lo!
load
  *a load of coal: to load the lorry with coal*
loaf
  *pl* loaves
loaf
  loafed
  loafing
loam
loan
  *a book on loan*
loath, loth
  *I am loath to go*
loathe
  *I loathe cruelty*
  loathed
  loathing
lob
  lobbed

lobbing
lobby
  *pl* lobbies
lobe
lobster
local
  *local people: drinking in his local*
locale
  *the locale of the film*
locality
localize, -ise
  localized
  localizing
locate
  located
  locating
location
loch
lock
locker
locket
lockjaw
locomotion
**locomotive**
locum
  *pl* locums
locust
lode
  *A lode is a vein in rock containing metal*
lodestar
lodestone
lodge
  lodged
  lodging

lodger
loftiness
lofty
  *adv* loftily
log
  logged
  logging
loganberry
  *pl* loganberries
logbook
loggerheads
logic
logical
  *adv* logically
loin
loincloth
loiter
  loitered
  loitering
loll
  lolled
  lolling
lone
  *a lone cottage: a lone star*
**loneliness**
lonely
lonesome
long
longevity
longing
**longitude**
loo
look
lookout
loom
  loomed
  looming
loop

looped
*The pilot looped the loop*

looping

loophole

loose
*a loose-fitting coat: This screw is loose: a loose end*

*adv* loosely

loosen

**loosened**

loosening

loot
*the burglar's loot*

lop

lopped
*He lopped a branch from the tree*

lopping

lope

loped
*The large dog loped along*

loping

lopped
*see* lop

lop-sided

**loquacious**

lord

lordly

lordship

lore

**lorgnette**

lorry
*pl* lorries

Los Angeles

lose
*to lose a glove: to*

*lose weight: to lose time*

lost

losing

loser

loss
*pl* losses

lost
*see* lose

lot

loth
*see* loath

lotion

lottery
*pl* lotteries

lotus

loud

loudness

loudspeaker

lounge

lounged

lounging

lour
*see* lower

louse
*pl* lice

lout

lovable

love

loved

loving

loveliness

lovely
*compar* lovelier
*superl* loveliest

lover

low

lower ['lōər]

lowered

lowering

lower, lour
['lowər]

lowland

lowliness

lowly

lowness

loyal
*adv* loyally

loyalist

loyalty

lozenge

lubricant

lubricate

lubricated

lubricating

lubrication

lucid

lucidity

luck

lucky
*compar* luckier
*superl* luckiest
*adv* luckily

**lucrative**

**lucre**

ludicrous

ludo

lug

lugged

lugging

**luggage**

**lugubrious**

lukewarm

lull

lulled

lulling

lullaby
*pl* lullabies

131

lumbago
lumbar
  *lumbar pain*
lumber
  *rubbish and*
  *lumber: Elephants*
  *lumber through the*
  *forests: to lumber*
  *him with the work*
lumbered
lumbering
lumberjack
luminosity
**luminous**
lump
lumpy
lunacy
lunar
lunatic
lunch
  *pl* lunches
**luncheon**
lung
lunge
  lunged
  lunging
lupin
lurch
lure
  lured
  luring
lurid
lurk
**luscious**
lush
lust
lustful
  *adv* lustfully
**lustre**

lustrous
lusty
  *adv* lustily
lute
  *to play a lute*
luxuriant
luxuriate
  luxuriated
  luxuriating
**luxurious**
luxury
  *pl* luxuries
lying
  *see* lie
lymph gland
lynch
lynx
  *pl* lynxes
lyre
  *A lyre is like a harp*
lyrebird
**lyric**
lyrical
  *adv* lyrically

# M

**macabre**
macaroni
  *macaroni cheese*
**macaroon**
  *biscuits and*
  *macaroons*
macaw
mace
machete
Machiavellian
machination
machine

machinery
**machinist**
Mach number
mackerel
mackintosh
  *pl* mackintoshes
mad
  *compar* madder
  *superl* maddest
madam
madden
  maddened
**maddening**
made
  *see* make
**Madeira**
madman
  *pl* madmen
madness
**Madonna**
madrigal
**maelstrom**
maestro
  *pl* maestros
**magazine**
magenta
maggot
maggoty
magic
magical
  *adv* magically
**magician**
magisterial
magistrate
magnanimity
**magnanimous**
magnate
  *He is a shipping*
  *magnate*

magnesia
magnesium
magnet
  *A magnet attracts
  iron*
magnetic
  *adv*
  magnetically
magnetism
magnetization,
  -isation
magnetize, -ise
  magnetized
  magnetizing
magnification
**magnificence**
magnificent
magnify
  magnified
  magnifying
magnitude
magnolia
magpie
**Maharajah**
**mahogany**
maid
  *a chamber-maid*
maiden
mail
  *first-class mail:
  mail the letter*
  mailed
  mailing
maim
  maimed
  maiming
main
  *the main points of
  his speech*

mainland
mainly
mainsail
mainstay
maintain
  **maintaining**
  maintained
**maintenance**
maize
  *fields of maize*
majestic
  *adv* majestically
majesty
  *pl* majesties
major
majority
  *pl* majorities
make
  made
  *She made a cake*
  making
maker
makeshift
make-up
maladjusted
malady
  *pl* maladies
**malaise**
malapropism
**malaria**
male
  *male and female*
malevolence
malevolent
malformation
malformed
malice
malicious
malign

**maligned**
maligning
**malignant**
**malinger**
  malingered
  malingering
  malingerer
mallard
malleable
mallet
**malnutrition**
malodorous
malpractice
malt
maltreat
maltreatment
mamma, mama
mammal
mammoth
man
  *pl* men
  manned
  manning
manacle
**manage**
  managed
  managing
**manageable**
**management**
manager
manageress
mandarin
mandate
mandatory
mandible
mandoline,
  mandolin
mane
  *a horse's mane*

manful
  adv manfully
mange
manger
mangle
  mangled
  mangling
mango
  pl mangoes
mangy
manhandle
  manhandled
  manhandling
manhood
mania
maniac
  The murderer was
  a maniac
maniacal
manic
  a manic depressive
manicure
manicurist
manifest
manifestation
manifesto
  pl manifestos,
    manifestoes
manifold
manipulate
  manipulated
  manipulating
manipulation
mankind
manna
manned
  see man
**mannequin**
manner

a manner of
speaking: a
pleasant manner

mannerism
mannerly
mannish
**manoeuvre**
manor
  the lord of the
  manor
manorial
manpower
manse
mansion
manslaughter
**mantelpiece**
mantilla
mantle
**manual**
  adv manually
manufacture
  manufactured
  manufacturing
**manufacturer**
manure
manuscript
Manx cat
many
map
  mapped
  mapping
maple
mar
  marred
  marring
maraud
**marauder**
marauding
marble

marcasite
March
march
  pl marches
marchioness
  pl
    marchionesses
mare
  a mare and her foal
**margarine**
margin
marginal
  adv marginally
**marguerite**
marigold
**marijuana**
marina
  yachts in the
  marina
marine
mariner
marionette
marital
maritime
marjoram
mark
marked
marker
market
  marketed
**marketing**
**marmalade**
maroon
  marooned
  marooning
**marquee**
marquess,
  marquis
  pls marquesses,

marquises
**marriage**
**marriageable**
marrow
marry
 married
 marrying
marsh
 *pl* marshes
marshal
 *an air marshal: a*
 *US marshal: to*
 *marshal the troops*
 marshalled
 marshalling
marshmallow
marshy
marsupial
martello tower
marten
 *the fur of a marten*
martial
 *martial music:*
 *martial law*
martin
 *a martin's nest*
martinet
**martyr**
 martyred
 martyring
martyrdom
marvel
 **marvelled**
 marvelling
**marvellous**
**marzipan**
mascot
masculine
masculinity

mash
mask
 *The surgeon wore*
 *a mask: The*
 *burglar wore a*
 *mask*
masochism
**masochist**
masochistic
 *adv*
 masochistically
mason
masonic
masonry
masque
 *The minstrels took*
 *part in the masque*
**masquerade**
 masqueraded
 masquerading
 masquerader
mass
 *pl* masses
Massachusetts
**massacre**
 massacred
 massacring
**massage**
 massaged
 massaging
masseur
masseuse
massive
mast
mastectomy
master
masterful
 *adv* masterfully
masterliness

masterly
masterpiece
mastery
masticate
 masticated
 masticating
mastication
mastiff
masturbate
 masturbated
 masturbating
mat
 *see* matt
mat
 *a mat by the front*
 *door: This material*
 *tends to mat*
matted
matting
matador
match
 *pl* matches
matchbox
 *pl* matchboxes
matchless
mate
 mated
 mating
material
 *adv* materially
materialism
materialistic
 *adv* materialisti-
 cally
materialization,
 -isation
materialize, -ise
 materialized
 materializing

135

maternal
  *adv* maternally
maternity
mathematical
  *adv*
    mathematically
mathematician
mathematics
**matinee**
matins
matriarch
matriarchal
matricide
matriculate
  matriculated
  matriculating
  matriculation
matrimonial
matrimony
matron
matronly
matt, matte, mat
  *matt paint*
matter
  **mattered**
  mattering
matter-of-fact
**mattress**
  *pl* mattresses
mature
  matured
  maturing
maturity
maudlin
maul
  mauled
  mauling
mausoleum
**mauve**

mawkish
maxim
maximum
  *pl* maxima
May
may
  might
maybe
mayday
**mayonnaise**
mayor
  *the Lord Mayor of*
  *London*
mayoress
maypole
maze
  *lost in a maze*
me
mead
meadow
**meagre**
  *adv* meagrely
meal
mean
  *a mean old miser:*
  *What does the*
  *word mean?*
  meant
  meaning
meander
  meandered
  meandering
meaning
meaningful
  *adv*
    meaningfully
meaningless
meanness
meant

  *see* mean
meanwhile
measles
measly
measure
  measured
  measuring
**measurement**
meat
  *Vegetarians don't*
  *eat meat*
meaty
**mechanic**
mechanical
  *adv*
    mechanically
mechanics
mechanism
mechanization,
  -isation
mechanize, -ise
  mechanized
  mechanizing
medal
  *a gold medal*
**medallion**
**medallist**
meddle
  *to meddle in*
  *people's affairs*
  meddled
  meddling
  meddler
media
  *see* medium
**mediaeval**,
  medieval
**mediate**
  *to mediate in a*

dispute
mediated
mediating
mediation
mediator
medical
*adv* medically
medicated
medication
medicinal
medicine
**medieval**
*see* mediaeval
**mediocre**
mediocrity
meditate
*to pray and
meditate*
meditated
meditating
meditation
meditative
Mediterranean
medium
*pl* media
*the mass media*
*pl* mediums
*Mediums are
psychic*
medley
*pl* medleys
meek
**meerschaum**
meet
*They meet in the
church hall*
met
meeting
megalomania

**megaphone**
megaton
Meissen
melancholic
**melancholy**
mellifluous
mellow
melodic
melodious
melodrama
melodramatic
*adv*
melodramatically
melody
*pl* melodies
melon
melt
meltdown
member
membership
membrane
memento
*pl* mementos
memo
memoir
memorable
*adv* memorably
memorandum
*pl* memoranda
memorial
**memorize, -ise**
memorized
memorizing
memory
*pl* memories
men
*see* man
menace
menaced

menacing
ménage
menagerie
mend
mendacious
mendacity
mendicant
menial
**meningitis**
menstrual
menstruate
menstruated
menstruating
menstruation
mental
*adv* mentally
mentality
*pl* mentalities
menthol
mention
**mentioned**
mentioning
mentor
menu
*pl* **menus**
mercantile
mercenary
*pl* mercenaries
merchandise
merchant
merciful
*adv* mercifully
merciless
mercurial
mercury
mercy
mere
*adv* merely
merge

merged
merging
merger
meridian
**meringue**
merino
*merino wool*
merit
merited
meriting
meritorious
mermaid
merman
**merriment**
merry
*compar* merrier
*superl* merriest
*adv* merrily
merry-go-
round
merrymaking
mesh
*pl* meshes
mesmerism
mesmerize, -ise
mesmerized
mesmerizing
mess
*pl* messes
message
**messenger**
met
*see* meet
metal
*a metal box*
metallic
metallurgical
**metallurgy**
**metamorphosis**

*pl* metamor-
phoses
metaphor
metaphorical
*adv*
metaphorically
metaphysical
metaphysics
meteor
meteoric
**meteorite**
**meteorological**
*adv* meteorolo-
gically
**meteorologist**
**meteorology**
mete out
*to mete out
punishment*
meted out
meting out
meter
*a gas meter*
method
methodical
*adv*
methodically
methylated
spirits
meticulous
metre
*a metre of cloth*
metric
metrical
metricate
metricated
metricating
metrication
metronome

metropolis
*pl* metropolises
**metropolitan**
mettle
*That horse has
plenty of mettle*
mew
mews
*a mews flat*
mezzo-soprano
**miaow**
mica
mice
*see* mouse
**Michaelmas
daisy**
microbe
microcosm
microfilm
**microphone**
microprocessor
microscope
microscopic
microwave
**midday**
middle
middle-aged
middle-class
middling
midge
midget
midnight
midriff
midst
midway
midwife
*pl* midwives
midwifery
mien

*a solemn mien*

might
  *see* may

might
  *the might of the army*

mightiness

mighty
  *compar* mightier
  *superl* mightiest
  *adv* mightily

**migraine**

migrant

migrate
  migrated
  migrating

migratory

mike

mild

mildew

mile

**mileage**

milestone

**milieu**

militant

military

militate
  militated
  militating

militia

milk

milky

mill

millennium
  *pl* millennia

miller

millet

milligramme

millilitre

**millimetre**

milliner

millinery

million

**millionaire**

millstone

mime
  mimed
  miming

mimic
  **mimicked**
  mimicking

**mimicry**

mimosa

minaret

mince
  minced
  mincing

mincemeat

mincer

mind

mindful

mindless

mine

miner
  *a coal miner*

mineral

**mineralogical**
  *adv*
    mineralogically

**mineralogist**

mineralogy

mingle
  mingled
  mingling

mini
  *pl* minis

**miniature**

minibus

*pl* minibuses

minimal

minimize, -ise
  minimized
  minimizing

minimum
  *pl* minima

minion

minister
  *a minister of the church: to minister to her needs*

  ministered
  ministering

ministerial
  *adv* ministerially

ministry
  *pl* ministries

mink

minnow

minor
  *of minor importance: legally, a minor*

minority
  *pl* minorities

minster
  *York Minster*

minstrel

mint

minuet

minus

minute

minx
  *pl* minxes

miracle

**miraculous**

mirage

mire

mirror
**mirrored**
mirroring
mirth
misadventure
misanthropist
misanthropy
misbehave
misbehaved
misbehaving
misbehaviour
**miscarriage**
miscarry
miscarried
miscarrying
**miscellaneous**
miscellany
*pl* miscellanies
mischance
**mischief**
**mischievous**
misconception
misconduct
miscreant
misdeed
**misdemeanour**
miser
miserable
*adv* miserably
miserly
misery
*pl* miseries
misfire
misfired
misfiring
misfit
misfortune
misgiving
misguided

**mishap**
mislay
mislaid
mislaying
mislead
misled
misleading
misnomer
**misogynist**
misprint
miss
*pl* misses
missed
missing
missal
*The choirboy carried a missal*
**misshapen**
missile
*a nuclear missile*
mission
missionary
*pl* missionaries
Mississippi
missive
**misspell**
misspelled,
misspelt
misspelling
**misspent**
mist
mistake
mistaken
*We were mistaken*
mistook
*I mistook her for you*
mistaking
mister

mistletoe
mistook
*see* mistake
mistress
*pl* mistresses
mistrust
misty
misunderstand
misunderstood
misunderstanding
misuse
mite
*a poor little mite*
mitigate
mitigated
**mitigating**
mitigation
mitre
mitt
mitten
mix
*pl* mixes
mixer
mixture
**mnemonic**
moan
moaned
moaning
moat
*a moat round the castle*
mob
mobbed
mobbing
mobile
mobility
mobilization,
-isation
mobilize, -ise

140

mobilized
mobilizing
moccasin
mock
mockery
mocking
modal
  *a modal verb*
mode
model
  *a model aeroplane*
**modelled**
modelling
moderate
  *adv* moderately
moderation
moderator
modern
modernity
modernization,
  -isation
modernize, -ise
  modernized
  modernizing
modernizer, -iser
modest
modesty
modicum
modification
modify
  modified
  modifying
modish
modulate
  modulated
  modulating
modulation
module
  *a space module*

mohair
**Mohammedan**
moist
moisten
  moistened
  moistening
moisture
moisturize, -ise
  moisturized
  moisturizing
molar
molasses
mole
molecular
molecule
molehill
molest
mollify
  mollified
  mollifying
mollusc
mollycoddle
  mollycoddled
  mollycoddling
molten
moment
momentary
  *a momentary
  pause*
  *adv*
    momentarily
momentous
  *a momentous
  discovery*
momentum
  *to gather
  momentum*
monarch
monarchy

*pl* monarchies
monastery
  *pl* monasteries
monastic
monasticism
Monday
**monetary**
money
moneyed,
  monied
mongoose
  *pl* mongooses
**mongrel**
monitor
  monitored
  monitoring
monk
monkey
  *pl* monkeys
  monkeyed
  monkeying
monocle
monogamous
monogamy
monogram
**monologue**
monopolize, -ise
  monopolized
  monopolizing
monopoly
  *pl* monopolies
monosyllabic
monosyllable
monotone
monotonous
monotony
monsoon
monster
**monstrosity**

*pl* monstrosities
monstrous
month
monthly
  *pl* monthlies
monument
monumental
moo
mood
moody
moon
moonbeam
moonlight
moor
  moored
  mooring
moorings
moose
  *the antlers of a moose*
  *pl* moose
**moot point**
mop
  mopped
  *She mopped the floor*
  mopping
mope
  moped
  *She moped and sulked*
  moping
moped ['mōped]
mopped
  *see* mop
moral
  *the moral of the story*
  *adv* morally

morale
  *Morale was low in the army*
morality
  *goodness and morality*
moralize, -ise
  moralized
  moralizing
morass
  *pl* morasses
morbid
morbidity
more
**moreover**
**morgue**
moribund
morn
morning
moron
moronic
morose
  *adv* morosely
**morphia**
morris dance
morrow
morse
morsel
mortal
  *adv* mortally
mortality
  *the mortality rate in car crashes*
mortar
**mortgage**
  mortgaged
  mortgaging
mortice
  *see* mortise

mortification
mortify
  mortified
  mortifying
mortise, mortice
mortuary
  *pl* mortuaries
**mosaic**
Moslem
mosque
**mosquito**
  *pl* mosquitos,
    mosquitoes
moss
  *pl* mosses
mossy
most
mostly
mote
  *a mote in the eye*
moth
mothball
moth-eaten
mother
  mothered
  mothering
motherhood
mother-in-law
  *pl* mothers-in-law
motherliness
motherly
motif
  *a motif of flowers*
motion
motionless
motivate
  motivated
  motivating

motive
*a motive for murder*

motley

motor

motor-bike

motorcycle

motorist

motorize, -ise

  motorized

  motorizing

motorway

mottled

motto

  *pl* mottoes

mould

moulder

mouldering

mouldy

moult

mound

mount

mountain

**mountaineer**

mountainous

mountebank

mourn

mourner

mournful

  *adv* mournfully

mourning

mouse

  *The cat ate the mouse: computer mouse*

  *pl* mice

mousse

  *lemon mousse*

**moustache**

mousy

mouth

  mouthed

  mouthing

**mouthful**

  *pl* mouthfuls

movable,

  moveable

move

  moved

  moving

movement

movie

  *pl* movies

moving

mow

  mowed

  mowing

mower

Mr

Mrs

Ms

much

muck

mucous

  *a mucous substance*

mucus

  *mucus from the nose*

muddle

  muddled

  muddling

muddy

mudguard

muff

muffin

muffle

  muffled

muffling

muffler

mufti

mug

  mugged

  mugging

mugger

muggy

mulatto

  *pl* mulattos

mulberry

  *pl* mulberries

mulch

mule

mulish

mull

mullet

multi-coloured

multicultural

**multifarious**

multimedia

multimillionaire

multinational

multiple

  *multiple injuries: 8 is a multiple of 4*

multiplication

multiplicity

multiply

  *x is the sign for multiply*

  multiplied

  multiplying

multitude

**multitudinous**

mumble

  mumbled

  mumbling

mumbo-jumbo

mummify
mummified
mummifying
mummy
  *pl* mummies
mumps
munch
mundane
municipal
municipality
  *pl*
    municipalities
munificence
munificent
munitions
mural
murder
  murdered
  murdering
  murderer
**murderous**
murky
murmur
  **murmured**
  murmuring
**muscle**
  *well-developed muscles*
**muscular**
muse
  *to muse on the beauty of nature*
  mused
  musing
**museum**
  *pl* museums
mush
mushroom
  mushroomed

mushrooming
mushy
music
musical
  *adv* musically
**musician**
musk
musket
musketeer
Muslim
**musquash**
mussel
  *I love fresh mussels*
must
mustard
muster
  mustered
  mustering
musty
mute
muted
mutilate
  mutilated
  mutilating
  mutilation
mutineer
mutinous
mutiny
  *pl* mutinies
  mutinied
  mutinying
mutter
  muttered
  muttering
mutton
**mutual**
  *adv* mutually
muzzle

muzzled
muzzling
muzzy
my
myopia
**myopic**
  *adv* myopically
myriad
**myrrh**
myrtle
myself
**mysterious**
mystery
  *pl* mysteries
mystic
  *mystic philosophy*
  *adv* mystically
**mystify**
  mystified
  mystifying
mystique
  *the mystique of the stage*
myth
**mythical**
  *adv* mythically
mythological
mythology
**myxomatosis**

N

nadir
nag
  nagged
  nagging
naiad
nail
  nailed

nailing
Nairobi
**naive**
naiveté
naked
namby-pamby
name
  named
  naming
namely
nanny
  *pl* nannies
nap
  napped
  napping
nape
**naphtha**
napkin
nappy
  *pl* nappies
**narcissus**
  *pl* narcissi
narcotic
narrate
  narrated
  narrating
narration
**narrative**
narrator
narrow
nasal
nastiness
**nasturtium**
nasty
  *adv* nastily
natal
nation
national
  *adv* nationally

nationalism
nationalistic
nationality
  *pl* nationalities
nationalization,
  -isation
**nationalize,** -ise
  nationalized
  nationalizing
nationwide
native
nativity
natty
  *adv* nattily
natural
  *adv* naturally
**naturalist**
naturalize, -ise
  naturalized
  naturalizing
nature
naught
  *He cared naught
  for her*
**naughtiness**
**naughty**
  *a naughty child*
  *adv* naughtily
**nausea**
nauseate
  nauseated
  nauseating
nauseous
**nautical**
naval
  *a naval battle*
nave
  *the nave of a
  church*

navel
  *The baby's navel
  has healed*
navigable
navigate
  navigated
  navigating
navigation
navigator
navvy
  *a navvy on a
  building site*
  *pl* navvies
navy
  *to join the navy*
  *pl* navies
nay
  *Nay, he will not
  come*
near
nearly
nearness
neat
nebulous
**necessary**
  *adv* necessarily
necessitate
  necessitated
  necessitating
**necessity**
  *pl* necessities
neck
necklace
necromancy
necropolis
  *pl* necropolises
nectar
nectarine
**née**

*Ann Smith née Jones*

need
  *Animals need water*
needful
needle
needless
needy
ne'er
ne'er-do-well
nefarious
negate
  negated
  negating
negative
neglect
neglectful
negligée
**negligence**
negligent
  *a careless, negligent mother*
**negligible**
  *a negligible amount*
  adv negligibly
negotiable
**negotiate**
  negotiated
  negotiating
  negotiation
**negotiator**
negro
  pl negroes
negroid
neigh
  *to neigh like a horse*

neighed
neighing
**neighbour**
**neighbourhood**
neighbouring
neighbourliness
neighbourly
**neither**
nemesis
neologism
neon lighting
nephew
nerve
nervous
nervousness
nervy
nest
nestle
  nestled
  nestling
net, nett
  *nett profit*
net
  *a ball in the net: to net a fish*
  netted
  netting
netball
nether
nethermost
nett
  *see* net
nettle
network
neuralgia
neurosis
**neurotic**
**neuter**
  neutered

neutering
**neutral**
  adv neutrally
neutrality
neutralize, -ise
  neutralized
  neutralizing
neutron
never
nevertheless
new
  *a new dress*
newfangled
newly
newness
news
newsagent
newspaper
newt
next
nib
nibble
  nibbled
  nibbling
nice
  adv nicely
nicety
  pl niceties
**niche**
nick
nickel
nickname
nicotine
**niece**
niggardly
niggling
nigh
night
  *a cold, dark night*

nightdress
nightfall
**nightingale**
nightly
  *a new show nightly*
nightmare
nil
nimble
  *adv* nimbly
nimbus
nincompoop
nine
nineteen
nineteenth
**ninetieth**
ninety
ninny
**ninth**
nip
  nipped
  nipping
nipple
nit
  *a stupid nit: nits in
  her hair*
nitrate
nitric
nitrogen
nitwit
no
  *We have no
  money: She
  answered 'No'*
  *pl* noes
nobility
noble
  *adv* nobly
nobody
**nocturnal**

*adv* nocturnally
nod
  nodded
  nodding
node
nodule
Noël, Nowell
noise
noisy
  *adv*
  **noisily**
nomad
nomadic
nom de plume
  *pl* noms de
  plume
nomenclature
nominal
  *adv* nominally
nominate
  nominated
  nominating
nomination
nominee
  = a person who
  has been
  nominated
nonagenarian
nonchalance
nonchalant
non-committal
nonconformist
nondescript
none
**nonentity**
  *pl* nonentities
nonplussed
nonsense
nonsensical

*adv*
  nonsensically
noodle
nook
no-one
noose
nor
norm
normal
  *adv* normally
north
northerly
  *in a northerly
  direction*
northern
  *northern lands*
Norwegian
nose
nosey, nosy
**nostalgia**
nostalgic
  *adv*
  nostalgically
nostril
not
  *He is not here*
notability
  *pl* notabilities
notable
  *adv* **notably**
notary public
  *pl* notaries
  public
notation
notch
  *pl* notches
note
  noted
  noting

noteworthy
nothing
nothingness
notice
  noticed
  noticing
**noticeable**
  adv **noticeably**
notifiable
notification
notify
  notified
  notifying
notion
**notoriety**
notorious
notwithstanding
nougat ['nōōgä]
  *This nougat is*
  *sticky*
nought
  *The telephone*
  *number contains*
  *two noughts*
noun
nourish
nourishment
novel
**novelist**
novelty
  pl novelties
November
novice
now
nowadays
Nowell
  *see* Noël
nowhere
noxious

nozzle
**nuance**
nuclear
nucleus
  pl nuclei
nude
**nudist**
nudity
nudge
  nudged
  nudging
nugget
  *a gold nugget*
**nuisance**
null
nullify
  nullified
  nullifying
**numb**
number
  **numbered**
  numbering
numeracy
numeral
**numerate**
numerical
  adv numerically
**numerous**
numismatics
numskull
nun
nunnery
  pl nunneries
**nuptial**
nurse
  nursed
  nursing
nursery
  pl nurseries

nurture
  nurtured
  nurturing
nut
nutcracker
nutmeg
**nutrient**
nutriment
**nutrition**
**nutritious**
nutshell
nutty
nuzzle
  nuzzled
  nuzzling
nylon
nymph

# O

o, oh
oaf
  pl oafs
oak
oar
  *an oar for a boat*
oasis
  pl oases
oath
  pl oaths
oats
obduracy
obdurate
  adv obdurately
obedience
**obedient**
obeisance
obelisk
**obese**

obesity
obey
  obeyed
  obeying
**obituary**
  *pl* obituaries
object
objection
objectionable
  *adv*
    objectionably
objective
  *adv* objectively
obligation
obligatory
  *adv* obligatorily
**oblige**
  obliged
  obliging
**oblique**
obliterate
  obliterated
  obliterating
oblivion
**oblivious**
oblong
**obnoxious**
oboe
  *pl* oboes
oboist
**obscene**
  *adv* obscenely
**obscenity**
  *pl* obscenities
obscure
  *adv* obscurely
obscurity
**obsequious**
observance

**observant**
observation
observatory
  *pl* observatories
observe
  observed
  observing
observer
obsess
obsession
**obsessive**
  *adv* obsessively
obsolescent
obsolete
obstacle
obstetrical
**obstetrician**
obstetrics
obstinacy
obstinate
  *adv* obstinately
**obstreperous**
obstruct
obstruction
obtain
  obtained
  obtaining
obtainable
obtrusive
  *adv* obtrusively
obtuse
  *adv* obtusely
obviate
  obviated
  obviating
obvious
obviously
**occasion**
occasional

*adv* **occasionally**
occult
**occupancy**
occupant
**occupation**
**occupier**
**occupy**
  **occupied**
  occupying
**occur**
  **occurred**
  occurring
**occurrence**
ocean
oceanic
ochre
octagonal
  *adv* octagonally
octave
octet
October
**octogenarian**
octopus
  *pl* octopuses
ocular
oculist
odd
oddity
  *pl* oddities
oddment
ode
odious
odium
**odour**
**odourless**
odyssey
of

  *a cup of tea: made*
  *of silver: to die of*

149

*hunger*

**off**

*to switch off a light: to run off: to finish off a job: badly off: The meat is off*

offal
off-chance
**offence**
offend
offender
offensive
 *adv* offensively
offer
 **offered**
 offering
offhand
office
officer
**official**
 *official action: official duties*
 *adv* officially
officiate
 officiated
 officiating
**officious**
 *rude and officious*
offing
off-licence
offset
 offset
 offsetting
offshoot
offside
offspring
oft
often

ogle
ogled
ogling
ogre
oh
 *see* o
oil
oiled
oiling
oilfield
oilrig
oily
ointment
OK
okay
okayed
okaying
old
old-fashioned
olive
ombudsman
omega
omelette, omelet
omen
**ominous**
**omission**
 *He apologized for the omission of her name from the list*
omit
 **omitted**
 omitting
omnibus
 *pl* omnibuses
omnipotent
omniscient
omnivorous
on
once

oncologist
oncology
oncoming
one
onerous
**oneself**
ongoing
onion
onlooker
only
onslaught
onus
onwards
onyx
ooze
oozed
oozing
opacity
opal
**opaque**
open
 **opened**
 opening
opener
openly
opera
 *see* opus
opera
operate
 operated
 operating
operatic
operation
operative
operator
operetta
**ophthalmic**
ophthalmologist
opiate

**opinion**
opinionated
opium
**opossum**
**opponent**
opportune
opportunism
opportunist
opportunistic
**opportunity**
  *pl* opportunities
oppose
  opposed
  opposing
**opposite**
opposition
oppress
oppression
oppressive
opprobrious
**opprobrium**
opt
optical
**optician**
optimism
optimist
optimistic
  *adv*
    optimistically
optimum
option
**optional**
  *adv* optionally
opulence
opulent
opus
  *pl* opera
or
oracle

oral
  *The dentist spoke
  about oral hygiene*
  *adv* orally
orange
orang-utan
oration
orator
oratorio
  *pl* oratorios
oratory
  *pl* oratories
orb
orbit
  orbited
  orbiting
orchard
**orchestra**
orchid
ordain
ordeal
order
  ordered
  ordering
orderly
  *pl* orderlies
ordinal
ordinance
**ordinary**
  *adv* ordinarily
ordination
Ordnance Survey
ore
  *iron ore*
oregano
organ
organdie
organic
  *adv* organically

organism
  *This poison kills all
  known organisms*
organist
organization,
  -isation
organize, -ise
  organized
  organizing
orgasm
  *sexual orgasm*
orgy
  *pl* orgies
orient
oriental
orientate
  orientated
  orientating
orienteering
orifice
origin
**original**
  *adv* originally
originate
  originated
  originating
ornament
ornamental
  *adv*
    ornamentally
ornate
ornithological
ornithologist
**ornithology**
**orphan**
orphanage
**orthodox**
orthodoxy
orthography

orthopaedic
oscillate
 oscillated
 oscillating
oscillation
osprey
 *pl* ospreys
ostensible
 *adv* ostensibly
ostentation
ostentatious
osteopath
ostracism
ostracize, -ise
 ostracized
 ostracizing
ostrich
 *pl* ostriches
other
otter
ottoman
ought
ounce
our
ours
ourselves
oust
out
outboard
outbreak
outcast
outcome
outcry
outdo
 outdid
 *She outdid her neighbours*
 outdone
 *She has outdone*

*them*
 outdoing
outdoor
outer
outermost
outfit
outfitter
 outing
outlandish
outlaw
outlay
outlet
outline
outlook
outlying
outnumber
 outnumbered
 outnumbering
out-patient
output
outrage
outrageous
outright
outset
outside
outsize
outskirts
outspoken
outstanding
outward
outwit
 outwitted
 outwitting
oval
ovary
 *pl* ovaries
ovation
oven
over

overall
overawe
 overawed
 overawing
overbearing
overcame
 *see* overcome
overcoat
overcome
 overcame
 *He overcame his enemies*
 overcome
 *He has overcome them*
 overcoming
overdo
 overdid
 *She overdid the meat*
 overdone
 *She has overdone it*
 overdoing
overdose
overdraft
overdrawn
overflow
overgrown
overheads
overhear
 overheard
 overhearing
overjoyed
overlap
 overlapped
 overlapping
overlook
overpowering

152

overran
  *see* overrun
**overrate**
  overrated
  overrating
**overreach**
overrun
  overran
  *The enemy overran the country*
  overrun
  *They have overrun the country*
  overrunning
overseas
overseer
overshadow
oversight
overstep
  overstepped
  overstepping
overt
overtake
  overtook
  *He overtook the car*
  overtaken
  *He has overtaken the car*
  overtaking
overthrow
  overthrew
  *He overthrew the king*
  overthrown
  *He has overthrown the king*
  overthrowing
overtime
overtook

*see* overtake
overture
overwhelm
**overwrought**
owe
  owed
  owing
owl
own
  owned
  owning
owner
ox
  *pl* oxen
**oxygen**
**oyster**
ozone

# P

pace
  paced
  pacing
Pacific
**pacifist**
pacify
  pacified
  pacifying
pack
  packed
  *We packed the cases: a packed hall*
  packing
package
packed
  *see* pack
packet
pact

*a pact between nations*
pad
  padded
  padding
paddle
  paddled
  paddling
paddock
padlock
paediatrician
paediatrics
paedophile
pagan
page
  paged
  paging
**pageant**
pageantry
pagoda
paid
  *see* pay
pail
  *a pail of water*
pain
  *a pain in his chest*
pained
painful
  *adv* painfully
painkiller
painless
painstaking
paint
painter
painting
pair
  *a pair of shoes*
  paired
  pairing

pal
palace
palatable
palate
  *the soft palate of*
  *the mouth*
palatial
palaver
pale
  *thin and pale: of a*
  *pale colour*
palette
  *an artist's palette*
palindrome
paling
palisade
pall
  palled
  palling
pallet
  *a straw pallet*
palliative
pallid
**pallor**
**palm**
palmist
palmistry
palpable
  *adv* palpably
palpitation
palsy
paltry
pampas
pamper
  pampered
  pampering
**pamphlet**
pan
  panned

panning
**panacea**
panache
pancake
panda
pandemonium
pander
  pandered
  pandering
pane
  *a pane of glass*
**panegyric**
panel
  panelling
pang
panic
  **panicked**
  panicking
pannier
panoply
**panorama**
pansy
  *pl* pansies
pant
**pantechnicon**
panther
**pantomime**
pantry
  *pl* pantries
pants
papa
papacy
papal
paper
  **papered**
  papering
paperback
paperweight
papier mâché

papoose
paprika
papyrus
par
  *not up to par: on a*
  *par with his*
  *brother*
parable
**parachute**
parachutist
parade
  paraded
  parading
paradigm
**paradise**
paradox
  *pl* paradoxes
paradoxical
  *adv*
    paradoxically
**paraffin**
paragon
**paragraph**
parakeet
**parallel**
parallelogram
**paralyse**
  paralysed
  paralysing
**paralysis**
paralytic
paramedic
paramilitary
paramount
paramour
parapet
**paraphernalia**
**paraphrase**
paraplegia

paraplegic
parasite
parasitic
parasol
**paratrooper**
paratroops
parboil
  parboiled
  parboiling
parcel
  **parcelled**
  parcelling
parch
parchment
pardon
  pardoned
  pardoning
pardonable
pare
  *to pare an apple: to pare one's toenails*
  pared
  paring
parent
parentage
parental
parenthesis
  *pl* parentheses
parenthetical
pariah
parish
  *pl* parishes
parishioner
parity
park
parka
Parkinsonism
parley
  *pl* parleys

parleyed
parleying
**parliament**
**parliamentary**
parlour
parlourmaid
parochial
parody
  *pl* parodies
  parodied
  parodying
parole
**paroxysm**
**parquet**
parr
  *A parr is a young salmon*
parrot
parry
  parried
  parrying
parse
  parsed
  parsing
**parsimonious**
parsimony
parsley
parsnip
parson
parsonage
part
partake
  partook
  partaken
  partaking
partial
  *adv* **partially**
partiality
**participant**

participate
  participated
  participating
participation
**participle**
**particle**
particular
particularly
partisan
**partition**
partly
**partner**
  partnered
  partnering
partook
  *see* partake
**partridge**
party
  *pl* parties
pass
  passed
  *He passed out of sight: The bus passed the house: The feeling soon passed*
  passing
passable
passage
passed
  *see* pass
**passenger**
passer-by
  *pl* passers-by
passion
passionate
  *adv* passionately
passive
  *adv* passively

passport
password
past
*The old think about the past: We walked past the church*

pasta
paste
pastel
*pastel colours*
pasteurization, -isation
pasteurize, -ise
  pasteurized
  pasteurizing
pastille
*a throat pastille*
**pastime**
pastor
pastoral
pastry
  *pl* pastries
pasturage
pasture
pasty ['pãsti]
pasty ['pasti]
  *pl* pasties
pat
  patted
  patting
patch
  *pl* patches
patchwork
patchy
pate
*a bald pate*
pâté
*pâté on toast*

patent
patently
paternal
  *adv* paternally
paternity
path
pathetic
  *adv* pathetically
**pathological**
pathologist
pathology
pathos
patience
patient
patio
  *pl* patios
patois
patriarch
patriarchal
patricide
patriot
patriotic
  *adv* patriotically
patriotism
patrol
  **patrolled**
  patrolling
patron
patronage
patronize, -ise
  patronized
  patronizing
patter
  pattered
  pattering
**pattern**
**patterned**
patty
*a mince patty*

*pl* patties
paucity
paunch
  *pl* paunches
pauper
pause
  paused
  **pausing**
pave
  paved
  paving
pavement
**pavilion**
paw
pawn
pawnbroker
pay
  paid
  paying
payable
payee
  = the person to whom money is paid
payment
pea
peace
*peace and quiet*
**peaceable**
  *adv* **peaceably**
peaceful
  *adv* peacefully
peach
  *pl* peaches
peacock
peak
*a mountain peak*
peaky
peal

a peal of bells:
Bells peal

pealed
pealing
peanut
pear
*an apple and a pear*

pearl
*a pearl necklace*

peasant
*a simple peasant*

peat
pebble
pebbly
pecan
peccadillo
*pl* peccadillos,
    peccadilloes

peck
peckish
**peculiar**
peculiarity
*pl* peculiarities
**pecuniary**
pedal
*to pedal a bicycle*

pedalled
pedalling
pedant
pedantic
*adv* pedantically
peddle
*to peddle one's wares*

peddled
peddling
pedestal
**pedestrian**

pedigree
**pedigreed**
pedlar
pedometer
peek
*a peek through the window*

peel
*to peel an apple*

peeled
peeling
peep
peeped
peeping
peer
*to peer through the window: a peer of the realm*

peered
peering
peerage
peerless
peevish
peewit
peg
pegged
pegging
**pejorative**
Pekinese,
    Pekingese
pelican
pellet
pell-mell
pelmet
pelt
pelvis
pen
penned
penning

penal
penalize, -ise
penalized
penalizing
penalty
penance
pence
*see* penny

penchant
pencil
**pencilled**
pencilling
pendant
*a silver pendant*

pendent
*a pendent light*

pending
pendulum
**penetrate**
penetrated
penetrating
penetration
pen-friend
penguin
**penicillin**
peninsula
penis
penitent
penitentiary
penknife
pen-name
pennant
pennies
*see* penny

**penniless**
penny
*pl* pence
*This costs ten pence*

*pl* pennies
*This machine takes pennies*
pension
pensioner
pensive
  *adv* pensively
pentagon
pentathlon
penthouse
pent-up
penultimate
penury
peony
  *pl* peonies
people
  peopled
  peopling
pepper
  **peppered**
  peppering
peppercorn
peppermint
peppery
pep-talk
perambulator
**perceive**
  perceived
  perceiving
per cent
percentage
**perceptible**
  *adv* perceptibly
perception
perceptive
perch
  *pl* perches
percolate
  percolated

percolating
percolator
percussion
perdition
peremptory
  *adv*
  peremptorily
**perennial**
  *adv* perennially
perfect
perfection
perfectionist
perfidious
perfidy
**perforate**
  perforated
  perforating
perform
performance
performer
perfume
perfunctory
  *adv*
  perfunctorily
perhaps
peril
**perilous**
perimeter
period
periodic
  *adv* **periodically**
periodical
peripatetic
**peripheral**
periphery
  *pl* peripheries
periscope
perish
perishable

periwinkle
perjure
  perjured
  perjuring
perjury
perk
perky
perm
permanence
permanency
**permanent**
permeable
permeate
  permeated
  permeating
**permissible**
permission
permissive
permissiveness
permit
  **permitted**
  permitting
permutation
**pernicious**
pernickety
peroxide
perpendicular
**perpetrate**
  perpetrated
  perpetrating
perpetrator
perpetual
  *adv* perpetually
perpetuate
  perpetuated
  perpetuating
perpetuity
perplex
perplexity

pl perplexities
perquisite
*A company car is one of the perquisites of the job*

persecute
persecuted
persecuting
persecution
persecutor
perseverance
persevere
persevered
persevering
persist
**persistence**
persistent
person
personable
personal
*She is his personal assistant: a personal letter*

adv personally
personality
pl personalities
personification
personify
personified
personifying
**personnel**
*the company's personnel officer*

perspective
Perspex ®
perspicacious
perspicacity
**perspiration**

perspire
perspired
perspiring
**persuade**
persuaded
persuading
**persuasion**
persuasive
adv persuasively
pert
pertain
pertained
**pertaining**
pertinacious
pertinacity
pertinence
pertinent
perturb
perturbation
**perusal**
peruse
perused
perusing
pervade
pervaded
pervading
perverse
adv perversely
perversion
perversity
pervert
peseta
**pessimism**
pessimist
pessimistic
adv
**pessimistically**
pest
pester

pestered
pestering
**pesticide**
pestilence
pestle
pet
petted
petting
**petal**
peter out
petered out
petering out
petite
**petition**
petrel
*a gull and a petrel*
petrify
petrified
petrifying
petrol
*two gallons of petrol*

**petroleum**
petticoat
pettiness
petty
adv pettily
petulance
petulant
pew
pewter
**phantom**
**Pharaoh**
pl Pharaohs
pharmaceutical
pharmacist
pharmacological
pharmacologist
pharmacology

**pharmacy**
  *pl* pharmacies
**pharyngitis**
**pharynx**
phase
  phased
  phasing
pheasant
  *pheasant feathers*
phenomenal
**phenomenon**
  *pl* phenomena
**phial**
philander
  philandered
  philandering
philanderer
philanthropic
  *adv*
    philanthropically
philanthropist
philanthropy
philatelist
**philately**
Philippines
philosopher
philosophic
  *adv*
    philosophically
philosophy
**phlegm**
phlegmatic
phlox
  *phlox growing in
  the garden*
**phobia**
  *pl* phobias
phobic
phoenix

phone
phonetics
phoney, phony
phosphate
phosphorescent
phosphorous
photocopy
  photocopied
  photocopying
Photofit ®
photogenic
  *adv*
    photogenically
photograph
photographer
photographic
  *adv* photo-
    graphically
photography
phrase
  phrased
  phrasing
phraseology
physical
  *adv* physically
**physician**
physicist
physics
physiological
  *adv*
    physiologically
physiologist
physiology
**physiotherapist**
physiotherapy
**physique**
pianist
piano
  *pl* pianos

piazza
  *a church in the
  piazza*
pibroch
Picasso
piccolo
  *pl* piccolos
pick
picket
  **picketed**
  picketing
pickle
  pickled
  pickling
pickpocket
picnic
  **picnicked**
  picnicking
pictorial
  *adv* pictorially
picture
**picturesque**
  *adv*
    picturesquely
pie
piebald
**piece**
  *a piece of paper*
piecemeal
piecework
pied
pier
  *the pier at the
  seaside*
pierce
  pierced
  piercing
pierrot
piety

piffle
pig
**pigeon**
pigeon-hole
piggery
pigment
pigmentation
pigmy
  see pygmy
pigsty
pigtail
pike
pilchard
pile
  piled
  piling
pilfer
  pilfered
  pilfering
pilgrim
**pilgrimage**
pill
pillage
**pillar**
pillion
pillory
  pl pillories
  pilloried
  pillorying
pillow
pilot
  piloted
  piloting
pimpernel
pimple
pimply
pin
  pinned
  flowers pinned to

her dress
  pinning
pinafore
pince-nez
pincers
pinch
  pl pinches
  pinched
pine
  pined
  The dog pined and
  died
  pining
pineapple
ping
ping-pong
pinion
  pinioned
  pinioning
pink
pinnacle
pinned
  see pin
pint
pioneer
  **pioneered**
  pioneering
**pious**
pip
  pipped
  He was pipped at
  the post
  pipping
pipe
  piped

a cake piped with
white icing: The
members of the
band piped away

all night
  piping
pipeline
piper
pipette
pipped
  see pip
piquancy
**piquant**
pique
  to resign out of
  pique: to pique
  one's curiosity

  piqued
  piquing
piracy
pirate
**pirouette**
  pirouetted
  pirouetting
pistachio
  pl pistachios
pistil
  the pistil of a
  flower
pistol
  shot by a pistol
piston
pit
  pitted
  pitting
pitch
  pl pitches
pitcher
**piteous**
pitfall
pith
pithy
pitiable

161

**pitiful**
  adv pitifully
pittance
pity
  pitied
  pitying
pivot
  pivoted
  pivoting
pixie, pixy
  pl pixies
pizza
  a tomato and
  cheese pizza

placard
placate
  placated
  placating
place
  a place in the sun:
  to place the book
  on the table
  placed
  placing
placebo
placenta
placid
plagiarism
plagiarize, -ise
  plagiarized
  plagiarizing
**plague**
plaice
  plaice and chips
plaid
plain
  Wheat grows on
  the plain: a plain
  dress

**plaintiff**
  The plaintiff lost
  the case
plaintive
  a plaintive cry
plait
  to plait hair
  plaited
  plaiting
plan
  planned
  planning
plane
  The plane landed:
  The joiner uses a
  plane: a plane-tree:
  a plane surface
planet
planetary
plank
plankton
plant
plantation
planter
**plaque**
plasma
plaster
  plastered
  plastering
plasterer
plastic
Plasticine ®
plasticity
plate
  a plate of food: to
  plate with silver
  plated
  plating
plateau

pl plateaux,
  plateaus
platform
platinum
platitude
platonic
platoon
platter
platypus
  pl platypuses
plaudit
plausibility
**plausible**
  adv plausibly
play
  played
  playing
player
playful
  adv playfully
playmate
playschool
playwright
plea
plead
pleasant
pleasantness
pleasantry
  pl pleasantries
please
  pleased
  pleasing
pleasurable
  adv pleasurably
pleasure
pleat
  pleated
  pleating
plebeian

plebiscite
plectrum
pledge
  pledged
  pledging
plenary
plenteous
plentiful
  *adv* plentifully
plenty
plethora
**pleurisy**
pliable
pliant
**pliers**
plight
plimsoll
plod
  plodded
  plodding
plop
  plopped
  plopping
plot
  plotted
  plotting
**plough**
  ploughed
  ploughing
plover
pluck
plucky
  *adv* pluckily
plug
  plugged
  plugging
plum
  *a red plum*
plumage

plumb
  *to plumb the
  depths*
  plumbed
  plumbing
plumber
plumbline
plume
plummet
plump
plunder
  plundered
  plundering
plunge
  plunged
  plunging
plural
plus
plush
plutocrat
plutocratic
ply
  plied
  plying
plywood
pneumatic
  *adv*
  pneumatically
**pneumonia**
poach
poacher
pocket
  pocketed
  pocketing
pockmark
pod
podgy
**poem**
poet

poetic
  *adv* poetically
poetry
poignance
**poignant**
point
pointed
pointer
pointless
poise
poised
poison
**poisonous**
poke
  poked
  poking
poker
poky
polar
pole
polecat
police
  policed
  policing
policeman
  *pl* policemen
policy
  *pl* policies
polio
**poliomyelitis**
polish
  *pl* polishes
polite
  *adv* politely
politeness
politic
  *It is politic to do as
  the king says*
political

*a political figure*
*adv* **politically**
**politician**
politics
polka
poll
  polled
  polling
pollen
pollinate
  pollinated
  pollinating
pollination
pollute
  polluted
  polluting
**pollution**
polo
**poltergeist**
polyester
polygamist
polygamous
polygamy
polyglot
polygon
polysyllabic
**polytechnic**
**polythene**
**pomegranate**
pommel
pomp
pompous
poncho
  *pl* ponchos
pond
ponder
  pondered
  pondering
ponderous

pontiff
**pontificate**
  pontificated
  pontificating
pontoon
pony
  *pl* ponies
**pony-trekking**
poodle
pool
  *a swimming pool:*
  *football pools: to*
  *pool their*
  *resources*
  pooled
  pooling
poop
poor
poorly
pop
  popped
  popping
pope
poplar
  *a poplar and a yew*
  *tree*
poplin
poppy
  *pl* poppies
populace
popular
  *a popular*
  *entertainer*
popularity
popularize, -ise
  popularized
  popularizing
populate
  populated

populating
population
**populous**
porcelain
porch
  *pl* porches
porcupine
pore
  *a blocked pore*
  pored
  *He pored over his*
  *books*
  poring
pork
pornographic
**pornography**
porous
porpoise
**porridge**
port
**portable**
portal
portcullis
  *pl* portcullises
portend
portent
portentous
porter
portfolio
  *pl* portfolios
port-hole
portico
  *pl* porticos,
  porticoes
portion
portly
portmanteau
  *pl*
    portmanteaux,

portmanteaus
**portrait**
portray
  portrayed
  portraying
**portrayal**
pose
  posed
  posing
poser
  *a poser before the camera: That question is quite a poser*
poseur
  *He is a poseur and a sham*
posh
position
  positioned
  positioning
**positive**
  *adv* positively
posse
possess
  possessed
  possessing
**possession**
possessive
  *adv* possessively
possessor
**possibility**
  *pl* possibilities
possible
  *adv* possibly
post
postage
postal

postcard
poster
posterior
posterity
postern
**posthumous**
postmortem
postpone
  postponed
  postponing
postponement
postscript
postulate
  postulated
  postulating
posture
postwar
posy
  *pl* posies
pot
  potted
  potting
potash
potassium
potato
  *pl* **potatoes**
potency
potent
potential
  *adv* potentially
pothole
potholing
potion
pot-pourri
potter
  pottered
  pottering
pottery
  *pl* potteries

pouch
  *pl* pouches
pouffe
poultice
**poultry**
pounce
  pounced
  pouncing
pound
pour
  *Did the rain pour down?*
  poured
  *She poured milk from the jug*
  pouring
pout
  pouted
  pouting
poverty
powder
  powdered
  powdering
powdery
power
  powered
  powerful
  *adv* powerfully
powerless
pow-wow
practicable
  *It is not practicable to try to make the journey in one day*
practical
  *a practical knowledge of carpentry: He is a dreamer but his wife is very*

*practical*
practically
practice
*She is at dancing practice: a doctor's practice*

practise
*You must practise your dance steps*

practised
practising
**practitioner**
pragmatic
pragmatist
prairie
praise
  praised
  praising
pram
prance
  pranced
  prancing
prank
prattle
  prattled
  prattling
prawn
pray
*I heard the minister pray*

  prayed
  praying
prayer
preach
preacher
preamble
prearrange
  prearranged
  prearranging

precarious
precaution
precautionary
**precede**
*She always precedes him into the room*

preceded
preceding
precedence
**precedent**
precept
**precinct**
precious
**precipice**
precipitate
  precipitated
  precipitating
precipitous
précis
  *pl* précis
**precise**
  *adv* precisely
precision
preclude
  precluded
  precluding
**precocious**
precocity
preconception
precursor
predator
predatory
**predecessor**
predicament
predict
predictable
  *adv* predictably
prediction

predilection
predominant
pre-eminent
preen
  preened
  preening
**prefabricated**
preface
prefect
prefer
**preferred**
preferring
preferable
**preference**
preferential
preferment
prefix
  *pl* prefixes
pregnancy
  *pl* pregnancies
pregnant
prehistoric
  *adv*
    prehistorically
prejudge
  prejudged
  prejudging
**prejudice**
  prejudiced
  prejudicing
prejudicial
prelate
**preliminary**
  *pl* preliminaries
prelude
premature
  *adv* prematurely
**premeditated**
premier

*Who is the Italian premier?*

première
*the première of the play*

premise
*pl* premises
*false premises*

premises
*They moved to new premises*

premium
*pl* premiums

**premonition**

preoccupation

**preoccupied**

prepaid
*see* prepay

preparation

preparatory

prepare
prepared
preparing

prepay
prepaid
prepaying

prepayment

preponderance

preposition

**prepossessing**

preposterous

**prerequisite**
*Patience is a prerequisite for teaching*

**prerogative**

presage
presaged
presaging

**Presbyterian**

prescribe
prescribed
prescribing

**prescription**

prescriptive

**presence**

present

presentable
*adv* presentably

presentation

presentiment

presently

preservation

**preservative**

preserve
preserved
preserving

preside
presided
presiding

**presidency**

president

press

pressgang

**pressure**

pressurize, -ise
pressurized
pressurizing

**prestige**

**prestigious**

**presumably**

presume
presumed
presuming

presumption

presumptuous

pretence

pretend

pretender

pretension

**pretentious**

preternatural
*adv*
preternaturally

pretext

prettiness

pretty
*adv* prettily

prevail
prevailed
prevailing

prevalence

**prevalent**

**prevaricate**
prevaricated
prevaricating

prevarication

prevent

preventive

preview

**previous**

previously

prey
*Mice are prey for owls: Owls prey on mice*

preyed
preying

price
*What is the price of that house?: I would price that hat at £15*

priced
pricing
priceless
prick

prickle
  prickled
  prickling
prickly
pride
  prided
  priding
**priest**
priesthood
priggish
prim
prima donna
primarily
primary
primate
prime
  primed
  priming
primer
primeval
**primitive**
  *adv* primitively
primrose
prince
princely
princess
  *pl* princesses
principal
  *the principal of the college*
principality
  *pl* principalities
principally
principle
  *the principle of the steam engine: a man of principle*
print
printer

prior
prioress
  *pl* prioresses
priority
  *pl* priorities
priory
  *pl* priories
prise
  *to prise open a lid*
  prised
  prising
prism
prison
**prisoner**
pristine
**privacy**
private
  *private information: a private secretary*
  *adv* privately
privateer
privation
privatization, -isation
privatize, -ise
privet
  *a privet hedge*
**privilege**
privileged
privy council
prize
  *to win a prize: to prize a possession dearly*
  prized
  prizing
probability
  *pl* probabilities

probable
  *adv* **probably**
probation
probe
  probed
  probing
probity
problem
problematic
proboscis
  *pl* proboscises
**procedure**
**proceed**
  *Proceed on your way!*
  proceeded
  proceeding
  proceeds
process
  *pl* processes
  processed
  processing
**procession**
proclaim
**proclamation**
proclivity
  *pl* proclivities
procrastinate
  procrastinated
  procrastinating
procrastination
procurator fiscal
procure
  procured
  procuring
prod
  prodded
  prodding
prodigal

prodigious
prodigy
  pl prodigies
produce
  produced
  producing
producer
product
production
productive
  adv productively
productivity
profane
  adv profanely
profanity
profess
**profession**
**professional**
  adv
    professionally
**professor**
**proffer**
proffered
proffering
**proficiency**
proficient
profile
profit
  *profit and loss*
**profited**
profiting
profitable
  adv profitably
profiteer
profiteered
**profiteering**
profligacy
profligate
profound

profuse
  adv profusely
profusion
progenitor
progeny
prognosticate
  prognosticated
  prognosticating
  prognostication
program
  *a computer*
  *program: to*
  *program a*
  *computer*

programmed
programming
programme
  *a theatre*
  *programme*

progress
progression
progressive
  adv
    progressively
**prohibit**
  prohibited
  prohibiting
  prohibition
**prohibitive**
  adv
    prohibitively
project
projectile
projection
projector
proletarian
proletariat
proliferate
  proliferated

proliferating
prolific
prolix
prolixity
prologue
prolong
**promenade**
prominence
**prominent**
promiscuity
**promiscuous**
promise
  pl promises
  promised
  promising
promontory
  pl promontories
promote
  promoted
  promoting
**promotion**
prompt
  adv promptly
prone
prong
pronoun
pronounce
  pronounced
  pronouncing
pronouncement
**pronunciation**
proof
  *Do they have proof*
  *of his guilt?: 70%*
  *proof spirit*

prop
  propped
  propping
**propaganda**

propagandist
**propagate**
  propagated
  propagating
  propagator
propel
  propelled
  propelling
**propeller**
propensity
  *pl* propensities
proper
properly
property
  *the lost property office*
  *pl* properties
prophecy
  *to make a prophecy*
  *pl* prophecies
prophesy
  *to prophesy about the future*
  prophesied
  prophesying
prophet
  *an Old Testament prophet*
propinquity
propitiate
  propitiated
  propitiating
propitious
**proportion**
proportional
  *adv* proportionally
proportionate

*adv*
  proportionately
**proposal**
propose
  proposed
  proposing
  proposition
propound
**proprietor**
proprietress,
  proprietrix
propriety
  *She behaved with dignity and propriety*
  *pl* proprieties
propulsion
**prosaic**
  *adv* prosaically
prose
**prosecute**
  prosecuted
  prosecuting
  prosecution
  prosecutor
prospect
prospective
prospector
prospectus
  *pl* prospectuses
prosper
  prospered
  prospering
prosperity
prosperous
prostate
  *the prostate gland*
**prostitute**
prostrate

*to prostrate with grief: He lay prostrate on the floor*

prostrated
prostrating
prostration
**protagonist**
protect
protection
protective
  *adv* protectively
protector
protégé
**protein**
protest
Protestant
protestation
**protocol**
proton
prototype
protract
protractor
protrude
  protruded
  protruding
protrusion
protuberance
protuberant
proud
prove
  *Can you prove that he murdered her?*
  proved
  proving
provender
proverb
proverbial
  *adv* proverbially

provide
　provided
　providing
providence
provident
providential
　*adv*
　　providentially
province
**provincial**
　*adv* provincially
provision
**provisional**
　*adv*
　　provisionally
proviso
　*pl* provisos
**provocation**
provocative
　*adv*
　　provocatively
**provoke**
　provoked
　provoking
prow
**prowess**
prowl
prowler
proximity
proxy
　*pl* proxies
prude
prudence
prudent
prudery
prudish
prune
　pruned
　pruning

pry
　pried
　prying
**psalm**
psalter
pseudo
**pseudonym**
**psychiatric**
psychiatrist
**psychiatry**
**psychic**
psychoanalysis
psychoanalyst
**psychological**
　*adv*
　　psychologically
psychologist
**psychology**
psychosomatic
ptarmigan
pterodactyl
pub
puberty
pubic
public
　*adv* **publicly**
publican
publication
**publicity**
publish
publisher
puce
pucker
　puckered
　puckering
pudding
puddle
puerile
puff

puffin
puffy
pugilist
pugnacious
pugnacity
pull
　*to pull a cart*
pullet
pulley
　*pl* pulleys
pullover
pulmonary
pulp
pulpit
pulsate
　pulsated
　pulsating
pulse
　pulsed
　pulsing
pulverize, -ise
　pulverized
　pulverizing
puma
**pumice stone**
pummel
　pummelled
　pummelling
pump
pumpkin
pun
　punned
　punning
punch
　*pl* punches
punctilious
punctual
　*adv* punctually
**punctuality**

171

punctuate
punctuated
punctuating
punctuation
puncture
punctured
puncturing
pundit
pungent
**punish**
punishable
punishment
punitive
punnet
punt
puny
pup
pupa
*pl* pupae
**pupil**
puppet
puppy
*pl* puppies
purchase
purchased
purchasing
purchaser
pure
purée
purely
purgative
purgatory
purge
purged
purging
purification
purify
purified
purifying

purist
puritan
puritanical
*adv* puritanically
purity
purl
*knit one, purl one*
purled
purling
purloin
purple
purport
purpose
purposeful
*adv* purposefully
**purposely**
purr
purred
purring
purse
purser
**pursue**
pursued
pursuing
pursuer
**pursuit**
pus
push
pushy
pusillanimous
put
*to put a cup on the table*
put
putting
putative
putrefaction
putrefy
putrefied

putrefying
putrid
putt
*to putt a ball*
putted
putting
putter
putty
puzzle
puzzled
puzzling
pygmy, pigmy
*pl* pygmies, pigmies
**pyjamas**
pylon
**pyramid**
pyre
Pyrex ®
Pyrrhic
python

**Q**

quack
quad
quadrangle
quadrangular
quadrant
quadrilateral
quadrille
**quadruped**
quadruple
quadruplet
quaff
quail
quailed
quailing
quaint

quake
 quaked
 quaking
**qualification**
qualify
 qualified
 qualifying
qualitative
quality
 *pl* qualities
qualm
quandary
 *pl* quandaries
quantitative
quantity
 *pl* quantities
**quarantine**
quarrel
 **quarrelled**
 quarrelling
**quarrelsome**
quarry
 *pl* quarries
 quarried
 quarrying
quart
quarter
quarterly
quartet
**quartz**
quasar
quash
 *to quash a*
 *rebellion*
quasi-
quaver
 quavered
 quavering
quay

*the boat tied to the*
*quay*
queasiness
queasy
 *adv* queasily
queen
 queenly
queer
quell
quench
querulous
**query**
 *pl* queries
 queried
 querying
quest
question
 **questioned**
 questioning
questionable
 *adv*
 questionably
**questionnaire**
**queue**
 *a cinema queue: to*
 *queue for the*
 *cinema*
 queued
 queuing,
 queueing
quibble
 quibbled
 quibbling
quick
quicken
 quickened
 quickening
quickness
quid

quiescent
quiet
 *a shy, quiet child*
**quieten**
 quietened
 quietening
quietness
quill
quilt
 quilted
quin
quince
quinine
quinquennial
quintessence
quintessential
**quintet**
quintuplet
quip
 quipped
 quipping
quire
 *a quire of paper*
quirk
quirky
quit
 quitted, quit
 quitting
quite
 *quite pretty*
quiver
 quivered
 quivering
quixotic
 *adv* quixotically
quiz
 *pl* quizzes
 **quizzed**
 quizzing

173

quizzical
  *adv* quizzically
quoits
quorum
quota
  *pl* quotas
**quotation**
quote
  quoted
  quoting
quotient

# R

rabbi
  *pl* rabbis
**rabbit**
rabble
**rabid**
**rabies**
raccoon, racoon
race
racecourse
**racial**
  *adv* racially
racialism
racialist
racism
racist
rack
racket, racquet
  *a tennis racket*
racket
  *a noisy racket: an illegal racket*
**racketeer**
raconteur
racoon
  *see* raccoon

racquet
  *see* racket
racy
radar
  *a radar beam*
radiance
radiant
radiate
  radiated
  radiating
radiation
**radiator**
radical
  *adv* radically
radio
  *pl* **radios**
  **radioed**
  radioing
radioactive
radiologist
radiology
radiotherapist
radiotherapy
radish
  *pl* radishes
radium
radius
  *pl* radii
raffia
**raffle**
  raffled
  raffling
raft
rafter
rag
  ragged
  *They ragged the new boy*
  ragging

ragamuffin
rage
  raged
  *He raged and swore*
  raging
ragged [ragd]
  *see* rag
ragged ['ragid]
  *ragged clothes*
raid
raider
  *The police caught the raider*
rail
**railing**
railway
raiment
rain
  *wind and rain: to rain heavily*
  rained
  raining
rainbow
rainy
raise
  *to raise a family: to raise one's arm*
  raised
  raising
**raisin**
rajah
rake
  raked
  raking
rakish
rally
  *pl* rallies
  rallied

rallying
am
rammed
ramming
Ramadan
amble
rambled
rambling
ambler
**amification**
amp
ampage
rampaged
rampaging
ampant
*the lion rampant:*
*Violence is*
*rampant*
ampart
*the rampart round*
*the castle*
an
*see* run
anch
*pl* ranches
ancid
ancorous
**ancour**
and
andom
ang
*see* ring
ange
ranged
ranging
anger
ank
ankle
rankled

rankling
**ransack**
ransom
ransomed
ransoming
rant
rap
rapped
*He rapped on the*
*door*
rapping
rapacious
rape
raped
*He raped and*
*murdered her*
raping
rapid
rapidity
rapier
rapist
rapped
*see* rap
rapt
*gazing with rapt*
*attention*
rapture
**rapturous**
rare
rarefied
rarely
raring
rarity
*pl* rarities
rascal
*adv* rascally
rash
rasher
rasp

raspberry
*pl* raspberries
rat
ratted
*The dog ratted: His*
*friends ratted on*
*him*
ratting
ratchet
rate
rated
*They rated him the*
*best pilot*
rating
rateable
rather
ratification
ratify
ratified
ratifying
rating
ratio
*pl* ratios
ration
rationed
**rationing**
**rational**
*adv* rationally
rationalization,
-isation
rationalize, -ise
rationalized
rationalizing
ratted
*see* rat
rattle
rattled
rattling
rattlesnake

ratty
raucous
ravage
　ravaged
　ravaging
rave
　raved
　raving
raven
**ravenous**
ravine
ravishing
ray
　*pl* rays
rayon
raze
　*to raze a city to the ground*
　razed
　razing
razor
reach
react
reaction
**reactionary**
read [rēd]
　*to read a book*
　read [red]
　*He read that book*
　reading
reader
readily
readiness
ready
real
　*a real diamond: a real friend*
realism
realist

realistic
　*adv* realistically
reality
　*pl* realities
realization,
　-isation
**realize, -ise**
　realized
　realizing
really
realm
ream
reap
　reaped
　reaping
　reaper
rear
　reared
　rearing
rearguard
reason
　reasoned
　**reasoning**
　**reasonable**
　*adv* reasonably
**reassurance**
reassure
　reassured
　reassuring
rebate
rebel
　**rebelled**
　rebelling
rebellion
**rebellious**
rebound
rebuff
rebuke
　rebuked

rebuking
rebut
　rebutted
　rebutting
rebuttal
recalcitrance
**recalcitrant**
recall
　recalled
　recalling
recant
recap
　recapped
　recapping
recapitulate
　recapitulated
　recapitulating
recapitulation
recapture
　recaptured
　recapturing
recede
　receded
　receding
**receipt**
**receive**
　received
　receiving
receiver
recent
recently
**receptacle**
reception
**receptionist**
receptive
recess
　*pl* recesses
recession
**recipe**

recipient
reciprocal
*adv* reciprocally
reciprocate
reciprocated
reciprocating
**recital**
recitation
recite
recited
reciting
reckless
reckon
reckoned
reckoning
reclaim
reclamation
recline
reclined
reclining
recluse
recognition
recognizable,
-isable
*adv*
recognizably
**recognize, -ise**
recognized
recognizing
recoil
recoiled
recoiling
recollect
recollection
**recommend**
recommendation
recompense
reconcile
reconciled

reconciling
**reconciliation**
recondite
**reconnaissance**
**reconnoitre**
reconnoitred
reconnoitring
record
recorder
recording
recount
recoup
recouped
recouping
recourse
recover
**recovered**
recovering
recovery
re-creation
*a skilful re-creation of the Victorian atmosphere in the film*
recreation
*She swims for recreation*
recrimination
recruit
recruited
recruiting
**recruitment**
rectangle
rectangular
rectify
rectified
rectifying
rectitude
rector

rectory
*pl* rectories
rectum
recumbent
recuperate
recuperated
recuperating
recuperation
recuperative
recur
recurred
recurring
**recurrence**
recurrent
red
*a red dress*
redden
reddened
reddening
redeem
Redeemer
redeeming
redemption
redeploy
redeployed
redeploying
red-handed
redness
redolent
redouble
redoubled
redoubling
redoubtable
redress
reduce
reduced
reducing
reduction
redundancy

pl redundancies
**redundant**
reed
*a broken reed: a
reed by the pond: a
reed of a musical
instrument*

reedy
reef
reefer
reek
reel
*a Scottish reel: to
reel drunkenly*

**reeled**
reeling
refectory
pl refectories
refer
**referred**
referring
**referee**
**reference**
referendum
pl referenda,
referendums
refine
refined
refining
refinement
refinery
pl refineries
reflect
reflection
reflective
adv reflectively
reflector
reflex
reflexive

reform
reformation
reformer
refraction
refractory
refrain
refrained
refraining
refresh
refresher course
refreshment
**refrigerator**
refuel
**refuelled**
refuelling
refuge
*to find refuge from
danger*

refugee
*He is a war refugee*
refund
**refusal**
refuse [rə'fūz]
*Did you refuse to
go?*

refused
refusing
refuse ['refūs]
*kitchen refuse*
refute
refuted
refuting
regain
regained
regaining
regal
*a stately and regal
carriage*

adv regally

regale
*to regale him with
humorous stories*

regaled
regaling
**regalia**
regard
regarding
regardless
**regatta**
pl regattas
regency
regeneration
regent
reggae
regicide
régime
regiment
regimental
regimentation
region
regional
adv regionally
register
registered
registering
registrar
registry
pl registries
regret
**regretted**
regretting
regretful
adv regretfully
**regrettable**
adv regrettably
regular
regularity
regulate

regulated
regulating
regulation
regulator
**regurgitate**
regurgitated
regurgitating
rehabilitate
rehabilitated
rehabilitating
**rehabilitation**
**rehearsal**
rehearse
rehearsed
rehearsing
**reign**
*How long did
Victoria reign?*
reigned
reigning
reimburse
reimbursed
reimbursing
rein
*the reins of a
horse: to rein in the
horse*
reined
reining
reincarnation
reindeer
*pl* reindeer
reinforce
reinforced
reinforcing
reinforcements
reinstate
reinstated
reinstating

reinstatement
**reiterate**
reiterated
reiterating
reiteration
reiterative
reject
rejection
**rejoice**
rejoiced
rejoicing
rejoinder
rejuvenate
rejuvenated
rejuvenating
relapse
relapsed
relapsing
relate
related
relating
relation
relationship
**relative**
*adv* relatively
relax
relaxation
relay
relayed
relaying
**release**
released
releasing
relegate
relegated
relegating
relegation
relent
relentless

**relevance**
**relevant**
reliable
*adv* reliably
reliance
reliant
relic
**relief**
*a sigh of relief*
**relieve**
*to relieve her pain*
relieved
relieving
religion
religious
relinquish
relish
*pl* relishes
reluctance
**reluctant**
rely
relied
relying
remain
remained
remaining
remainder
remand
remark
remarkable
*adv* remarkably
remedy
*pl* remedies
remedied
remedying
**remember**
remembered
remembering
remembrance

remind
reminder
**reminisce**
  reminisced
  reminiscing
**reminiscence**
reminiscent
remiss
remission
remit
  remitted
  remitting
**remittance**
remnant
remonstrance
remonstrate
  remonstrated
  remonstrating
remorse
remorseful
  *adv*
    remorsefully
remorseless
remote
  *adv* remotely
**removal**
remove
  removed
  removing
remunerate
  remunerated
  remunerating
**remuneration**
remunerative
renal
render
  rendered
  rendering
**rendezvous**

*pl* rendezvous
renegade
renew
**renewal**
rennet
renounce
  renounced
  renouncing
renovate
  renovated
  renovating
renovation
renown
renowned
rent
rental
**renunciation**
reorganization,
  -isation
reorganize, -ise
  reorganized
  reorganizing
rep
repaid
  *see* repay
repair
  **repaired**
  repairing
**reparation**
repartee
repast
repatriate
  repatriated
  repatriating
repatriation
repay
  **repaid**
  repaying
repayment

repeal
  repealed
  repealing
repeat
  repeated
  repeating
repeatedly
repel
  repelled
  repelling
repellent,
  repellant
repent
repentance
**repentant**
repercussion
**repertoire**
repertory
repetition
repetitious
**repetitive**
  *adv* repetitively
replace
  replaced
  replacing
replacement
replenish
replete
replica
  *pl* replicas
reply
  *pl* replies
  replied
  replying
report
reporter
repose
repository
  *pl* repositories

reprehensible
*adv*
  reprehensibly
represent
representation
representative
repress
repression
repressive
**reprieve**
  reprieved
  reprieving
reprimand
**reprisal**
reproach
  *pl* reproaches
reproachful
  *adv*
  reproachfully
reprobate
reproduce
  reproduced
  reproducing
reproduction
reproof
  *a look of reproof*
reprove
  *to reprove the*
  *naughty child*
  reproved
  reproving
reptile
reptilian
republic
republican
**repudiate**
  repudiated
  repudiating
repudiation

repugnance
**repugnant**
repulsive
  *adv* repulsively
**reputable**
reputation
repute
reputed
reputedly
request
requiem
**require**
  required
  requiring
  requirement
**requisite**
**rescind**
rescue
  rescued
  **rescuing**
research
  *pl* researches
  researcher
**resemblance**
resemble
  resembled
  resembling
resent
resentful
  *adv* resentfully
resentment
reservation
reserve
  reserved
  reserving
  reserved
**reservoir**
reside
  resided

residing
residence
resident
residential
residual
residue
**resign**
  resigned
  resigning
**resignation**
resilience
**resilient**
resin
resinous
resist
**resistance**
resolute
  *adv* resolutely
**resolution**
resolve
  resolved
  resolving
resonance
resonant
resonate
  resonated
  resonating
resort
resounding
resource
**resourceful**
respect
respectability
**respectable**
  *adv* respectably
respectful
  *a respectful salute*
  *adv* respectfully
respective

*They went to their respective homes*

adv respectively
respiration
respirator
respite
resplendent
respond
response
**responsibility**
  pl
  responsibilities
**responsible**
  adv responsibly
responsive
rest
  *take a rest: rest in peace*

**restaurant**
restaurateur
restful
  adv restfully
restitution
restive
  adv restively
restless
**restoration**
restore
  restored
  restoring
restrain
  restrained
  restraining
restraint
restrict
restriction
restrictive
result
resultant

resume
resumed
resuming
résumé
resumption
resurgence
resurgent
resurrect
**resurrection**
**resuscitate**
  resuscitated
  resuscitating
  resuscitation
retail
  retailed
  retailing
**retailer**
retain
  retained
  retaining
retainer
retaliate
  retaliated
  retaliating
retaliation
retarded
retch
  *The sight of blood makes him retch*
retention
retentive
reticence
reticent
retina
  pl retinas,
  retinae
retinue
**retiral**
retire

retired
retiring
retirement
retort
retrace
  retraced
  retracing
retract
retractable
retraction
retreat
  retreated
  retreating
retribution
**retrieve**
  retrieved
  retrieving
retriever
**retrograde**
retrospect
retrospective
  adv
  retrospectively
return
returnable
**reunion**
reunite
  reunited
  reuniting
**reveal**
  revealed
  revealing
**reveille**
revel
  revelled
  revelling
revelation
reveller
**revelry**

revenge
  revenged
  revenging
**revenue**
reverberate
  reverberated
  reverberating
reverberation
revere
  revered
  revering
reverence
Reverend
reverent
reverential
  *adv* reverentially
reverie
reversal
reverse
  reversed
  reversing
**reversible**
reversion
revert
review
  *the review of his
  new play: to review
  a novel*
reviewer
revile
  reviled
  reviling
revise
  revised
  revising
revision
**revival**
revive
  revived

reviving
revoke
  revoked
  revoking
revolt
  revolting
**revolution**
**revolutionary**
  *pl*
    revolutionaries
revolutionize,
  -ise
  revolutionized
  revolutionizing
revolve
  revolved
  revolving
revolver
revue
  *a musical revue*
revulsion
reward
rhapsodize, -ise
  rhapsodized
  rhapsodizing
**rhapsody**
  *pl* rhapsodies
rhetoric
rhetorical
  *adv* rhetorically
rheumatic
**rheumatism**
**rhinoceros**
  *pl* rhinoceroses
**rhododendron**
**rhubarb**
**rhyme**

  *Cat is a rhyme for
  rat: Do these words*

*rhyme?*
  rhymed
  rhyming
**rhythm**
rhythmic,
  rhythmical
  *adv* rhythmically
rib
ribald
ribbed
ribbon
rice
rich
riches
richness
rickets
rickety
rickshaw
**ricochet**
  ricocheted
  ricocheting
rid
  rid
  ridding
riddance
ridden
  *see* ride
riddle
  riddled
  riddling
ride
  rode
  *He rode on a horse*
  ridden
  *He has ridden on a
  horse*
  riding
rider
ridge

ridicule
  ridiculed
  ridiculing
  **ridiculous**
rife
riff-raff
rifle
  rifled
  rifling
rift
rig
  rigged
  rigging
right
  *the road on the
  right: the right
  answer: the right to
  vote*

**righteous**
righteousness
rightful
  *adv* rightfully
rigid
rigmarole
**rigorous**
rigour
rim
rime
  *the rime on the
  grass*
rind
ring
  *an engagement
  ring: to ring a
  racing pigeon*
  ringed
  *He ringed the
  pigeons*
  ringing

ring
  *to ring the bells*
  rang
  *The bell rang*
  rung
  *I have rung the bell*
  ringing
ringed
  *see* ring
rink
rinse
  rinsed
  rinsing
riot
  rioted
  rioting
  rioter
**riotous**
rip
  ripped
  ripping
ripe
ripen
  ripened
  ripening
  ripeness
ripple
  rippled
  rippling
rip-roaring
rise
  rose
  *The sun rose*
  risen
  *The sun has risen*
  rising
risk
risky
**risotto**

**rissole**
rite
  *to perform a
  religious rite*
ritual
  *adv* ritually
rivet
  **riveted**
  riveting
rivulet
road
  *a main road*
roam
  roamed
  roaming
roar
  roared
  roaring
roast
rob
  robbed
  robbing
robbery
  *pl* robberies
robe
robin
robot
robust
rock
rocker
rockery
  *pl* rockeries
rocket
  **rocketed**
  rocketing
rocky
rode
  *see* ride
rodent

184

roe
*a roe deer: cod roe*
**rogue**
roguish
role
*the role of Hamlet*
roll
*a roll of carpet: to roll a ball*
roller
rollicking
Roman
romance
romantic
*adv* romantically
romp
roof
*pl* roofs
rook
rookery
*pl* rookeries
roomy
root
rooted
rooting
rope
roped
roping
ropy
rosary
*pl* rosaries
rose
*see* rise
rose
rosemary
**rosette**
roster
rostrum
*pl* rostrums,

rostra
rosy
rot
rotted
rotting
rota
*pl* rotas
rotary
rotate
rotated
rotating
**rotation**
rote
*He learnt the answers by rote*
rotten
rotter
rotund
rouge
rough
*a rough surface: a rough sea*
**roughage**
roughen
roughened
roughening
**roulette**
round
rounders
rouse
roused
rousing
rout
*the rout of Napoleon's army*
route
*the quickest route to Edinburgh*
**routine**

*adv* routinely
rove
roved
roving
rover
row [rō]
*a row of cabbages: to row a boat*
rowed
*He rowed the boat*
rowing
row [row]
*a noisy row*
rowan
rowdy
rowdyism
rowed
*see* row
rower
rowing boat
rowlock
royal
*adv* royally
royalist
**royalty**
*pl* royalties
rub
rubbed
rubbing
rubber
rubbish
rubble
ruby
*pl* rubies
**rucksack**
rudder
ruddy
rude
*adv* rudely

rudeness
rudimentary
rudiments
rue
  rued
  ruing
rueful
  *adv* ruefully
ruff
  *a ruff round the
  neck*
**ruffian**
ruffle
  ruffled
  ruffling
rug
Rugby
rugged
ruin
  ruined
  ruining
ruination
**ruinous**
ruinously
rule
  ruled
  ruling
ruler
rum
rumble
  rumbled
  rumbling
ruminant
ruminate
  ruminated
  ruminating
**rummage**
  rummaged
  rummaging

**rumour**
rump
rumple
  rumpled
  rumpling
rumpus
run
  ran
  *He ran away*
  run
  *He has run away*
  running
rune
rung
  *see* ring
rung
  *the rung of the
  ladder*
runner
runner-up
  *pl* runners-up
runway
rupee
rupture
  ruptured
  rupturing
rural
ruse
rush
  *pl* rushes
rusk
russet
rust
rustic
rustle
  rustled
  rustling
rustler
rusty

rut
  rutted
  rutting
ruthless
ruthlessness
rye
  *rye bread*

**S**

Sabbath
sable
**sabotage**
sabre
**saccharine**
sachet
sack
sacrament
sacred
**sacrifice**
  sacrificed
  sacrificing
sacrificial
**sacrilege**
sacrilegious
sacrosanct
sad
  *compar* sadder
  *superl* saddest
  *adv* sadly
sadden
  **saddened**
  saddening
saddle
  saddled
  saddling
saddler
sadism
sadist

sadistic
  adv sadistically
sadness
safari
safe
  adv safely
**safeguard**
safety
saffron
sag
  sagged
  sagging
saga
  pl sagas
sagacious
sagacity
sage
  adv sagely
sago
said
  see say
sail
  a sail round the
  bay: to sail a boat
  sailed
  sailing
sailor
saint
saintly
sake
salaam
**salad**
**salami**
salary
  pl salaries
sale
  a furniture sale
salesman
salient

saline
saliva
salivary
salivate
  salivated
  salivating
sallow
sally
  pl sallies
  sallied
  sallying
**salmon**
salon
  a hairdressing
  salon
saloon
  a saloon car: a
  saloon bar
salt
salty
**salubrious**
salutary
salutation
salute
  saluted
  saluting
**salvage**
  salvaged
  salvaging
salvation
salve
  salved
  salving
salver
salvo
  pl salvos,
  salvoes
same
sameness

sample
  sampled
  sampling
sampler
sanatorium
  pl sanatoriums,
  sanatoria
sanctify
  sanctified
  sanctifying
sanctimonious
**sanction**
  sanctioned
  sanctioning
sanctity
**sanctuary**
  pl sanctuaries
sand
sandal
sandpaper
**sandwich**
  pl sandwiches
sandy
sane
  adv sanely
saneness
sang
  see sing
sanguine
  adv sanguinely
**sanitary**
sanitation
sanity
sank
  see sink
sap
  sapped
  sapping
sapling

sapphire
sarcasm
sarcastic
  *adv* sarcastically
sarcophagus
  *pl* sarcophagi,
    sarcophaguses
sardine
sardonic
  *adv* sardonically
sari
sarong
sartorial
sash
  *pl* sashes
sat
  *see* sit
Satan
satanic
satchel
sated
**satellite**
satiate
  satiated
  satiating
satiety
satin
satire
satirical
  *adv* satirically
satirist
satisfaction
**satisfactory**
  *adv*
    satisfactorily
satisfy
  satisfied
  satisfying
saturate

saturated
saturating
saturation
**Saturday**
saturnine
satyr
sauce
saucepan
saucer
saucy
  *adv* saucily
sauerkraut
saunter
  sauntered
  sauntering
**sausage**
savage
  *adv* savagely
savagery
save
  saved
  saving
  savings
saviour
  *Christ the Saviour*
savour
  *to savour the*
    *delicious wine*
savoury
  *pl* savouries
saw
  *see* see
saw
  sawed
  *He sawed the tree*
    *down*
  sawn
  *He has sawn off*
    *the branch*

sawing
saxophone
say
  said
  saying
scab
scabbard
scabby
scabies
scaffold
**scaffolding**
scald
scale
scallop
scalloped
scallywag
scalp
scalpel
scaly
scamp
scamper
  scampered
  scampering
scampi
scan
  scanned
  scanning
scandal
scandalize, -ise
  scandalized
  scandalizing
scandalmonger
**scandalous**
scansion
scant
scanty
  *adv* scantily
scapegoat
scar

scarred
*His cheek is scarred*
scarring
scarce
scarcely
scarcity
*pl* scarcities
scare
scared
*She was scared of the dark*
scaring
scarf
*pl* scarves, scarfs
scarlet
scarred
*see* scar
**scathing**
scatter
scattered
scattering
scavenger
scene
*the first scene of the play: the scene of the crime*
scenery
**scenic**
scent
*the scent of spring flowers*
sceptic
*A sceptic doesn't believe anyone*
sceptical
*adv* sceptically
scepticism

**sceptre**
**schedule**
**scheme**
schemed
scheming
schism
**schizophrenia**
schizophrenic
scholar
scholarly
scholarship
scholastic
*adv* scholastically
school
schooled
schooling
schoolfellow
**schooner**
**sciatica**
**science**
scientific
*adv* scientifically
scientist
scintillate
scintillated
scintillating
**scissors**
scoff
scold
scolding
scone
scoop
scooped
scooping
scooter
scope
scorch
score

scored
scoring
scorer
scorn
scornful
*adv* scornfully
scorpion
scoundrel
scour
scoured
scouring
**scourge**
scourged
scourging
scout
scowl
scrabble
scrabbled
scrabbling
scraggy
scramble
scrambled
scrambling
scrap
scrapped
*They have scrapped the plans*
scrapping
scrape
scraped
*She scraped her arm on the stone wall*
scraping
scrapped
*see* scrap
scratch
*pl* scratches
scrawl

scrawny
scream
  screamed
  screaming
scree
screech
  *pl* screeches
screed
screen
  screened
  screening
screw
  screwed
  screwing
scribble
  scribbled
  scribbling
scripture
scroll
scrub
  scrubbed
  scrubbing
scruff
  *adv* scruffily
scruffy
**scruple**
**scrupulous**
  *adv* scrupulously
scrutinize, -ise
  scrutinized
  scrutinizing
scrutiny
scuffle
scullery
  *pl* sculleries
sculptor
  *He is an artist and
  a sculptor*
sculpture

  *a beautiful piece of
  sculpture*
scum
scupper
  scuppered
  scuppering
**scurrilous**
scurry
  scurried
  scurrying
scurvy
scuttle
  scuttled
  scuttling
**scythe**
sea
  *ships on the sea*
seagull
seal
  sealed
  sealing
  *the sealing of the
  envelope: sealing
  wax*
seam
  *to sew a seam: a
  coal seam*
seamy
séance
sear
  *to sear meat*
  seared
  searing
search
  *pl* searches
season
  seasoned
  seasoning
seasonable

**seasonal**
  *adv* seasonally
seat
  seated
  seating
seaweed
secateurs
secede
  seceded
  seceding
secession
secluded
seclusion
second
**secondary**
second-hand
secrecy
secret
  *They kept their
  marriage a secret:
  a secret plan*
**secretarial**
**secretary**
  *pl* secretaries
secrete
  *to secrete a dagger
  under a cloak*
  secreted
  secreting
secretion
**secretive**
  *adv* secretively
sect
sectarian
section
sector
secular
secure
  *adv* securely

190

secured
securing
security
*pl* securities
sedate
*adv* sedately
sedation
**sedative**
**sedentary**
sediment
sedition
seditious
seduce
seduced
seducing
seduction
seductive
*adv* seductively
see
*Did you see him?:*
*to see clearly*
saw
*I saw you*
seen
*I have seen him*
seeing
seed
seedling
seedy
seek
**sought**
seeking
seem
*They seem friendly*
seemed
seeming
seemingly
seemly
seen

*see* see
seep
seeped
seeping
seer
*The seer foretold*
*her death*
seesaw
seethe
seethed
seething
segment
segregate
segregated
segregating
segregation
seismic
**seize**
seized
seizing
seizure
seldom
select
selection
selective
self
*pl* selves
self-assured
self-effacing
selfish
sell
*to sell flowers from*
*a stall*
sold
selling
Sellotape ®
selvage
semblance
seminar

**semolina**
senate
senator
send
sent
*I sent a letter*
sending
**senile**
senility
senior
seniority
sensation
sensational
*adv*
sensationally
sense
sensed
sensing
senseless
**sensible**
*adv* sensibly
**sensitive**
*adv* sensitively
sensitivity
sensory
sensual
*a sensual face*
*adv* sensually
sensuous
*the sensuous qual-*
*ity of the sculpture*
sent
*see* send
sentence
sentenced
sentencing
**sentimental**
*adv*
sentimentally

sentimentality
sentinel
Seoul
**separate**
  adv separately
  separated
  separating
**separation**
**September**
septic
  a septic wound: a
  septic tank
septuagenarian
sepulchral
sepulchre
sequel
sequence
sequestered
sequin
seraph
  pl seraphs,
    seraphim
seraphic
sere
  withered and sere
**serenade**
serene
  adv serenely
serenity
serf
serge
**sergeant**
serial
  a television serial:
  a magazine serial
**series**
  a series of plays
  pl series
serious

in a serious mood
sermon
serpent
**serrated**
serried
serum
servant
serve
  served
  serving
service
**serviceable**
**serviette**
servile
  adv servilely
servility
session
set
  set
  setting
**settee**
setter
settle
  settled
  settling
settlement
settler
seven
seventeen
seventeenth
seventh
seventieth
seventy
sever
  severed
  severing
**several**
severance
severe

adv severely
severity
sew
  to sew a seam
  sewed
  She sewed the
  seam
  sewn
  She has sewn it
  sewing
sewage
sewed
  see sew
sewer ['sūər]
sewer ['sōər]
  a sewer and a
  knitter
sewn
  see sew
sex
sexagenarian
sextant
  a ship's sextant
sexton
  The sexton tolled
  the bell
**sexual**
  adv sexually
shabby
  adv shabbily
shackles
shade
  shaded
  shading
shadow
shady
shaft
shaggy
shake

192

shook
*She shook the child*

shaken
*She has shaken the child*

shaking

shaky
*adv* shakily

shall
  should

**shallot**

shallow

sham
  shammed
  shamming

shambles

shame
  shamed
  shaming

shameful
  *adv* shamefully

shameless

shammy
  *see* chamois

shampoo
  **shampooed**
  shampooing

shamrock

shape
  shaped
  shaping

shapeless

shapely

share
  shared
  sharing

sharp

sharpen

sharpened

sharpening

sharpener

shatter
  **shattered**
  shattering

shave
  shaved
  shaving

shawl

sheaf
  *pl* sheaves

shear
  *to shear sheep*

  sheared
  *He sheared the sheep*

  shorn
  *He has shorn the sheep*

  shearing

  shears

sheath

shed

sheep

**sheepish**

sheer
  *a sheer drop: sheer delight*

  sheered
  *The car sheered off the road*

  sheering

sheet

**sheikh**

shekel

shelf
  *a wooden shelf*
  *pl* shelves

shell

shelter
  sheltered
  sheltering

shelve
  *to shelve the problem: The cliff shelves slightly*

**shepherd**

sherbet

**sheriff**

sherry

shied
  *see* shy

**shield**

shier, shiest
  *see* shy

shift

shiftless

shifty
  *adv* shiftily

shilling

shimmer
  shimmered
  shimmering

shin

shine
  shone
  shining

shingles

shiny

ship
  shipped
  shipping

shipwreck

shire

shirk

shirker

shirt

shiver
  shivered
  shivering
shoal
shock
shocking
shod
  see shoe
shoddy
  adv shoddily
shoe
  to shoe a horse
  shod
  shoeing
shone
  see shine
shoo
  to shoo the birds
  away
  shooed
  shooing
shook
  see shake
shoot
  to shoot dead
  shot
  shooting
shop
  shopped
  shopping
shopper
shore
shorn
  see shear
short
shortage
shortcoming
shorten
  **shortened**

shortening
shorthand
shortly
shot
  see shoot
should
  see shall
shoulder
  shouldered
  shouldering
shout
shove
  shoved
  shoving
shovel
  **shovelled**
  shovelling
show
  showed
  He showed me the
  book
  shown
  He has shown me
  the book
  showing
shower
  showered
  showering
showery
shown
  see show
showy
  adv showily
shrank
  see shrink
shrapnel
shred
  shredded
  shredding

shrew
**shrewd**
shrewish
**shriek**
  shrieked
  shrieking
shrill
  adv **shrilly**
shrimp
shrine
shrink
  shrank
  That dress shrank
  shrunk
  That dress has
  shrunk
  shrinking
shrivel
  shrivelled
  shrivelling
shroud
shrub
shrubbery
  pl shrubberies
shrug
  shrugged
  shrugging
shrunk
  see shrink
shrunken
shudder
  **shuddered**
  shuddering
shuffle
  shuffled
  shuffling
shun
  shunned
  shunning

shunt
shut
  shut
  shutting
shutter
shuttle
shy
  *compar* shyer,
    shier
  *superl* shyest,
    shiest
  *adv* shyly
shy
  shied
  shying
shyness
sibilant
Sibyl
sick
sicken
  sickened
  sickening
sickle
sickly
side
  sided
  siding
sideboard
sideways
siding
sidle
  sidled
  sidling
**siege**
siesta
**sieve**
  sieved
  sieving
sift

**sigh**
  sighed
  sighing
sight
  *What a sight he is
  in that hat!: The
  sight of him made
  her cry: to sight
  land from the ship*

  sighted
  sighting
sightseeing
sign
  signed
  signing
signal
  **signalled**
  signalling
signatory
  *pl* signatories
signature
signet
  *a signet ring*
significance
**significant**
signify
  signified
  signifying
Sikh
silage
silence
  silenced
  silencing
silencer
silent
**silhouette**
  silhouetted
  silhouetting
silicon

  *Silicon is a
  common element*
silicone
  *silicone polish*
silk
silky
sill
silly
silo
  *pl* silos
silt
silver
silvery
similar
similarity
  *pl* similarities
simile
simmer
  simmered
  simmering
simper
  simpered
  simpering
simple
  *adv* simply
**simpleton**
**simplicity**
simplification
simplify
  simplified
  simplifying
simply
simulate
  simulated
  simulating
simulation
**simultaneous**
sin
  sinned

sinning
since
sincere
  *adv* **sincerely**
sincerity
sinecure
sinew
sinful
  *adv* sinfully
sing
  sang
  *He sang a song*
  sung
  *He has sung a song*
  singing
  *singing a song*
singe
  singed
  singeing
  *singeing the shirt with the iron*
single
  *adv* singly
  singled
  singling
singleness
singlet
singular
singularity
sinister
sink
  sank
  *The ship sank*
  sunk
  *The ship has sunk*
  sinking
sinner
Sinn Fein

**sinuous**
  *sinuous curves*
sinus
  *He has sinus trouble*
  *pl* sinuses
sip
  sipped
  sipping
siphon
  siphoned
  siphoning
sir
sire
siren
**sirloin**
sisal
sister
sister-in-law
  *pl* sisters-in-law
sisterly
sit
  sat
  sitting
site
  *the site of the new factory*
  sited
  siting
sit-in
sitting-room
situated
situation
six
sixteen
sixteenth
sixth
**sixtieth**
sixty

size
  sized
  sizing
sizeable, sizable
sizzle
  sizzled
  sizzling
skate
  skated
  skating
**skein**
skeletal
**skeleton**
sketch
  *pl* sketches
sketchy
  *adv* sketchily
skew
skewer
  skewered
  skewering
ski
  *pl* skis
  *He fastened on his skis*
  skied
  skiing
skid
  skidded
  skidding
skiff
**skilful**
  *adv* skilfully
skill
  skilled
skim
  skimmed
  skimming
skimp

skimpy
  *adv* skimpily
skin
  skinned
  skinning
skinny
skip
  skipped
  skipping
skipper
skirmish
  *pl* skirmishes
skirt
skirting
skittish
skittle
skulk
skull
skunk
sky
  *pl* skies
  *blue skies*
skylark
skylight
slack
slacken
  slackened
  slackening
slag
slain
  *see* slay
slake
  slaked
  slaking
slalom
slam
  slammed
  slamming
slander

slandered
slandering
**slanderous**
slang
slant
slap
  slapped
  slapping
slapdash
slash
  *pl* slashes
slat
slate
  slated
  *The roof is slated:*
  *His book was*
  *slated by the critics*
  slating
slatted
  *a slatted wooden*
  *fence*
**slaughter**
  slaughtered
  slaughtering
slave
slaver
  slavered
  slavering
slavery
**slavish**
slay
  *to slay the enemy*
  slew
  *He slew his enemy*
  slain
  *He has slain the*
  *enemy*
  slaying
sledge

sledged
sledging
sleep
  slept
  sleeping
sleeper
sleepy
  *adv* sleepily
sleet
sleeve
sleeveless
**sleigh**
  *a sleigh in the*
  *snow*
**sleight-of-hand**
slender
slept
  *see* sleep
**sleuth**
slew
  *see* slay
slew
  *The car began to*
  *slew round*
  slewed
  slewing
slice
  sliced
  slicing
slick
slide
  slid
  sliding
slight
slightly
slightness
slim
  slimmed
  slimming

slimy
sling
  slung
  slinging
slink
  slunk
  slinking
slinky
  *adv* slinkily
slip
  slipped
  slipping
slipper
slippery
slit
  slit
  slitting
slither
  slithered
  slithering
sliver
slobber
  slobbered
  slobbering
sloe
  *a ripe sloe*
slog
  slogged
  slogging
**slogan**
slop
  slopped
  *The water slopped
  in the pail*
  slopping
slope
  sloped
  *The hill sloped
  down*

sloping
slopped
  *see* slop
sloppy
  *adv* sloppily
slot
  slotted
  slotting
**slothful**
  *adv* slothfully
slouch
slough [slow]
  = a marsh
  *the slough of
  despond*
slough [sluf]
  *to slough off skin*
  sloughed
  sloughing
slovenly
slow
  *a slow train: to
  slow down*
sludge
slug
  sluggish
**sluice**
slum
slumber
  slumbered
  slumbering
slump
slung
  *see* sling
slunk
  *see* slink
slur
  slurred
  slurring

slush
slushy
slut
sluttish
sly
  *adv* **slyly**
slyness
smack
small
smallness
smart
smash
  *pl* smashes
**smattering**
smear
  smeared
  smearing
smell
  smelled, smelt
  *They smelled
  smoke: It smelt of
  fish*
  smelling
smelly
smelt
  *see* smell
smelt
  *to smelt ore*
  smelted
  smelting
smile
  smiled
  smiling
smirk
**smithereens**
smithy
smitten
smock
smocking

smog
smoke
  smoked
  smoking
smokeless
smoker
smoky
smooth
  smoothed
  smoothing
smother
  smothered
  smothering
smoulder
  smouldered
  smouldering
smudge
  smudged
  smudging
smug
smuggle
  smuggled
  smuggling
**smuggler**
smut
smutty
snack
snag
  snagged
  snagging
snail
snake
  snaked
  snaking
snap
  snapped
  snapping
snappy
  *adv* snappily

snare
  snared
  snaring
snarl
snatch
  *pl* snatches
sneak
sneaky
sneer
  sneered
  sneering
sneeze
  sneezed
  sneezing
sniff
snigger
  sniggered
  sniggering
snip
  snipped
  *She snipped the thread*
  snipping
snipe
  sniped
  *They sniped at the enemy*
  sniping
sniper
snipped
  *see* snip
snippet
snivel
  **snivelled**
  snivelling
snob
snobbery
snobbish
**snooker**

snoop
  snooped
  snooping
snooze
  snoozed
  snoozing
snore
  snored
  snoring
snorkel
snort
snout
snow
  snowed
  snowing
snowball
snowy
snub
  snubbed
  snubbing
snuff
snuffle
  snuffled
  snuffling
snug
snuggle
  snuggled
  snuggling
so
  *so beautiful: so much*
soak
so-and-so
soap
soapiness
soapy
soar
  *to soar high in the air*

soared
soaring
sob
  sobbed
  sobbing
sober
  sobered
  sobering
soberness
**sobriety**
**soccer**
sociability
**sociable**
  *He is friendly and sociable*
  *adv* sociably
sociableness
social
  *social history: a social occasion: social class*
  *adv* socially
socialism
socialist
socialistic
sociological
sociology
sock
socket
sod
soda
sodden
sofa
soft
soften
  softened
  softening
software
soggy

soil
  soiled
  soiling
**sojourn**
  sojourned
  sojourning
solace
  solaced
  solacing
**solar**
sold
  *see* sell
solder
  *to solder metal*
  soldered
  soldering
soldier
  *The soldier left the army*
  soldiered
  soldiering
sole
  *the sole of the foot: lemon sole: He is the sole survivor*
  *adv* solely
**solemn**
  *adv* solemnly
**solemnity**
sol-fa
solicit
  solicited
  soliciting
**solicitor**
solicitous
solid
solidarity
solidify
  solidified

solidifying
solidity
**soliloquy**
  *pl* soliloquies
solitary
solitude
solo
  *pl* solos
**soloist**
solstice
solubility
**soluble**
solution
solve
  solved
  solving
solvency
solvent
**sombre**
  *adv* sombrely
sombreness
sombrero
  *pl* sombreros
some
  *some people*
somebody
someone
**somersault**
something
somnolence
somnolent
son
  *a son and a daughter*
son-in-law
  *pl* sons-in-law
sonata
song
songster

songstress
  pl songstresses
sonic
sonnet
sonorous
soon
**sooner**
soot
  *soot in the
  chimney*
soothe
  soothed
  soothing
sooty
**sophisticated**
sophistication
soporific
sopping
soprano
  pl sopranos
sorcerer
sorcery
sordid
sore
  *a sore leg*
  adv sorely
soreness
sorrel
sorrow
sorrowful
  adv sorrowfully
sorry
sort
sortie
SOS
sotto voce
soufflé
sought
  *see* seek

soul
  *spirit and soul: the
  soul of kindness: a
  dear old soul: soul
  music*
**soulful**
  adv soulfully
sound
soup
sour
source
souse
  soused
  sousing
southerly
  *a southerly wind*
southern
  *the southern seas*
**sovereign**
sovereignty
sow [sow]
  *a sow in the pigsty*
sow [sō]
  *to sow seeds*
  sowed
  *He sowed seeds*
  sown
  *He has sown seeds*
  sowing
sower
  *a sower of seeds*
soya
spa
space
  spaced
  spacing
spacecraft
**spacious**
spaciousness

spade
**spaghetti**
span
  spanned
  spanning
spangle
**spaniel**
spank
spanking
spanner
spar
  sparred
  *He sparred with his
  opponent*
  sparring
spare
  spared
  *They spared his life*
  sparing
**sparing**
  adv sparingly
spark
sparkle
  sparkled
  sparkling
sparred
  *see* spar
sparrow
sparse
  adv sparsely
spartan
spasm
spasmodic
  adv
    spasmodically
spastic
spat
  *see* spit
spate

spatial
spats
spatter
  spattered
  spattering
**spatula**
spawn
speak
  spoke
  *She spoke to me*
  spoken
  *He has spoken at last*
  speaking
spear
special
  *adv* specially
**specialist**
speciality
  *Cream cakes are their speciality*
  *pl* specialities
specialization, -isation
specialize, -ise
  specialized
  specializing
specialty
  *Which medical specialty is he in?*
  *pl* specialties
species
  *pl* species
  *animals of different species*
specific
  *adv* specifically
specification
specify

specified
  specifying
specimen
specious
  *a specious argument*
speck
speckled
spectacle
**spectacles**
spectacular
  *adv*
    spectacularly
spectator
spectral
**spectre**
spectrum
  *pl* spectrums, spectra
speculate
  speculated
  speculating
speculation
speculative
  *adv*
    speculatively
sped
  *see* speed
speech
  *pl* speeches
speechless
speed
  speeded
  *The driver always speeded*
  sped
  *They sped along the path*
  speeding

**speedometer**
speedy
  *adv* speedily
spell
  spelled, spelt
  spelling
spend
  spent
  spending
sperm
spew
sphagnum
sphere
**spherical**
**sphinx**
spice
spiciness
spick-and-span
**spicy**
spider
spidery
spiel
spike
spiked
spiky
spill
  spilled, spilt
  spilling
spillage
spin
  spun
  spinning
**spinach**
spinal
spindle
spindly
spin-drier
spine
spineless

spinet
spinner
spinney
  *pl* spinneys
spinster
spiral
  spiralled
  spiralling
spire
spirit
  spirited
  spiriting
spiritual
  *adv* spiritually
**spiritualism**
spiritualist
spit
  spat
  spitting
spite
spiteful
  *adv* spitefully
spittle
spittoon
splash
  *pl* splashes
splay
splay-footed
spleen
splendid
**splendour**
splice
  spliced
  splicing
splint
splinter
  splintered
  splintering
split

split
splitting
splutter
  spluttered
  spluttering
spoil
  spoilt, spoiled
  spoiling
spoke
  *see* speak
spoke
spoken
  *see* speak
spokesman
sponge
  sponged
  sponging
sponger
spongy
**sponsor**
  sponsored
  sponsoring
**spontaneity**
**spontaneous**
spoof
spooky
spool
spoon
  spooned
  spooning
spoonerism
spoonful
  *pl* spoonfuls
sporadic
  *adv* sporadically
**sporran**
sport
sporting
sportsman

  *pl* sportsmen
sportsmanlike
spot
  spotted
  spotting
spotless
spotlight
spotty
spouse
spout
  spouted
  spouting
sprain
  sprained
  spraining
sprang
  *see* spring
sprawl
spray
  **sprayed**
  spraying
spread
  spread
  spreading
spread-eagled
spree
sprig
sprightliness
**sprightly**
  *adv* sprightlily
spring
  sprang
  *He sprang to his feet*
  sprung
  *He had sprung to his feet*
  springing
sprinkle

sprinkled
sprinkling
sprinkler
sprint
sprinter
sprite
sprocket
sprout
  sprouted
  sprouting
spruce
  *adv* sprucely
sprung
  *see* spring
spry
  *adv* spryly
spun
  *see* spin
spur
  spurred
  spurring
**spurious**
spurn
spurt
sputter
  sputtered
  sputtering
sputum
spy
  *pl* spies
  spied
  spying
**squabble**
  squabbled
  squabbling
squad
squadron
squalid
squall

squally
**squalor**
**squander**
  squandered
  squandering
square
  *adv* squarely
squash
  *to squash under foot: to squash the fruit*
squash (rackets)
**squat**
  squatted
  squatting
**squatter**
squaw
**squawk**
  squawked
  squawking
**squeak**
  squeaked
  squeaking
  squeaky
**squeal**
  squealed
  squealing
**squeamish**
squeeze
  squeezed
  squeezing
squelch
squib
squid
squiggle
squiggly
squint
squire
squirm

**squirrel**
squirt
stab
  stabbed
  stabbing
stability
stabilize, -ise
  stabilized
  stabilizing
stabilizer, -iser
**stable**
**staccato**
stack
stadium
  *pl* stadiums
staff
  staffed
  staffing
stag
stage
  staged
  staging
stagger
  **staggered**
  staggering
stagnant
stagnate
  stagnated
  stagnating
stagnation
staid
  *She is staid and respectable*
stain
  stained
  staining
stainless
stair
  *a winding stair*

staircase

stake

*a wooden stake: a stake in the firm: to stake a claim*

staked

staking

stalactite

stalagmite

stale

stalemate

stalk

*the stalk of the flower: to stalk off angrily: to stalk deer*

stalker

stall

**stallion**

**stalwart**

stamen

**stamina**

stammer

  **stammered**

  stammering

stamp

stampede

  stampeded

  stampeding

stance

stanch, staunch

*to stanch the blood*

stand

  stood

  standing

standard

standardization, -isation

standardize, -ise

standardized

standardizing

standby

stand-in

**stand-offish**

standstill

stank

*see* stink

stanza

staple

star

  starred

*Who starred in that film?*

  starring

starboard

starch

*pl* starches

starchy

stardom

stare

*a disapproving stare: to stare in amazement*

  stared

*She stared in amazement at him*

  staring

stark

starling

starred

*see* star

starry

start

startle

  startled

  startling

**startling**

starvation

starve

  starved

  starving

state

  stated

  stating

stately

statement

state-of-the-art

statesman

*pl* statesmen

statesmanlike

**static**

station

stationary

*The car was stationary*

stationer

stationery

*pens, pencils and other stationery*

statistical

*adv* statistically

statistician

**statistics**

statue

*a statue of Nelson*

statuesque

statuette

stature

status

status quo

statute

*by statute of Parliament*

**statutory**

staunch

*a staunch supporter*

staunch
  *see* stanch
stave
  staved, stove
  staving
stay
  stayed
    *We stayed at that hotel: She stayed unmarried*
  staying
**steadfast**
steadiness
steady
  *adv* steadily
  steadied
  steadying
steak
  *steak and chips*
steal
  *Did he steal the jewels?*
  stole
    *He stole the ring*
  stolen
    *He has stolen the ring*
  stealing
**stealth**
stealthy
  *adv* stealthily
steam
  steamed
  steaming
steamer
steamy
steed
steel
  *iron and steel*

steely
steep
  steeped
  steeping
steeple
steeplechase
steeplejack
steer
  steered
  steering
stem
  stemmed
  stemming
stench
stencil
  **stencilled**
  stencilling
stentorian
step
  *He climbed the wooden steps*
  stepped
  stepping
stepmother
steppe
  *the steppes of Russia*
**stereo**
**stereophonic**
stereotype
  stereotyped
sterile
sterility
sterilization, -isation
**sterilize, -ise**
  sterilized
  sterilizing
sterling

stern
sternness
stertorous
stethoscope
stevedore
stew
steward
stewardess
  *pl* stewardesses
stick
  stuck
  sticking
stickiness
stickler
sticky
stiff
stiffen
  stiffened
  stiffening
**stifle**
  stifled
  stifling
stigma
stile
  *Climb over the stile into the other field*
stiletto
  *pl* stilettos
still
stillborn
stillness
stilted
stilts
stimulant
  *Is that drug a stimulant?*
stimulate
  stimulated
  stimulating

stimulus
*the stimulus provided by competing against others*

*pl* stimuli
sting
  stung
  stinging
stingy
stink
  stank
  *The pigsty stank*
  stunk
  *It has stunk for days*
  stinking
stint
stipend
stipulate
  stipulated
  stipulating
stipulation
stir
  stirred
  stirring
**stirrup**
stitch
  *pl* stitches
stoat
stock
  *He comes of noble stock: a stock of tinned food: stocks and shares: Criminals used to be put in the stocks: We do not stock newspapers*
  stocked

*He stocked many brands of whisky*
  stocking
stockade
stockbroker
stocked
  *see* stock
stockiness
stocking
stocktaking
stocky
  *adv* stockily
  *stockily-built*
stodginess
stodgy
stoic
stoical
  *adv* stoically
**stoicism**
stoke
  stoked
  *He stoked the fire*
  stoking
stoker
stole
  *see* steal
stolen
  *see* steal
stolid
stolidity
**stomach**
stone
stony
  *adv* stonily
stood
  *see* stand
stooge
stool
stoop

stooped
stooping
stop
  stopped
  stopping
stoppage
stopper
**storage**
store
  stored
  storing
storey
  *a four-storey building*
  *pl* storeys
stork
storm
stormy
  *adv* stormily
story
  *a fairy story*
  *pl* stories
stout
stoutness
stove
  *see* stave
stove
stow
**stowaway**
straddle
  straddled
  straddling
straggle
  straggled
  straggling
straggly
straight
  *a straight line: a straight actor*

straighten
  straightened
    *The dentist straightened her teeth*
  straightening
straightness
strain
  strained
  straining
strainer
strait
  *a strait between pieces of land*
straitened
  *in straitened circumstances*
**straitjacket**
straitlaced
strand
strange
  *adv* strangely
strangeness
stranger
strangle
  strangled
  strangling
stranglehold
strangulation
strap
  strapped
  strapping
stratagem
**strategic**
  *adv* strategically
strategist
strategy
  *pl* strategies
stratification

stratified
stratosphere
stratum
  *a stratum of rich ore: a stratum of society*
  *pl* strata
stratus
  *stratus clouds*
straw
strawberry
  *pl* strawberries
stray
  strayed
  straying
streak
streakiness
**streaky**
stream
  streamed
  streaming
streamer
streamline
  streamlined
  streamlining
street
**strength**
**strengthen**
  strengthened
  strengthening
**strenuous**
stress
  *pl* stresses
  stressed
  stressing
stressful
stretch
  *pl* stretches
stretcher

strew
  strewed
    *They strewed the flowers*
  strewn
    *strewn with wild flowers*
  strewing
stricken
strict
stricture
stride
  strode
  striding
stridency
strident
strife
  *quarrelling and strife*
strike
  struck
  striking
string
  strung
  stringing
stringency
  *pl* stringencies
stringent
stringy
strip
  stripped
    *He stripped the wood: They stripped the wallpaper off*
  stripping
striped
  *red and white striped*

stripling
stripped
  *see* strip
**stripy**
strive
  *to strive to do
  better*
  strove
  *He strove to do
  well*
  striven
  *He has striven*
  striving
strode
  *see* stride
stroke
  stroked
  stroking
stroll
strong
stroppy
strove
  *see* strive
struck
  *see* strike
**structural**
  *adv* structurally
structure
structured
struggle
  struggled
  struggling
strum
  strummed
  strumming
strung
  *see* string
strut
  strutted

strutting
**strychnine**
stub
  stubbed
  stubbing
stubble
**stubborn**
stubbornness
stubby
stucco
stuck
  *see* stick
stud
  studded
  studding
student
studio
  *pl* studios
**studious**
studiousness
study
  *pl* studies
  studied
  studying
stuff
  stuffing
stuffy
stultify
  stultified
  stultifying
stumble
  stumbled
  stumbling
stump
stumpy
stun
  stunned
  stunning
stung

  *see* sting
stunk
  *see* stink
stunt
stunted
stupefaction
stupefy
  stupefied
  stupefying
stupendous
stupid
stupidity
**stupor**
sturdiness
sturdy
  *adv* sturdily
sturgeon
stutter
  stuttered
  stuttering
sty
  *a pig in a sty*
  *pl* sties
stye, sty
  *a stye on the eye*
  *pl* sties, styes
style
  *style of dress:
  literary style*
  styled
  styling
**stylish**
**stylus**
  *pl* styluses
**suave**
  *adv* suavely
suavity
subaltern
subcommittee

subconscious
**subdue**
  subdued
  subduing
subject
subjective
  *adv* subjectively
subjectiveness
subjectivity
subjugate
  subjugated
  subjugating
  subjugation
**sublieutenant**
sublime
  *adv* sublimely
sublimity
submarine
submerge
  submerged
  submerging
submersion
submission
**submissive**
  *adv*
    submissively
submit
  submitted
  submitting
subordinate
  subordinated
  subordinating
suborn
  suborned
  suborning
subpoena
  **subpoenaed**
  subpoenaing
subscribe

subscribed
subscribing
subscription
**subsequent**
subservience
subservient
subside
  subsided
  subsiding
**subsidence**
subsidiary
  *pl* subsidiaries
subsidize, -ise
  subsidized
  subsidizing
subsidy
  *pl* subsidies
subsist
subsistence
subsoil
substance
**substantial**
  *adv*
    substantially
substantiate
  substantiated
  substantiating
substantive
**substitute**
  substituted
  substituting
substitution
subterfuge
**subterranean**
subtitle
**subtle**
  *adv* subtly
**subtlety**
  *pl* subtleties

subtract
subtraction
suburb
**suburban**
suburbia
subversive
  *adv* subversively
subway
**succeed**
  succeeded
  succeeding
success
  *pl* successes
**successful**
  *adv* successfully
succession
successive
  *adv* successively
**successor**
**succinct**
  *adv* succinctly
succour
  succoured
  succouring
succulence
**succulent**
**succumb**
  succumbed
  succumbing
such
suck
sucker
suckle
  suckled
  suckling
suction
sudden
suddenly
**suddenness**

suds
sue
 **sued**
 suing
 **suede**
  *a suede jacket*
suet
suffer
 suffered
 suffering
 **sufferance**
suffice
 sufficed
 sufficing
 **sufficient**
suffix
 *pl* suffixes
 **suffocate**
 suffocated
 suffocating
suffocation
suffrage
suffragette
suffuse
 suffused
 suffusing
suffusion
sugar
sugar-beet
sugared
sugary
suggest
suggestible
 **suggestion**
suggestive
 *adv* suggestively
suicidal
 **suicide**
suit [sōot]

*a suit of clothes:
This will suit you*
 suited
 suiting
suitability
suitable
 *adv* suitably
suitcase
suite [swēt]
 *a suite of rooms: a
 bedroom suite*
suitor
sulk
sulky
 *adv* sulkily
sullen
 **sullenness**
sully
 sullied
 sullying
sulphur
sulphuric
sultan
sultana
sultry
 *adv* sultrily
sum
 *a difficult sum*
 summed
 summing
summarily
summarize, -ise
 summarized
 summarizing
summary

*a summary of our
plans: a short
summary of the
plot of the play*

 *pl* summaries
summer
summery
 *a summery day: a
 summery dress*
summit
summon
 **summoned**
 summoning
summons
 *pl* summonses
 **sumptuous**
sun
 *The sun shone
 brightly*
 sunned
 sunning
sunbathe
 sunbathed
 sunbathing
sunburn
sunburned,
 sunburnt
sundae
 *an ice cream
 sundae*
Sunday
 *They went to
 church on Sunday*
sundial
sundries
sundry
sung
 *see* sing
sunk
 *see* sink
sunken
 *sunken cheeks*
sunny

*adv* sunnily
suntan
  suntanned
  suntanning
sup
  supped
  supping
super
  *a super holiday*
superannuated
**superannuation**
superb
**supercilious**
**superficial**
  *adv* superficially
superfluity
**superfluous**
superhuman
superintend
superintendence
**superintendent**
superior
**superiority**
superlative
  *adv*
  superlatively
supermarket
supernatural
  *adv*
  supernaturally
**supersede**
  superseded
  superseding
supersonic
superstition
**superstitious**
  *adv*
  superstitiously
**supervise**

supervised
supervising
supervision
**supervisor**
supine
supper
  *They had supper at 9 pm*
supplant
supple
  *adv* supply
supplement
**supplementary**
suppleness
suppliant
supplication
supply
  *pl* supplies
  supplied
  supplying
support
supporter
suppose
  supposed
  **supposing**
supposedly
supposition
suppress
suppression
suppurate
  suppurated
  suppurating
supremacy
supreme
  *adv* supremely
surcharge
sure
surely
surety

*pl* sureties
surf
surface
  surfaced
  surfacing
surfeit
surfing
surge
  surged
  surging
**surgeon**
surgery
  *pl* surgeries
surgical
  *adv* surgically
surliness
surly
  *adv* surlily
surmise
  surmised
  surmising
surmountable
surname
surpass
surplice
  *a priest's surplice*
surplus
  *a surplus of butter*
surprise
  surprised
  surprising
surrender
  surrendered
  surrendering
surreptitious
surround
**surroundings**
surtax
**surveillance**

survey
surveyed
surveying
**surveyor**
**survival**
survive
survived
surviving
survivor
susceptibility
**susceptible**
suspect
suspend
suspender
suspense
suspension
suspicion
**suspicious**
sustain
sustained
sustaining
**sustenance**
swab
swabbed
swabbing
swaddle
swaddled
swaddling
swagger
swaggered
swaggering
swain
swallow
swam
  *see* swim
swamp
swan
swank
swanky

swap, swop
swapped,
  swopped
swapping,
  swopping
swarm
swarthy
swashbuckling
swat
swatted
swatting
swathed
sway
swayed
swaying
swear
swore
  *He swore to be true*
sworn
  *He has sworn to be true*
swearing
sweat
sweated
sweating
sweater
sweaty
swede
  *The farmer grows swedes*
Swedish
sweep
swept
sweeping
sweet
  *a sweet smile: a sweet orange: to suck a sweet*
sweeten

sweetened
sweetening
**sweetener**
sweetheart
sweetness
swell
swelled
  *His leg swelled*
swollen
  *His leg has swollen*
swelling
swelter
sweltered
sweltering
swept
  *see* sweep
swerve
swerved
swerving
swift
swiftness
swig
swigged
swigging
swill
swim
swam
  *She swam a length*
swum
  *She has swum a length*
swimming
swimmer
swimmingly
swindle
swindled
swindling
swindler
swine

swing
 swung
 swinging
 *swinging on a gate*
swingeing
 *swingeing cuts*
swinish
swipe
 swiped
 swiping
swirl
swish
switch
 *pl* switches
switchboard
swivel
 swivelled
 swivelling
swollen
 *see* swell
swoon
swoop
 swooped
 swooping
swop
 *see* swap
sword
swordfish
swore, sworn
 *see* swear
swum
 *see* swim
swung
 *see* swing
**sycamore**
sycophant
syllabic
syllable
syllabus

214

*pl* syllabuses,
 syllabi
sylph
symbol
 *a mathematical
 symbol: a symbol
 of the king's
 authority*
symbolic
 *adv*
 symbolically
symbolism
symbolize, -ise
 symbolized
 symbolizing
symmetrical
 *adv*
 symmetrically
**symmetry**
sympathetic
 *adv*
 sympathetically
**sympathize, -ise**
 sympathized
 sympathizing
sympathy
**symphony**
 *pl* symphonies
symposium
 *pl* symposia,
 symposiums
symptom
symptomatic
**synagogue**
**synchronize, -ise**
 synchronized
 synchronizing
syncopate
 syncopated

syncopating
syncopation
**syndicate**
synod
**synonym**
synonymous
synopsis
 *pl* synopses
syntax
synthesis
synthesize, -ise
 synthesized
 synthesizing
**synthetic**
 *adv*
 synthetically
**syringe**
syrup
syrupy
**system**
systematic
 *adv*
 systematically


T

tab
tabard
tabby
 *pl* tabbies
tabernacle
table
 tabled
 tabling
**tableau**
 *pl* tableaux
tablespoonful
 *pl*
 tablespoonfuls

tablet
tabloid
**taboo**
tabor
tabulate
  tabulated
  tabulating
tacit
**taciturn**
taciturnity
tack
  *pl* tacks
  *tin tacks: shoe tacks*
tackle
  tackled
  tackling
tacky
tact
tactful
  *adv* tactfully
tactical
  *adv* tactically
tactician
tactics
tactless
tadpole
**taffeta**
tag
  tagged
  tagging
tail
  *a dog's tail: the tail of his coat: Did the police tail him?*
  tailed
  tailing
tailor
  tailored

**tailoring**
taint
take
  took
  *He took a book*
  taken
  *He has taken a book*
  taking
**talc**
talcum (powder)
tale
  *a fairy tale*
**talent**
talented
talisman
talk
**talkative**
tall
tallness
tallow
tally
  *pl* tallies
  tallied
  tallying
tally-ho
talon
tambourine
tame
  *adv* tamely
  tamed
  taming
tamper
  tampered
  tampering
tampon
tan
  tanned
  tanning

tandem
tang
tangent
**tangerine**
**tangible**
  *adv* tangibly
tangle
  tangled
  tangling
tango
  *pl* tangos
tank
tankard
tanker
tannery
  *pl* tanneries
tannin
tantalize, -ise
  tantalized
  tantalizing
tantamount to
tantrum
tap
  tapped
  *The enemy tapped the telephone line: She tapped the table*
  tapping
tape
  taped
  *They taped the music*
  taping
taper
  *a lighted taper*
  tapered
  tapering
tape recorder

tapestry
  *pl* tapestries
tapeworm
tapioca
tapir
  *A tapir resembles a pig*
tapped
  *see* tap
tar
  tarred
  tarring
tarantula
tardy
  *adv* tardily
tare
  *Tare is the weight of an empty truck: weeds and tares*
target
  targeted
  targeting
**tariff**
tarmac
tarmacadam
tarnish
**tarpaulin**
tarragon
tarry
  tarried
  tarrying
tart
tartan
tartar
task
tassel
**tasselled**
taste
  tasted

tasting
tasteful
  *adv* tastefully
tasteless
tasty
tattered
tatters
tattle
**tattoo**
tattooed
tattooing
taught
  *see* teach
taunt
taut
  *The string is taut*
tauten
  tautened
  tautening
tautological
  *adv* tautologically
tautology
tavern
tawdry
tawny
tax
  *income tax*
taxation
taxi
  *pl* taxis
  taxied
  **taxiing**
taxidermist
taxidermy
tea
  *a cup of tea*
teach
  taught

*She taught French*
teaching
teacher
teak
teal
team
  *football team*
team (up) with
  teamed (up) with
  teaming (up) with
teapot
tear [tēr]
  *a tear of grief*
tear [tăr]
  *to tear one's coat*
  tore
  *She tore her coat*
  torn
  *She has torn her coat*
  tearing
tease
  teased
  teasing
teaser
teaspoonful
  *pl* teaspoonfuls
**teat**
**technical**
  *adv* technically
technicality
  *pl* technicalities
technician
**technique**
**technological**
  *adv* technologically

216

technologist
technology
  *pl* technologies
teddy-bear
**tedious**
tedium
tee
  *a golf tee: to tee a
  golf-ball*

  **teed**
teeing
teem
  *to teem with rain:
  to teem with fish*

teemed
teeming
teenage
**teenager**
teens
teeth
  *see* tooth
teethe
  *When do babies
  teethe?*

teethed
teething
teetotal
**teetotaller**
telegram
telegraph
telegraphic
telepathic
  *adv*
    telepathically
telepathy
telephone
telephoned
telephoning
**telephonist**

telephoto lens
telescope
  telescoped
  telescoping
telescopic
  *adv*
    telescopically
**televise**
  televised
  televising
television
tell
  told
  telling
teller
temerity
temper
  tempered
  tempering
temperament
**temperamental**
  *adv*
    temperamentally
temperance
temperate
**temperature**
tempest
**tempestuous**
temple
tempo
  *pl* tempos,
    tempi
temporal
  *temporal, not
  spiritual*

temporary
  *a temporary job*
temporize, -ise
  temporized

temporizing
tempt
**temptation**
tempting
ten
tenable
tenacious
tenacity
**tenancy**
  *pl* tenancies
tenant
tenanted
tend
**tendency**
  *pl* tendencies
tender
  tendered
  tendering
tendon
  *a damaged tendon
  in his leg*

tendril
tenet
**tennis**
tenon
  *mortise and tenon*
tenor
  *a tenor and a
  soprano*

tense
  *adv* tensely
tension
tent
tentacle
tentative
  *adv* tentatively
tenterhooks
tenth
**tenuous**

217

tenure
  *land tenure*
tepid
tercentenary
term
termagant
**terminal**
terminate
  terminated
  terminating
termination
terminology
terminus
  *pl* terminuses,
  termini
termite
tern
**terrace**
terracing
terracotta
terra firma
terrain
**terrestrial**
terrible
  *adv* **terribly**
terrier
terrific
  *adv* **terrifically**
**terrify**
  terrified
  terrifying
territorial
**territory**
  *pl* territories
terror
terrorism
**terrorist**
terrorize, -ise
  terrorized

terrorizing
terse
  *adv* tersely
terseness
test
**testament**
testicle
testify
  testified
  testifying
testimonial
  *Did her previous
  employer give her
  a testimonial?*
testimony
  *the testimony of
  the witness*
  *pl* testimonies
testy
  *adv* testily
**tetanus**
tête-à-tête
tether
  tethered
  tethering
text
textile
textual
texture
Thailand
than
thank
thankful
  *adv* thankfully
thankless
thanksgiving
that
**thatch**
  thatched

thatching
thaw
the
theatre
theatrical
  *adv* theatrically
thee
theft
their
  *They lost their
  gloves*
theirs
them
theme
themselves
then
thence
theodolite
theologian
theological
theology
theorem
theoretic,
  theoretical
  *adv* theoretically
theorize, -ise
  theorized
  theorizing
theory
  *pl* theories
**therapeutic**
therapist
therapy
there
  *There is no-one
  there: I saw it there*
thereabouts
**therefore**
therm

thermal
Thermos ® (flask)
**thermostat**
thesaurus
these
thesis
  *pl* theses
they
they'd
  = they had, they
  would
they'll
  = they will
they're
  = they are
  *They're coming
  today*
thick
thicken
  thickened
  thickening
thicket
thickness
  *pl* thicknesses
**thief**
  *pl* thieves
thievish
thigh
thimble
thin
  *compar* thinner
  *superl* thinnest
  thinned
  thinning
thine
thing
think
  thought
  thinking

**thinness**
third
third-rate
thirst
thirsty
  *adv* thirstily
thirteen
thirteenth
**thirtieth**
thirty
this
thistle
thong
thorax
thorn
thorny
**thorough**
  *a thorough search*
**thoroughfare**
thoroughgoing
those
thou
though
thought
thought
  *see* think
thoughtful
  *adv* thoughtfully
thoughtfulness
thoughtless
thousand
thousandth
thrall
thrash
  *Did he thrash that
  child?: to thrash
  out the problem*
thread
threadbare

threadworn
threat
threaten
  **threatened**
  threatening
three
thresh
  *to thresh corn*
**threshold**
threw
  *see* throw
thrice
thrift
thrifty
  *adv* thriftily
thrill
thriller
thrilling
thrive
  thrived
  thriving
throat
throb
  throbbed
  throbbing
throes
  *in the throes of
  moving house*
**thrombosis**
throne
  *the king's throne*
throng
throttle
  throttled
  throttling
through
  *through the door*
**throughout**
throw

pl throws
*three throws of the dice*

threw
*He threw a stone*

thrown
*He has thrown a stone*

throwing

thrush
pl thrushes

thrust
thrust
thrusting

thud
thudded
thudding

thug

thumb

thump

thunder
thundered
thundering
thunderstruck
thundery

Thursday

thus

**thwart**
thwarted
thwarting

thy

thyme
*to season the sauce with thyme*

thyroid

tiara

tic
*a nervous tic*

tick

*in a tick: a dog tick: a tick at each answer: the tick of a clock*

ticket

tickle
tickled
tickling
ticklish
tickly

tidal

tide

tidiness

tidings

tidy
*compar* tidier
*superl* tidiest
*adv* tidily
tidied
tidying

tie
tied
**tying**

tier
*two tiers of the wedding cake*

tiger

tigress
pl tigresses

tight

tighten
**tightened**
tightening
tightness

tights

tile
tiled
*He tiled the floor*
tiling

till
tilled
*He tilled the land*
tilling

tiller

tilt

timber
*The timber is rotting*

timbre
*the timbre of his voice*

time
*What time is it?: to time a race*

timed
timing
timeless
timely
timetable

timid

timidity

**timorous**

timpani, tympani

tin
tinned
tinning

tincture

tinder

tinfoil

tinge
**tinged**
tinging

tingle
tingled
tingling

tinker
tinkered
tinkering

220

tinkle
  tinkled
  tinkling
tinsel
tint
tiny
tip
  tipped
  tipping
tipple
tipsy
tiptoe
  **tiptoed**
  tiptoeing
tirade
tire
  *The runner began to tire: Did the journey tire you?*
  tired
  tiring
tireless
tiresome
**tissue**
tit
titbit
tithe
**titivate**
  titivated
  titivating
**title**
titled
titter
  tittered
  tittering
tittle-tattle
titular
to
  *to go to town*

toad
toadstool
toady
  toadied
  toadying
toast
toaster
tobacco
**tobacconist**
Tobago
**toboggan**
today
toddler
to-do
toe
  *the toe of her shoe*
**toffee**
together
togs
toil
  toiled
  toiling
toilet
token
told
  *see* tell
tolerable
  *adv* tolerably
tolerance
tolerate
  tolerated
  tolerating
toleration
toll
tomahawk
tomato
  *pl* **tomatoes**
tomb
  *the tomb of the late*

*king*
tombola
tomboy
tombstone
tomcat
tome
  *a learned Latin tome*
tomfoolery
**tomorrow**
tomtom
ton
  *a ton of coal*
tone
  toned
  toning
tongs
**tongue**
tongue-tied
tonic
tonight
tonnage
tonne [tun]
  *a tonne is a metric ton*
**tonsilitis,
  tonsillitis**
tonsils
tonsure
too
  *I am going too*
took
  *see* take
tool
toot
  tooted
  tooting
tooth
  *pl* teeth

*She had two teeth filled*

top
topaz
toper
topi, topee
  *A topi is a sun-helmet*
topiary
topic
topical
  *adv* topically
topmost
topography
topping
topple
  toppled
  toppling
topsyturvy
torch
  *pl* torches
tore
  *see* tear
torment
tormentor
torn
  *see* tear
tornado
  *pl* tornadoes
torpedo
  *pl* torpedoes
  torpedoed
  torpedoing
torpid
torpor
**torrent**
torrential
torrid
torso

*pl* torsos
tortoise
**tortoiseshell**
**tortuous**
torture
  tortured
  torturing
Tory
  *pl* Tories
toss
tot
total
  *adv* totally
  **totalled**
  totalling
totalitarian
tote
totem pole
totter
  tottered
  tottering
tot up
  totted up
  totting up
touch
touchiness
touching
touchy
  *adv* touchily
tough
**toughen**
  toughened
  toughening
toupee
  *toupees and wigs*
tour
  toured
  touring
tourism

tourist
**tournament**
**tourniquet**
tousled
tout
  touted
  touting
tow
  *to tow a car*
  towed
  towing
toward
towards
towel
  towelled
  **towelling**
tower
  towered
  towering
town
toxic
toxicity
toxin
toy
trace
  traced
  tracing
traceable
tracery
track
tract
traction
tractor
trade
  traded
  trading
trademark
trader
tradesman

trade union
trade unionist
tradition
**traditional**
 adv traditionally
traffic
 **trafficked**
 trafficking
trafficker
**tragedy**
 pl tragedies
tragic
 adv
 **tragically**
rail
 trailed
 trailing
railer
rain
 trained
 training
rainee
rainer
rait
 *Patience is not one
 of his traits*
raitor
**raitorous**
ram
rammel
 trammelled
 trammelling
ramp
rample
 trampled
 trampling
rampoline
rance
ranquil

 adv tranquilly
**tranquillity**
**tranquillizer, -iser**
transaction
transatlantic
**transcend**
 transcended
 transcending
transcription
transept
transfer
 **transferred**
 transferring
**transferable**
transference
transfiguration
transfix
transform
 transformation
transfuse
 transfusion
transgression
transience
transient
**transistor**
transit
 transition
 transitional
 transitive
 transitory
 adv transitorily
translate
 translated
 translating
translation
translator
translucence
translucent
transmission

transmit
 transmitted
 transmitting
**transmitter**
transparency
 pl
 transparencies
**transparent**
transpire
 transpired
 transpiring
transplant
transport
 transportation
transpose
 transposed
 transposing
transposition
transverse
transvestite
trap
 trapped
 trapping
**trapeze**
trapper
trappings
trash
trauma
**traumatic**
travel
 **travelled**
 travelling
 traveller
traverse
 traversed
 traversing
travesty
trawl
 trawled

trawling
trawler
tray
*cups and saucers on a tray*
**treacherous**
treachery
treacle
tread
trod
*He trod on her toe*
trodden
*He has trodden on it*
treadle
treason
treasonable
treasure
treasurer
**treasury**
*pl* treasuries
treat
treatise
*a philosophical treatise*
treatment
treaty
*pl* treaties
*treaties signed after the war*
treble
tree
**trek**
trellis
*pl* trellises
tremble
trembled
trembling
tremendous

**tremor**
tremulous
trench
*pl* trenches
trenchant
trencherman
trend
trendy
trepidation
trespass
*pl* trespasses
tress
*pl* tresses
trestle
trews
trial
triangle
**triangular**
tribal
tribe
tribulation
**tribunal**
tribune
tributary
*pl* tributaries
tribute
trice
trick
trickery
trickle
trickled
trickling
trickster
tricky
tricolour
tricycle
trident
tried
*see* try

triennial
tries
*see* try
trifle
trifled
trifling
trifling
trigger
triggered
triggering
trigonometry
trill
**trilogy**
*pl* trilogies
trim
trimmed
trimming
Trinity
trinket
trio
*pl* trios
trip
tripped
tripping
tripe
triple
triplet
triplicate
**tripod**
tripper
trite
**triumph**
triumphed
triumphing
triumphal
**triumphant**
trivial
triviality
*pl* trivialities

trod, trodden
  *see* tread
troll
trolley
  *pl* trolleys
trollop
trombone
troop
  *a troop of soldiers:*
  *a cavalry troop: to*
  *troop out of the*
  *hall*

trooped
trooping
trooper
**trophy**
  *pl* trophies
tropic
tropical
trot
  trotted
  trotting
trotters
troubadour
trouble
  troubled
  troubling
**troublesome**
trough
trounce
  trounced
  trouncing
troupe
  *a troupe of actors*
trousers
**trousseau**
  *pl* trousseaux,
  trousseaus
trout

trowel
truancy
**truant**
truce
truck
truculent
trudge
  trudged
  trudging
true
truffle
**truism**
truly
trump
trumpet
  trumpeted
  trumpeting
truncated
truncheon
trundle
  trundled
  trundling
trunk
truss
  *pl* trusses
  trussed
  trussing
trust
**trustee**
trustful
  *adv* trustfully
trusting
trustworthy
trusty
truth
truthful
  *adv* truthfully
truthfulness
try

  *pl* tries
  tried
  **trying**
**tryst**
tsar, tzar, czar
**tsetse**
tub
tuba
tubby
tube
tuber
**tuberculosis**
tubing
tubular
tuck
**Tuesday**
tuft
tug
  tugged
  tugging
tug-of-war
**tuition**
**tulip**
tulle
tumble
  tumbled
  tumbling
tumbler
tumbrel, tumbril
tummy
  *pl* tummies
**tumour**
tumult
tumultuous
tun
  *A tun is a large*
  *cask*
tuna
tune

tuned
tuning
tuneful
  *adv* tunefully
tuneless
tunic
tunnel
  **tunnelled**
  tunnelling
turban
  *He wore a turban on his head*
turbine
  *a turbine engine*
turbot
turbulence
turbulent
**tureen**
turf
**turgid**
turkey
  *pl* turkeys
Turkish
turmoil
turn
turning
turnip
turnover
**turnstile**
turntable
turpentine
**turquoise**
turret
turreted
turtle
turtleneck
tusk
tussle
tutor

tutorial
tutu
twaddle
twang
tweak
tweed
**tweezers**
**twelfth**
twelve
**twentieth**
twenty
twice
twiddle
  twiddled
  twiddling
twig
**twilight**
twin
twine
  twined
  twining
twinge
twinkle
  twinkled
  twinkling
twirl
twist
twister
twitch
  *pl* twitches
twitter
  twittered
  twittering
two
  *two apples*
twofold
**tycoon**
  *a business tycoon*
tympani

  *see* timpani
type
  typed
  typing
typewriter
typhoid
**typhoon**
  *The ship was sunk in a typhoon*
typhus
**typical**
  *adv* typically
typify
  typified
  typifying
typist
**tyrannical**
  *adv* tyrannically
tyrannize, -ise
  tyrannized
  tyrannizing
tyrannous
**tyranny**
tyrant
tyre
  *a tyre for the car*
tzar
  *see* tsar

## U

**ubiquitous**
udder
ugliness
ugly
  *compar* uglier
  *superl* ugliest
ukelele, ukulele
ulcer

ulterior
ultimate
  *adv* **ultimately**
ultimatum
  *pl* ultimatums,
  ultimata
ultrasonic
ultraviolet
umbilical
umbrage
**umbrella**
umpire
  umpired
  umpiring
unable
unaccountable
  *adv*
  unaccountably
unadulterated
unanimity
**unanimous**
unapproachable
unassuming
unaware
  *I was unaware of*
  *his presence*
unawares
  *The blow took him*
  *unawares*
unbalanced
unbend
  unbent
  unbending
unbridled
unburden
  unburdened
  unburdening
uncalled for
uncanniness

uncanny
  *adv* uncannily
uncared for
uncertain
uncharted
uncle
uncoil
  uncoiled
  uncoiling
uncommon
uncompromising
unconscionable
  *He has been an*
  *unconscionable*
  *time doing that job*

**unconscious**
  *He was knocked*
  *unconscious: He*
  *was unconscious*
  *of the trouble*

  *adv*
  unconsciously
uncouth
undaunted
undeniable
  *adv* undeniably
under
undercarriage
underclothes
undercover
undercurrent
undercut
  undercut
  undercutting
**underdeveloped**
underdog
underdone
underestimate
  underestimated

underestimating
underfoot
undergo
  underwent
  undergone
  undergoing
undergraduate
underground
**undergrowth**
underhand
underline
  underlined
  underlining
underlying
undermine
  undermined
  undermining
underneath
underpin
  underpinned
  underpinning
**underprivileged**
**underrate**
  underrated
  underrating
undersigned
underskirt
understand
  understood
  understanding
understandable
  *adv*
  understandably
understate
  understated
  understating
understatement
understood
  *see* understand

understudy
  understudied
  **understudying**
undertake
  undertook
  undertaken
  undertaking
undertaker
undertone
undertook
  *see* undertake
undervalue
  undervalued
  undervaluing
underwear
underwent
  *see* undergo
underworld
underwrite
  underwrote
  underwritten
  underwriting
underwriter
undo
  undid
  *He undid his coat*
  undone
  *His coat is undone*
  undoing
**undoubted**
undress
undue
undulate
  undulated
  undulating
**unduly**
unearth
unearthly
uneasy

*adv* uneasily
unemployed
unemployment
unequal
**unequalled**
unequivocal
*adv*
  unequivocally
unerring
uneven
unexpected
unfailing
unfair
unfaithful
unfasten
  unfastened
  unfastening
unfit
  unfitted
unflagging
unflinching
unfold
unforgettable
  *adv* **unforgettably**
unfortunate
  *adv*
    **unfortunately**
unfounded
unfurl
ungainly
**ungracious**
ungrateful
  *adv* ungratefully
**unguarded**
unhappiness
unhappy
  *adv* unhappily
unhealthy
  *adv* unhealthily

unhinge
  unhinged
  unhinging
unicorn
unification
uniform
uniformity
unify
  unified
  unifying
**uninterrupted**
union
**unique**
  *adv* uniquely
unison
unit
unitary
unite
  united
  uniting
unity
**universal**
  *adv* universally
universe
university
  *pl* universities
unkempt
unkind
unleash
unless
unlikely
unload
  unloaded
  unloading
unlooked for
unloose
  unloosed
  unloosing
unlucky

*adv* unluckily
unmanly
unmask
unmentionable
unmistakable
*adv*
  unmistakably
unmitigated
unmoved
**unnecessary**
  *adv*
    unnecessarily
unobtrusive
  *adv*
    unobtrusively
unpack
unpalatable
unparalleled
unpick
unprecedented
unpremeditated
unprepossessing
unpretentious
unprincipled
unravel
  **unravelled**
  unravelling
**unremitting**
**unrequited**
unrest
**unrivalled**
unruliness
unruly
**unsavoury**
unscathed
unscrew
unseasonable
unseen
unsettled

unsightly
**unsophisticated**
unsound
unspeakable
  *adv* unspeakably
unstudied
unsuspecting
unthinkable
**until**
untimely
unto
untold
untoward
untrue
untruth
untruthful
  *adv* untruthfully
**unusual**
  *adv* unusually
unvarnished
unveil
  unveiled
  unveiling
unwanted
  *unwanted children*
**unwieldy**
unwitting
unwonted
  = not usual
  *unwonted*
  *generosity*
unworthy
up
upbraid
  upbraided
  upbraiding
upbringing
upgrade
  upgraded

upgrading
**upheaval**
uphill
uphold
upheld
upholding
upholder
upholster
  upholstered
  upholstering
upholsterer
upholstery
upkeep
upland
upmost
upon
upper
**uppermost**
upright
uprising
uproar
**uproarious**
uproot
  uprooted
  uprooting
upset
  upset
  upsetting
upshot
upside-down
upstairs
upstanding
upstart
upstream
uptake
up-to-date
uranium
urban
  *an urban motorway*

urbane
  *an urbane young
  man*
urbanities
urchin
Urdu
urge
  urged
  urging
urgency
urgent
urinary
urinate
  urinated
  urinating
urine
urn
Uruguay
us
usage
use
  used
  using
useful
  *adv* usefully
usefulness
useless
user-friendly
usher
  ushered
  ushering
**usherette**
usual
  *adv* **usually**
usurp
usurper
utensil
uterus
utility

*pl* utilities
utilization,
  -isation
utilize, -ise
  utilized
  utilizing
utmost
utter
  uttered
  uttering
utterance
**utterly**
U-turn

**V**

**vacancy**
  *pl* vacancies
vacant
vacate
  vacated
  vacating
vacation
  *a summer vacation
  in Spain*
**vaccinate**
  vaccinated
  vaccinating
vaccine
vacillate
  vacillated
  vacillating
vacuous
**vacuum**
vagabond
vagary
  *pl* vagaries
vagina
vagrancy

vagrant
**vague**
  *adv* vaguely
vagueness
vain
  *conceited and vain*
valance
vale
  *the Vale of
  Evesham*
valency
  *pl* valencies
**valentine**
valet
valiant
**valid**
validity
valley
  *pl* valleys
valorous
valour
**valuable**
valuation
valuator
value
  valued
  valuing
valuer
valve
vamp
vampire
van
vandal
**vandalism**
vandalize, -ise
  vandalized
  vandalizing
vane
  *a weather vane*

vanguard
**vanilla**
vanish
vanity
  *pl* vanities
vanquish
vantage
vapid
vaporize, -ise
  vaporized
  vaporizing
vaporizer, -iser
vapour
variable
  *adv* variably
variance
variant
variation
varicose
varied
**variegated**
variety
  *pl* **varieties**
**various**
varnish
  *pl* varnishes
vary
  varied
  varying
vase
Vaseline ®
vassal
vast
vat
vaudeville
vault
vaunt
veal
veer

veered
veering
vegan
vegetable
**vegetarian**
vegetate
  vegetated
  vegetating
vegetation
vehemence
**vehement**
**vehicle**
vehicular
veil
  *a bride's veil: to
  veil in mystery*
veiled
veiling
vein
  *a clot of blood in a
  vein: a vein of
  cheerfulness*
veined
vellum
velocity
  *pl* velocities
velvet
velveteen
velvety
venal
  *corrupt and venal
  lawyers*
**vendetta**
vending
vendor
**veneer**
venerable
venerate
  venerated

venerating
veneration
**venereal disease**
Venetian blind
vengeance
vengeful
venial
  *venial sins*
venison
venom
**venomous**
vent
ventilate
  ventilated
  ventilating
ventilation
**ventilator**
ventricle
ventriloquism
**ventriloquist**
venture
  ventured
  venturing
venue
veracity
  *They doubted the
  veracity of his
  statement*
verandah,
  veranda
verb
verbal
  *adv* verbally
verbatim
verbose
verbosity
verdant
verdict
verdigris

231

verdure
verge
  verged
  verging
verger
verification
verify
  verified
  verifying
verily
veritable
  *adv* veritably
vermicelli
**vermilion**
vermin
verminous
vermouth
vernacular
vernal
**verruca**
**versatile**
versatility
verse
version
versus
vertebra
  *pl* vertebrae
**vertebrate**
vertex
  *the vertex of a cone*
  *pl* vertices
**vertical**
  *adv* **vertically**
vertigo
verve
very
vespers
vessel

vest
**vestibule**
vestige
vestigial
vestry
  *pl* vestries
vet
  vetted
  vetting
veteran
**veterinary surgeon**
veto
  *pl* vetoes
**vetoed**
  vetoing
vex
  vexed
  vexing
vexation
vexatious
via
**viable**
viaduct
viands
vibrant
vibrate
  vibrated
  vibrating
vibration
vicar
vicarious
vice
viceroy
vice versa
vicinity
**vicious**
**vicissitude**
victim

victimization, -isation
victimize, -ise
  victimized
  victimizing
victor
**victorious**
victory
  *pl* victories
victuals
video
  *pl* videos
  videoed
  videoing
videotape
vie
  vied
  vying
view
viewpoint
vigil
vigilance
vigilant
  *to keep a vigilant watch*
vigilante
  *The vigilantes helped the police*
vignette
**vigorous**
vigour
Viking
vile
vilify
  vilified
  vilifying
villa
**village**
villager

232

villain
villainous
villainy
  pl villainies
vindicate
  vindicated
  vindicating
**vindictive**
  adv vindictively
vine
vinegar
vineyard
vintage
viola
violate
  violated
  violating
violation
**violence**
violent
violet
violin
violinist
violoncello
viper
virago
  pl viragos
virgin
virginal
virginity
virile
virility
**virtual**
  adv virtually
virtue
virtuosity
**virtuoso**
  pl virtuosos
virtuous

virulence
virulent
**virus**
  pl viruses
visa
  pl visas
visage
vis-à-vis
viscera
viscid
viscosity
**viscount**
viscountess
  pl viscountesses
viscous
**visibility**
visible
  adv visibly
vision
visionary
  pl visionaries
visit
  visited
  visiting
visitation
**visitor**
visor
vista
  pl vistas
**visual**
  adv visually
visualize, -ise
  visualized
  visualizing
vital
  adv vitally
vitality
**vitamins**
vitreous

vitrified
vitriol
vituperation
vituperative
**vivacious**
vivacity
viva voce
vivid
vividness
vivisection
vixen
viz
vizier
**vocabulary**
  pl vocabularies
vocal
  adv vocally
vocation
  a vocation to be a
  priest
vocational
**vociferous**
vodka
vogue
voice
  voiced
  voicing
void
**volatile**
volcanic
volcano
  pl volcanoes
vole
volition
volley
  pl volleys
volt
voltage
volubility

voluble
  *adv* volubly
volume
**voluminous**
**voluntary**
  *adv* voluntarily
**volunteer**
  **volunteered**
  volunteering
voluptuous
vomit
  vomited
  vomiting
voracious
voracity
  *the voracity of his appetite*
vortex
  *the vortex of a whirlpool*
  *pl* vortices, vortexes
vote
  voted
  voting
vouch
voucher
vow
  vowed
  vowing
vowel
**voyage**
  voyaged
  voyaging
vulgar
vulgarity
**vulnerable**
vulture

# W

wad
wadding
waddle
  waddled
  waddling
wade
  waded
  wading
wader
wafer
  *an ice cream wafer*
waffle
  waffled
  waffling
waft
wag
  wagged
  *The dog wagged his tail*
  wagging
wage
  waged
  *He waged war*
  waging
wagged
  *see* wag
waggle
  waggled
  waggling
waggon
waif
  *a poor little waif*
wail
  wailed
  wailing
waist
  *She has a tiny*

*waist*
wait
waiter
waiting-room
waitress
waive
  *to waive the right to the throne*
  waived
  waiving
wake
  woke, waked
  *He woke up in the night*
  woken, wakened
  *You've woken him*
  waking
wakeful
waken
  wakened
  wakening
walk
**walkie-talkie**
wall
wallaby
  *pl* wallabies
wallet
wallop
  **walloped**
  walloping
wallow
wallpaper
**walnut**
walrus
  *pl* walruses
**waltz**
  *pl* waltzes
wan

wand
wander
  wandered
  wandering
**wanderer**
wanderlust
wane
  waned
  waning
wangle
  wangled
  wangling
want
  *dying of want: for*
  *want of money:*
  *They want money*

wanton
war
  warred
  warring
warble
  warbled
  warbling
warbler
ward
  warded
  warding
warden
  *warden of the*
  *hostel*
warder
  *a prison warder*
**wardrobe**
ware
  *earthenware,*
  *stoneware*
warehouse
wares
  *He sold his wares*

*at the fair*
warfare
wariness
warlike
warm
**warmth**
warn
warp
warpath
**warrant**
warren
**warrior**
warship
wart
wary
  *adv* warily
was
  *see* be
wash
washer
wash-hand basin
wasp
**wastage**
waste
  *a waste of food: to*
  *waste food*
  wasted
  wasting
wasteful
  *adv* wastefully
waster
wastrel
wastepaper
  basket
watch
  *pl* watches
watchful
  *adv* watchfully
watchman

*pl* watchmen
water
  **watered**
  watering
waterfall
waterlogged
waterproof
**watery**
watt
wattage
wattle
wave
  *He gave a friendly*
  *wave: a heat wave:*
  *Did he wave to*
  *you?*

  waved
  waving
wavelength
waver
  *to waver and*
  *hesitate*

  wavered
  wavering
wavy
wax
waxy
way
  *the way home: the*
  *way she wears her*
  *hair*

wayfarer
waylay
  waylaid
  waylaying
wayside
wayward
we
weak

*a weak child*
weaken
**weakened**
weakening
weakling
weakly
*a sick and weakly child*
weakness
**wealth**
wealthy
*compar*
wealthier
*superl* wealthiest
wean
weaned
weaning
weapon
wear
*She often wears an apron*
wore
*She wore the dress*
worn
*She's worn that before*
wearing
wearable
wearer
**wearisome**
weary
*adv* wearily
wearied
wearying
weasel
weather
weathered
weathering
weatherbeaten

weathervane
weave
wove
*She wove cloth*
woven
*She has woven a rug*
weaving
weaver
web
webbed
webbing
wed
wedded
wedding
we'd
= we had, we would
wedding
wedge
wedged
wedging
wedlock
**Wednesday**
weed
weedy
week
*two days a week*
weekday
weekend
weekly
*a weekly paper: He visits his mother weekly*
weep
wept
weeping
weigh
*to weigh the*

*potatoes*
weighed
weighing
**weight**
weighty
weir
**weird**
welcome
welcomed
welcoming
weld
welder
welfare
well
*compar* better
*superl* best
we'll
= we shall, we will
**wellingtons**
well-off
well-to-do
well up
welled up
welling up
Welsh rarebit
welt
welter
wench
*pl.* wenches
wend
went
*see* go
wept
*see* weep
were
*see* be
we're
= we are

weren't
= were not
werewolf
west
westerly
*a westerly wind*
western
*western ideas*
westward
westwards
wet
*a wet day: to wet the carpet*
*compar* wetter
*superl* wettest
wet
wetting
wetness
we've
= we have
whack
whale
whaler
wharf
*pl* wharves,
wharfs
what
whatever
whatsoever
wheat
**wheaten**
wheedle
wheedled
wheedling
wheel
wheeled
wheeling
wheelbarrow
wheelchair

wheeze
wheezed
wheezing
whelk
whelp
when
whence
whenever
where
**whereabouts**
whereas
wherefore
whereupon
**wherever**
**wherewithal**
whet
*to whet the appetite*
whetted
whetting
**whether**
which
whichever
whiff
while
while away
whiled away
whiling away
**whilst**
whim
whimper
whimpered
whimpering
whimsical
*adv* whimsically
whimsy
*pl* whimsies
whine
whined

whining
whinge
whinged
whingeing
whinny
*pl* whinnies
whinnied
whinnying
whip
whipped
whipping
whippet
whirl
whirr
whisker
whisky
*pl* whiskies
whisper
whispered
whispering
whist
whistle
whistled
whistling
whit
*not a whit*
white
whiten
whitened
whitening
whiteness
whitewash
whither
**whiting**
Whitsun, Whit
whittle
whittled
whittling
whizz

237

who
whodunnit
whoever
whole
*a whole orange:*
*the whole*
*household*

*adv* **wholly**
**wholesale**
**wholesome**
who'll
= who will
**whom**
whoop
*She gave a whoop*
*of joy: to whoop*
*with joy*

whooped
whooping
whooping-cough
whore
*the whore of*
*Babylon*

whose
why
wick
wicked
wickedness
wicker
wicket
wide
*adv* widely
widen
**widened**
widening
widespread
widow
widower
**width**

**wield**
wielded
wielding
wife
*pl* wives
wig
wiggle
wiggled
wiggling
wiggly
wigwam
wild
wilderness
wildness
wile
wilful
*adv* wilfully
will
would
*I would go if I*
*could*

will
willed
*She willed him to*
*win: He willed her*
*all his money*

willing
will-o'-the-wisp
willow
willowy
willynilly
wilt
wily
win
won
winning
wince
winced
wincing

winch
*pl* winches
wind [wind]
winded
*The blow winded*
*him*

winding
wind [wīnd]
wound
*He wound the*
*bandage round her*
*arm*

winding
windfall
windmill
window
windscreen
windy
wine
wing
winged
wink
winkle
**winnings**
winsome
winter
wintered
wintering
**wintry**
wipe
wiped
wiping
wiper
wire
wired
wiring
wireless
**wiry**
wisdom

wise
*adv* wisely
wish
*pl* wishes
wishbone
wishful
wishywashy
wisp
wistful
*adv* wistfully
wistfulness
wit
*cleverness and wit*
witch
*pl* witches
witchcraft
with
withdraw
withdrew
*He withdrew his application*
withdrawn
*He has withdrawn his application*
withdrawing
**withdrawal**
wither
withered
withering
**withhold**
withheld
withholding
within
without
withstand
withstood
withstanding
witness
*pl* witnesses

**witticism**
wittingly
*He did not wittingly deceive her*
witty
*adv* wittily
*He spoke wittily and interestingly*
wizard
**wizened**
wobble
wobbled
wobbling
wobbly
woe
*sadness and woe*
**woebegone**
woeful
*adv* woefully
woke, woken
*see* wake
wolf
*pl* wolves
wolfed
wolfing
wolfish
woman
*pl* women
womanhood
womanly
**womb**
won
*see* win
wonder
wondered
wondering
**wonderful**
*adv* wonderfully
wonderland

wonderment
**wondrous**
wont
*as he was wont to do*
won't
= will not
woo
*to woo a girl and marry her*
wooed
*He wooed her ardently*
wooing
wood
*a beech wood: wood for the fire*
wooded
**wooden**
woodland
woodpecker
woodwork
woody
wooed
*see* woo
wooer
wool
**woollen**
woolly
word
wording
wordy
wore
*see* wear
work
workable
worker
workman
*pl* workmen

workmanship
world
worldly
worm
worn
  *see* wear
worry
  *pl* worries
worried
worrying
worse
worsen
  **worsened**
  worsening
worship
  **worshipped**
  worshipping
worshipful
  *adv* worshipfully
worst
worsted
worth
worthless
worthy
  *adv* worthily
would
  *see* will
would-be
wound [wōōnd]
  *a bullet wound*
wound [wownd]
  *see* wind
wove, woven
  *see* weave
wraith
wrangle
  wrangled
  wrangling
wrap

*to wrap in paper*
wrapped
  *The book was wrapped in brown paper*
wrapping
**wrapper**
**wrath**
wrathful
  *adv* wrathfully
**wreak**
  *to wreak vengeance: to wreak havoc*
wreaked
wreaking
wreath
  *a wreath of flowers*
wreathe
  *to wreathe in flowers: to wreathe in smiles*
wreathed
wreathing
wreck
  *a wreck on the sea-bed: to wreck the car*
wrecked
wrecking
**wreckage**
wren
wrench
  *pl* wrenches
wrest
  *to wrest it from his grasp*
wrestle
wrestled

wrestling
wrestler
wrestling
wretch
  *a poor wretch*
  *pl* wretches
**wretched**
wriggle
wriggled
wriggling
wring
  *to wring the clothes: to wring a promise from her*
wrung
  *She wrung the clothes*
wringing
wringer
wrinkle
wrinkled
wrinkling
**wrist**
writ
write
  *to write neatly*
wrote
  *He wrote a letter*
written
  *He has written a letter*
writing
**writhe**
writhed
writhing
wrong
**wrongdoer**
wrongful
  *adv* wrongfully

wrote
  *see* write
**wrought-iron**
wrung
  *see* wring
wry
  *a wry smile: a wry
  neck*

# X

X-ray
  **X-rayed**
  X-raying
xenophobia
xenophobic
Xerox ®
**xylophone**

# Y

**yacht**
yachting
yachtsman
yak
yank
yap
  yapped
  yapping
yard
yardstick
yarn
**yashmak**
yawn
year
yearling
yearly
yearn
yeast
yell
**yellow**

yelp
yen
**yeoman**
yes
yesterday
yet
Yeti
yew
  *a yew tree*
**yield**
yodel
  yodelled
  yodelling
yoga
**yoghurt**
yoke
  *the yoke of a
  plough: the yoke of
  a dress*
yokel
yolk
  *the yolk of an egg*
yonder
yore
  *days of yore*
you
  *you and I*
you'd
  = you had, you
    would
you'll
  = you will
young
youngster
your
  *your house*
you're
  = you are
yourselves

youth
youthful
  *adv* youthfully
you've
  = you have
Yo-Yo ®
Yule

# Z

Zaire
zany
zeal
zealot
**zealous**
zebra
zenith
**zephyr**
zero
zest
zestful
  *adv* zestfully
zigzag
  **zigzagged**
  zigzagging
zinc
zip
  zipped
  zipping
zither
zodiac
zone
zoo
**zoological**
zoologist
zoology
zoom
  zoomed
  zooming

# Appendix

# Words liable to be confused

a
an

aboard
abroad

accept
except

access
excess

acme
acne

ad
add

adapter
adaptor

addition
edition

adverse
averse

advice
advise

aesthetic
ascetic

affect
effect

affluent
effluent

aid
aide

ail
ale

air
heir

aisle
isle

ale
ail

all
awl

allay
alley

allegory
allergy

alley
allay

alliterate
illiterate

allude
elude

allusion
delusion
illusion

altar
alter

alteration
altercation

alternately
alternatively

amateur
amateurish

amend
emend

amiable
amicable

among
between

amoral
immoral
immortal

an
a

angel
angle

annals
annuals

annex
annexe

annuals
annals

ant
aunt

antiquated
antique

arc
ark

arisen
arose

arose
arisen

artist
artiste

ascent
assent

ascetic
aesthetic

assay
essay

assent
ascent

astrology
astronomy

ate
eaten

aunt
ant

aural
oral

averse
adverse

awl
all

axes
axis

bad
bade

bade
bid

bail
bale
bale out

baited
bated

245

bale
bale out
bail

ball
bawl

ballet
ballot

banns
bans

bare
bear

barn
baron
barren

base
bass

bass (*pl*)
basses

bated
baited

bath
bathe

baton
batten

bawl
ball

bazaar
bizarre

be
bee

beach
beech

bean
been
being

bear
bare

beat
beaten

beat
beet

beau
bow

became
become

bee
be

beech
beach

been
bean

being

beer
bier

beet
beat

befallen
befell

began
begun

being
bean
been

belief
believe

bell
belle

bellow
below

beret
berry
bury

berth
birth

beside
besides

between
among

bid
bade

bier
beer

bight
bite

birth
berth

bit
bitten

bite
bight

bizarre
bazaar

blew
blown

blew
blue

bloc
block

blond
blonde

blown
blew

blue
blew

boar
boor
bore

board
bored

boast
boost

bonny
bony

bookie
bouquet

boor
boar
bore

boost
boast

bootee
booty

bore
boar
boor

bore
born
borne

borough
burgh

bough
bow

bound
bounded

bouquet
bookie

bow
beau

bow
bough

boy
buoy

brae
bray

brake
break

brassière
brazier

246

bray
brae

brazier
brassière

breach
breech

bread
bred

break
brake

breath
breathe

bred
bread

breech
breach

bridal
bridle

broach
brooch

broke
broken

brooch
broach

buffet ['bufit]
buffet ['bʊofã]

buoy
boy

burgh
borough

bury
beret
berry

but
butt

buy
by
bye

cache
cash

caddie
caddy

calf
calve

callous
callus

calve
calf

came
come

canned
could

cannon
canon

can't
cant

canvas
canvass

carat
carrot

cart
kart

cartilage
cartridge

carton
cartoon

cartridge
cartilage

cash
cache

cast
caste

cavalier
cavalry

ceiling
sealing

cell
sell

cellular
cellulose

censor
censure

cent
scent
sent

centenarian
centenary

cereal
serial

chafe
chaff

charted
chartered

chased
chaste

cheap
cheep

check
cheque

checked
chequered

cheep
cheap

cheque
check

chilli
chilly

choir
quire

choose
chose
chosen

chord
cord

chose
choose
chosen

chute
shoot

cite
sight
site

clothes
cloths

coarse
course

collage
college

coma
comma

come
came

comma
coma

commissionaire
commissioner

complement
compliment

complementary
complimentary

concert
consort

confidant
confidante
confident

247

conscience
conscientious
conscious

consort
concert

consul
council
counsel

continual
continuous

coop
coup

coral
corral

cord
chord

co-respondent
correspondent

cornet
coronet

cornflour
cornflower

coronet
cornet

corps
corpse

corral
coral

correspondent
co-respondent

cost
costed

could
canned

council
counsel
consul

councillor
counsellor

coup
coop

course
coarse

courtesy
curtsy

creak
creek

crevasse
crevice

crochet
crotchet

cue
queue

curb
kerb

currant
current

curtsy
courtesy

cygnet
signet

cymbal
symbol

dairy
diary

dam
damn

dammed
damned

damn
dam

dear
deer

decry
descry

deer
dear

delusion
allusion
illusion

dependant
dependent

deprecate
depreciate

descendant
descendent

descry
decry

desert
dessert

device
devise

devolution
evolution

dew
due
Jew

diary
dairy

did
done

die
dye

died
dyed

dinghy
dingy

disbelief
disbelieve

discus
discuss

doe
dough

doily
dolly

done
did

dough
doe

draft
draught

dragon
dragoon

draught
draft

drawn
drew

drank
drunk

drew
drawn

driven
drove

drunk
drank

dual
duel

ducks
dux

dudgeon
dungeon

due
dew
Jew

duel
dual

dully
duly

dungeon
dudgeon

dux
ducks

dye
die

dyed
died

dyeing
dying

earthly
earthy

easterly
eastern

eaten
ate

eclipse
ellipse

economic
economical

edition
addition

eerie
eyrie

effect
affect

effluent
affluent

elder
eldest

elicit
illicit

eligible
legible

ellipse
eclipse

elude
allude

emend
amend

emigrant
immigrant

emigration
immigration

emission
omission

emphasis
emphasize

employee
employer

ensure
insure

entomologist
etymologist

envelop
envelope

epigram
epitaph
epithet

ere
err

erotic
erratic

err
ere

erratic
erotic

escapement
escarpment

essay
assay

etymologist
entomologist

evolution
devolution

ewe
yew
you

except
accept

excess
access

executioner
executor

exercise
exorcise

expand
expend

expansive
expensive

expatiate
expiate

expend
expand

expensive
expansive

expiate
expatiate

extant
extinct

eyrie
eerie

faerie
fairy

fain
feign

faint
feint

fair
fare

fairy
faerie

fallen
fell
felled

fare
fair

fate
fête

faun
fawn

feat
feet

feign
fain

feint
faint

fell
fallen
felled

ferment
foment

fête
fate

fiancé
fiancée

filed
filled

final
finale

fir
fur

fission
fissure

flair
flare

flammable
inflammable

flare
flair

flea
flee

flew
flu
flue

flew
flown

flocks
phlox

floe
flow

flour
flower

floury
flowery

flow
floe

flower
flour

flowery
floury

flown
flew

flu
flue
flew

foment
ferment

font
fount

forbade
forbidden

fore
four

foregone
forgone

foresaw
foreseen

foreword
forward

forgave
forgiven

forgone
foregone

forgone
forwent

forgot
forgotten

forsaken
forsook

forswore
forsworn

fort
forte
forty

forth
fourth

forty
fort
forte

forward
foreword

forwent
forgone

foul
fowl

found
founded

fount
font

four
fore

fourth
forth

fowl
foul

franc
frank

freeze
frieze

froze
frozen

funeral
funereal

fur
fir

gabble
gable

gaff
gaffe

gait
gate

galleon
gallon

gamble
gambol

gaol
goal

gate
gait

gave
given

genie
genius
genus

genteel
gentile
gentle

genus
genie
genius

gild
guild

gilt
guilt

given
gave

glacier
glazier

glutinous
gluttonous

goal
gaol

gone
went

gorilla
guerrilla

gourmand
gourmet

gradation
graduation

grate
great

grew
grown

grief
grieve

grill
grille

| | | | |
|---|---|---|---|
| griped | hart | hole | immoral |
| gripped | heart | whole | amoral |
| grisly | heal | honorary | immortal |
| gristly | heel | honourable | immorality |
| grizzly | | | immortality |
| | hear | hoop | |
| grope | here | whoop | impetuous |
| group | | | impetus |
| | heart | hoped | |
| ground | hart | hopped | impracticable |
| grounded | | | impractical |
| | heel | horde | |
| grown | heal | hoard | in |
| grew | | | inn |
| | heir | horse | |
| guerrilla | air | hoarse | inapt |
| gorilla | | | inept |
| | here | hue | |
| guild | hear | hew | incredible |
| gild | | | incredulous |
| | heroin | human | |
| guilt | heroine | humane | indigenous |
| gilt | | | indigent |
| | heron | humiliation | |
| hail | herring | humility | industrial |
| hale | | | industrious |
| | hew | hung | |
| hair | hue | hanged | ineligible |
| hare | | | illegible |
| | hewed | hymn | |
| half | hewn | him | inept |
| halve | | | inapt |
| | hid | idle | |
| hallo | hidden | idol | inflammable |
| hallow | | | flammable |
| halo | higher | illegible | |
| | hire | ineligible | ingenious |
| halve | | | ingenuous |
| half | him | illicit | |
| | hymn | elicit | inhuman |
| hangar | | | inhumane |
| hanger | hire | illiterate | |
| | higher | alliterate | inn |
| hanged | | | in |
| hung | hoar | illusion | |
| | whore | allusion | insure |
| hanger | | delusion | ensure |
| hangar | hoard | | |
| | horde | immigrant | intelligent |
| hare | | emigrant | intelligible |
| hair | hoarse | | |
| | horse | immigration | interment |
| | | emigration | internment |

251

invertebrate
inveterate

isle
aisle

it's
its

jam
jamb

Jew
dew
due

jib
jibe

judicial
judicious

junction
juncture

kart
cart

kerb
curb

key
quay

knave
nave

knead
kneed
need

knew
known

knight
night

knightly
nightly

knit
nit

knot
not

knotty
naughty

know
no

known
knew

lade
laid
lay
lied

lain
lane

lair
layer

lama
llama

lane
lain

laterally
latterly

lath
lathe

latterly
laterally

lay
lade
laid
lied

layer
lair

lea
lee

lead
led

leak
leek

led
lead

lee
lea

leek
leak

legible
eligible

lemming
lemon

leopard
leper

lessen
lesson

liable
libel

liar
lyre

libel
liable

licence
license

lied
lade
laid
lay

lightening
lightning

lineament
liniment

liqueur
liquor

literal
literary
literate

llama
lama

load
lode

loan
lone

loath
loathe

local
locale

lode
load

lone
loan

looped
loped
lopped

loose
lose

loot
lute

loped
lopped
looped

lose
loose

loth
loathe

lumbar
lumber

lute
loot

lyre
liar

| | | | |
|---|---|---|---|
| macaroni | mat | minister | muscle |
| macaroon | matt | minster | mussel |
| made | mayor | missal | muse |
| maid | mare | missile | mews |
| magnate | maze | mistaken | mussel |
| magnet | maize | mistook | muscle |
| maid | mean | mite | mystic |
| made | mien | might | mystique |
| mail | meat | moat | naught |
| male | meet | mote | nought |
| main | mete out | modal | naughty |
| mane | medal | model | knotty |
| maize | meddle | module | naval |
| maze | mediate | momentary | navel |
| male | meditate | momentous | nave |
| mail | meet | momentum | knave |
| mane | meat | moose | navel |
| main | mete out | mouse | naval |
| maniac | merino | mousse | navvy |
| manic | marina | moped | navy |
| manner | metal | mopped | nay |
| manor | mettle | moral | née |
| mare | mete out | morale | neigh |
| mayor | meat | morality | need |
| marina | meet | mortality | knead |
| merino | meter | mote | kneed |
| marshal | metre | moat | negligent |
| martial | mettle | motif | negligible |
| marten | metal | motive | neigh |
| martin | mews | mouse | nay |
| martial | muse | moose | née |
| marshal | mien | mousse | net |
| martin | mean | mucous | nett |
| marten | might | mucus | new |
| mask | mite | multiple | knew |
| masque | miner | multiply | night |
| | minor | | knight |

nightly
knightly

nit
knit

no
know

northerly
northern

not
knot

nougat
nugget

nought
naught

nugget
nougat

oar
ore

of
off

official
officious

omission
emission

oral
aural

ore
oar

organism
orgasm

outdid
outdone

overcame
overcome

overdid
overdone

overran
overrun

overtaken
overtook

overthrew
overthrown

packed
pact

pail
pale

pain
pane

pair
pare
pear

palate
palette
pallet

pale
pail

palette
palate
pallet

pane
pain

par
parr

pare
pear
pair

parr
par

passed
past

pastel
pastille

pate
pâté
patty

peace
piece

peak
peek
pique

peal
peel

pear
pair
pare

pearl
purl

peasant
pheasant

pedal
peddle

peek
peak
pique

peel
peal

peer
pier

pence
pennies

pendant
pendent

pennies
pence

perquisite
prerequisite

personal
personnel

petrel
petrol

pheasant
peasant

phlox
flocks

piazza
pizza

piece
peace

pier
peer

pined
pinned

piped
pipped

pique
peak
peek

pistil
pistol

pizza
piazza

place
plaice

plain
plane

plaintiff
plaintive

plait
plate

plane
plain

plate
plait

plum
plumb

politic
political

pool
pull

poplar
popular

pore
pour

pored
poured

poser
poseur

pour
pore

poured
pored

practicable
practical

practice
practise

pray
prey

precede
proceed

premier
première

prerequisite
perquisite

prey
pray

price
prise
prize

principal
principle

prise
price
prize

private
privet

prize
prise
price

proceed
precede

profit
prophet

program
programme

proof
prove

property
propriety

prophecy
prophesy

prophet
profit

propriety
property

prostate
prostrate

prove
proof

pull
pool

purl
pearl

put
putt

quash
squash

quay
key

queue
cue

quiet
quite

quire
choir

quite
quiet

racket
racquet

radar
raider

raged
ragged

raider
radar

rain
reign
rein

raise
raze

rampant
rampart

ran
run

rang
ringed
rung

rap
wrap

raped
rapped

rapped
rapt
wrapped

rated
ratted

raze
raise

read
red

read
reed

real
reel

red
read

reed
read

reel
real

refuge
refugee

regal
regale

reign
rain
rein

relief
relieve

reproof
reprove

respectful
respective

rest
wrest

retch
wretch

review
revue

rhyme
rime

ridden
rode

| | | | |
|---|---|---|---|
| right | ruff | sea | series |
| rite | rough | see | serious |
| write | | sealing | sew |
| rime | run | ceiling | so |
| rhyme | ran | | sow |
| | rung | seam | |
| ring | wrung | seem | sewed |
| wring | | | sewn |
| | rye | sear | |
| ringed | wry | seer | sewer |
| rang | | sere | sower |
| rung | sail | | |
| | sale | secret | sewn |
| risen | | secrete | sewed |
| rose | salon | | |
| | saloon | see | sewn |
| rite | | sea | sown |
| right | sang | | |
| write | sung | seem | sextant |
| | | seam | sexton |
| road | sank | | |
| rode | sunk | seen | shaken |
| rowed | sunken | saw | shook |
| | | | |
| rode | saviour | seen | shear |
| ridden | savour | scene | sheer |
| | | | |
| roe | saw | seer | sheared |
| row | seen | sear | sheered |
| | | sere | shorn |
| rôle | sawed | | |
| roll | sawn | sell | shelf |
| | | cell | shelve |
| rose | scared | | |
| risen | scarred | sensual | shoe |
| | | sensuous | shoo |
| rote | scene | | |
| wrote | seen | sent | shook |
| | | cent | shaken |
| rough | scent | scent | |
| ruff | cent | | shoot |
| | sent | septic | chute |
| rout | | sceptic | |
| route | sceptic | | shorn |
| | septic | sere | sheared |
| row | | sear | sheered |
| roe | scraped | seer | |
| | scrapped | | showed |
| rowed | | serial | shown |
| road | sculptor | cereal | |
| rode | sculpture | | shrank |
| | | | shrunk |

sight
cite
site

signet
cygnet

silicon
silicone

singeing
singing

sinuous
sinus

site
cite
sight

skies
skis

slain
slew

slated
slatted

slay
sleigh

slew
slain

sloe
slow

sloped
slopped

slow
sloe

smelled
smelt

sniped
snipped

so
sew
sow

soar
sore

sociable
social

solder
soldier

sole
soul

some
sum

son
sun

soot
suit

sore
soar

soul
sole

southerly
southern

sow
sew
so

sowed
sown

sower
sewer

sown
sewn

spared
sparred

speciality
specialty

species
specious

sped
speeded

spoke
spoken

sprang
sprung

squash
quash

staid
stayed

stair
stare

stake
steak

stalk
stock

stanch
staunch

stank
stunk

stare
stair

stared
starred

stationary
stationery

statue
statute

staunch
stanch

stayed
staid

steak
stake

steal
steel

step
steppe

stile
style

stimulant
stimulus

stock
stalk

stocked
stoked

storey
story

straight
strait

straightened
straitened

stratum
stratus

strewed
strewn

strife
strive

striped
stripped

strive
strife

striven
strove

stunk
stank

sty
stye

style
stile

suede
swede

suit
soot

| | | | |
|---|---|---|---|
| suite | tacks | tendon | tiled |
| sweet | tax | tenon | tilled |
| sum | tail | tenor | timber |
| some | tale | tenure | timbre |
| summary | taken | testimonial | time |
| summery | took | testimony | thyme |
| sun | tale | their | tire |
| son | tail | there | tyre |
| | | they're | |
| sundae | taped | | to |
| Sunday | tapped | thorough | too |
| | | through | two |
| sung | taper | | |
| sang | tapir | thrash | toe |
| | | thresh | tow |
| sunk | tapped | | |
| sank | taped | threw | tomb |
| sunken | | through | tome |
| | tare | | |
| super | tear | threw | ton |
| supper | | thrown | tonne |
| | taught | | tun |
| surplice | taut | throes | |
| surplus | | throws | too |
| | tax | | to |
| swam | tacks | throne | two |
| swum | | thrown | |
| | tea | | took |
| swede | tee | through | taken |
| suede | | thorough | |
| | team | | topi |
| sweet | teem | through | toupee |
| suite | | threw | |
| | tear | | tore |
| swelled | tare | thrown | torn |
| swollen | | threw | |
| | tear | | tow |
| swingeing | tier | thrown | toe |
| swinging | | throne | |
| | tee | | trait |
| swollen | tea | throws | tray |
| swelled | | throes | |
| | teem | | treaties |
| swore | team | thyme | treatise |
| sworn | | time | |
| | teeth | | trod |
| swum | teethe | tic | trodden |
| swam | | tick | |
| | temporal | | troop |
| symbol | temporary | tier | troupe |
| cymbal | | tear | |

258

tun
ton
tonne

turban
turbine

two
to
too

tycoon
typhoon

tyre
tire

unaware
unawares

unconscionable
unconscious

undid
undone

unwanted
unwonted

urban
urbane

vacation
vocation

vain
vane
vein

vale
veil

venal
venial

veracity
voracity

vertex
vortex

vigilant
vigilante

vocation
vacation

voracity
veracity

vortex
vertex

wafer
waver

waged
wagged

waif
waive

wave

waist
waste

want
wont

warden
warder

ware
wear

waste
waist

wave
waif

waver
wafer

way
weigh

weak
week

wear
ware

weekly
weakly

weigh
way

went
gone

westerly
western

wet
whet

whit
wit

whole
hole

whoop
hoop

whore
hoar

willed
would

winded
wound

wit
whit

withdrawn
withdrew

wittily
wittingly

woe
woo

woke
woken

wont
want

woo
woe

wore
worn

would
willed

would
wood
wooed

wove
woven

wrap
rap

wrapped
rapped
rapt

wreak
wreck

wreath
wreathe

wrest
rest

wretch
retch

wring
ring

write
right
rite

wrote
rote

wrote
written

wrung
rung

wry
rye

yew
ewe
you

yoke
yolk

yore
your

259